Africa in the New Millennium

ABOUT THIS SERIES

The books in this new series are the result of an initiative by CODESRIA, the Council for the Development of Social Science Research in Africa, to encourage African scholarship relevant to the multiple intellectual, policy and practical problems and opportunities confronting the African continent in the twenty-first century.

CODESRIA in association with Zed Books

Titles in preparation:

Africa and Development Challenges in the New Millennium: The NEPAD Debate
Edited by J. O. Adesina, Yao Graham and A. Olukoshi

Urban Africa: Changing Contours of Survival in the City
Edited by A. M. Simone and A. Abouhani

Liberal Democracy and Its Critics in Africa: Political Dysfunction and the Struggle for Social Progress
Edited by Tukumbi Lumumba-Kasongo

Negotiating Modernity: Africa's Ambivalent Experience
Edited by Elísio Salvado Macamo

Insiders and Outsiders: Citizenship and Xenophobia in Contemporary Southern Africa
Francis B. Nyamnjoh

About CODESRIA

The Council for the Development of Social Science Research in Africa (CODESRIA) is an independent organization whose principal objectives are facilitating research, promoting research-based publishing and creating multiple forums geared towards the exchange of views and information among African researchers. It challenges the fragmentation of research through the creation of thematic research networks that cut across linguistic and regional boundaries.

CODESRIA publishes a quarterly journal, *Africa Development*, the longest-standing Africa-based social science journal; *Afrika Zamani*, a journal of history; the *African Sociological Review*, *African Journal of International Affairs* (AJIA), *Africa Review of Books* and *Identity, Culture and Politics: An Afro-Asian Dialogue*. It co-publishes the *Journal of Higher Education in Africa*, and *Africa Media Review*. Research results and other activities of the institution are disseminated through 'Working Papers', 'Monograph Series', 'CODESRIA Book Series', and the CODESRIA Bulletin.

THANDIKA MKANDAWIRE | editor

African intellectuals

Rethinking politics, language, gender
and development

CODESRIA Books
DAKAR

in association with

Zed Books
LONDON | NEW YORK

African intellectuals: Rethinking politics, language, gender and development
was first published by Zed Books Ltd, 7 Cynthia Street, London N1 9JF, UK
and Room 400, 175 Fifth Avenue, New York, NY 10010, USA in 2005

www.zedbooks.co.uk

and in South Africa by UNISA Press, PO Box 392, Pretoria RSA 003

www.unisa.ac/za

in association with CODESRIA, Avenue Cheikh Anta Diop, x Canal IV,
BP3304 Dakar, 18524 Senegal

www.codesria.org

Editorial copyright © CODESRIA, 2005
Individual chapters © individual contributors, 2005

CODESRIA would like to express its gratitude to the Swedish International
Development Cooperation Agency (SIDA/SAREC), the International Develop-
ment Research Centre (IDRC), Ford Foundation, MacArthur Foundation,
Carnegie Corporation, the Norwegian Ministry of Foreign Affairs, the Danish
Agency for International Development (DANIDA), the French Ministry of
Cooperation, the United Nations Development Programme (UNDP), the
Netherlands Ministry of Foreign Affairs, Rockefeller Foundation, FINIDA,
NORAD, CIDA, IIEP/ADEA, OECD, IFS, OXFAM America, UN/UNICEF and the
Government of Senegal for supporting its research, training and publication
programmes.

Cover designed by Andrew Corbett
Set in Arnhem and Futura Bold by Ewan Smith, London
Index: ed.emery@britishlibrary.net
Printed and bound in Malta by Gutenberg Press Ltd

Distributed in the USA exclusively by Palgrave Macmillan, a division of
St Martin's Press, LLC, 175 Fifth Avenue, New York, NY 10010.

A catalogue record for this book is available from the British Library.
US CIP data are available from the Library of Congress.

CODESRIA editionISBN 2 86978 145 8 cased
Zed Books edition ISBN 1 84277 620 7 hb
                  ISBN 1 84277 621 5 pb

Contents

1 | Introduction

THANDIKA MKANDAWIRE

The papers in this volume were presented at the conference held in Dakar in December 2003 to mark the thirtieth anniversary of CODESRIA. The theme of the conference was 'Intellectuals, Nationalism and the Pan-African Idea'. The conference was both a celebration of an institution that has played a vital role in the sustenance and promotion of intellectual activities in Africa and also an occasion for sombre reflection, for looking back and for self-re-examination. It was an occasion for drawing up a new road map for tomorrow. It was a meeting of the old and the young, covering four 'generations' of African intellectuals. The inter-generational encounter suggested that the torch was being passed, dimmed perhaps but definitely not extinguished by the travails and tribulations the African intellectual enterprise has lived through during the last half-century. The papers (and the companion volume in French) have been selected because together they capture the intellectual genesis and institutional and intellectual contexts within which the social sciences have developed in Africa and the turbulent climate that each generation has lived through.

In this introduction I will not follow the traditional way of presenting the contents of each chapter sequentially. This is partly because of the recurring and cross-cutting nature of the themes that the authors tackle. In addition, as it turns out, I cover elsewhere some of the issues that would have constituted natural elements of an introduction in my paper in this volume. Instead I will highlight these themes and indicate how various authors deal with them. The themes touched upon in the volume are obviously not exhaustive, but they are broad enough to capture African intellectual life and ferment.

Intellectuals, pan-Africanism and nationalism

Intellectual work is quintessentially the labour of the mind and soul. Not surprisingly intellectuals have played a major role in shaping passions, ideologies and societal visions. The relationship between African intellectuals and pan-Africanism and nationalism has been both a symbiotic and a fraught one. If I were to select a single motif for this volume, it would be the importance of pan-Africanism as the context within which African nations have been imagined. Few movements have stirred the minds of

African intellectuals as much as pan-Africanism. In their turn, intellectuals have played an important role in shaping this pan-African concept, by reconstructing the past, interpreting the present and mapping out visions of the future. Ali Mazrui argues that while we can imagine intellectualism without pan-Africanism, we cannot envisage pan-Africanism without intellectualism. In a similar vein Joseph Ki-Zerbo highlights the dialectical cross-fertilization of the two, 'given that nationalism without pan-Africanism is meaningless and pan-Africanism without a liberation dimension is also an absurdity'. It is thus impossible to discuss pan-Africanism without bringing in the intellectuals who conceived it, while on the other hand the intellectual endeavours have attained full meaning only through their grounding in the pan-Africanist political projects and have only become valorized through the actions of other social actors. And consequently the world-views and the rise and dissipation of social movements have enormous implications for intellectual work in Africa.

Concern for the emancipation of the continent from the ravages of foreign domination and underdevelopment and the building of a new Africa that would assume its rightful place in the comity of nations have grounded much of the progressive thought of African intellectuals. Ki-Zerbo, whose own committed intellectual life is an illustration of the fact, advances the view that African intellectuals' involvement in the nationalist struggle was 'structurally programmed as a dialectic and antagonistic break with the realities, interest and values of colonial rule'. He insists not only on engagement by intellectuals (not in the sense of belonging to political parties) but also on their being able to 'develop an active neutrality, a positive autonomy, as opposed to one that is inert, amorphous and mute'. For him 'African intellectuals have to be at the forefront of responsible citizenship'. This, it turns out, is a message that has had considerable resonance among African intellectuals. Amina Mama and I myself note that generally African intellectuals have accepted their social responsibility and in most cases have also accepted both the nation-building and developmentalist projects espoused by the political class. For a whole number of reasons, however, recounted by Ki-Zerbo, Mazrui and myself, such heroic attempts to be relevant have often proven forlorn and quixotic. The barriers have included authoritarianism, dependence, the pettiness of state projects driven by power hunger and self-aggrandizement, etc. What governments wanted was not critical support but subservience and sycophancy. With their ears finely tuned to the voices of foreign experts and deaf to local voices, African states simply didn't care about local debates, except when they threatened state authority. And too many intellectuals allowed themselves to be 'yoked to power', and to accept the injunction: 'silence: we are developing', as Ki-Zerbo puts it.

One key determinant of both the conditions for the flourishing of intellectuals and the autonomy of the spaces in which they have operated has been the state. The African state has posed a serious dilemma for African intellectuals, at once seductive and menacing. On the one hand, its strengthening has always been deemed necessary both for safeguarding the sovereignty of the new states and for steering the nation-building project; on the other hand, this has posed the problem of creating what Ki-Zerbo refers to as the 'tropical Leviathan'. And it is a Leviathan which has been insistent that intellectual endeavour be nationally relevant. As Amina Mama points out, however, with hindsight it is easy to see that 'national relevance' remained unproblematized, and insensitive to the fact that African nations are deeply marked by class, ethnicity, gender, religion and other dimensions of difference and inequality. In addition, relevance in the context of authoritarian rule meant an uncritical acceptance of the state's interpretation of these objectives and what was required to achieve them. Ki-Zerbo reminds us (as I attempt to do myself) how development was used to justify authoritarian rule and how intellectuals often accepted the Faustian bargain of being part of the exhilarating project in exchange for remaining silent, since one could only be 'organic' by not being intellectual.

Much of the conflict between intellectuals and nationalism arises from the fact that while intellectuals have often drawn the ideational contours of pan-Africanism, the shaping of its political projects has been carried out by other actors, some of whom were intellectuals who had metamorphosed into not always recognizably intellectual actors. In many countries, qualities that had made intellectuals the kingpin of nationalism became the original sin in the post-colonial era. And indeed, all too often the word 'intellectuals' has moved from being a badge of pride to a term of abuse and derision. The capacity of intellectuals to 'speak truth to power', and their penchant for puncturing myths which was prized in the struggle for independence, were now perceived as divisive and thus inimical to the new nation-state. In most cases, states wanted intellectuals to confine their critical faculties to foreign powers. Continued criticism of the machinations of our erstwhile colonial masters and the new imperial order could be turned against African intellectuals by diverting their attention from a number of domestic issues. It was safer to talk about such entities as the 'centre' and the 'periphery' without incurring the wrath of any particular national potentate. Indeed the anti-imperialism of most governments in Africa meant that such discourse was quite palatable and usable.

In a paper on one of the most heroic movements of the struggle for national liberation, the African National Congress, Raymond Suttner argues that if one takes the Gramscian notion of intellectuals as 'people who,

3

broadly speaking, create for a class or people ... a coherent and reasoned account of the world', intellectuals are crucial to the emergence of a new culture, representing the world-view of an emerging class or people. Suttner uses the notion of the 'collective organic intellectual' to account for the ANC educating its followers, interpreting the historical experience and shaping the collective memory, rendering visible what is opaque, exposing the mystifications of those in power and giving meaning to events. The notion of collective intellectual is not that of a simple aggregation of individuals, 'but comprises a multiplicity of individuals, unity and cohesion among whom is by no means automatic'. Few movements in Africa illustrate this point as forcefully as the African National Congress, and its story is reflected in other African movements, albeit not as illustriously. This is not only a case where intellectuals played a central role in the struggle but also where men and women made enormous personal sacrifices in the fight against the scourge of apartheid.

Liberation movements, by their very nature, accommodated a broad range of views. Such accommodation was often facilitated by the exigencies of the struggle and the unity of purpose that characterized these movements. During this phase, the intellectual hegemony of the liberation movement was often sustained by the persuasiveness of its message and its resonance with the aspirations of compatriots and the appeals to unity in the face of the recalcitrant enemy. Consequently, differences were often voluntarily or tactically muted. It is often after liberation that the muted voices become louder, and it also in this phase that we see the conflation of power with truth.

The usual spartan intellectual certainty of the leaders of the triumphant movements, and its moral prestige, often enhanced by years of personal sacrifice, has always posed problems for African intellectuals following liberation. Suttner hints at the beginnings in South Africa of a process whereby the pronouncements of the leadership have an air of finality that does not encourage engagement in intellectual debates. He also observes how the patronage of the state may be contributing to the silencing of dissent or critical support through co-option. Many African countries have travelled this path before. It is important that South African intellectuals insist on autonomy and a critical distance from the state, even where the liberation movement's commitment to democracy is impeccable. Such a demand for autonomous spaces for intellectual activities may be vilified as elitist, aloof and self-indulgent, but these spaces are essential to any productive role for intellectuals in the new democratic South Africa, specifically, as I argue in my paper, as the post-colonial national project's Achilles heel was its failure to forge an organic link with the emerging intelligentsia.

Nationalism and developmentalism were not only restrictive in the political sense of censorship, however, but also epistemologically, by blinding intellectuals to other social concerns, a fact reflected in Amina Mama's discussion of feminism, in which she suggests that in intellectual terms the developmental nexus has been responsible for as many constraints as opportunities. Because of their confinement to developmentalist concerns, gender studies in Africa have tended to avoid the controversial issue of sexuality. Reliance on donor funding, whose *raison d'être* is putatively development, has made gender studies vulnerable to the vagaries of the development industry and shifting donor interests. Gender studies also reflect poignantly some of the problems that progressive thought has faced in Africa in negotiations over unequal power and authority; such negotiation 'has ensured a dynamic appropriation and incorporation that constantly subverts and challenges more transformative feminist ideas'.

Amina Mama reminds us that nationalism, as a homogenizing discourse that fulfilled valuable unifying functions, did not take full cognizance of the diverse composition of most African nations. In its quest for unity, it tended to occult or ride roughshod over other social identities such as class, gender or ethnicity. The resulting blind spot with respect to each of these has had an enormous impact on nation-building and development, in most cases leading to fatal errors and social injustice. These weaknesses have also permeated African scholarship, where historically, with perhaps the exception of the issue of class in Marxist-inspired literature, gender and ethnicity have not received the necessary attention let alone become core concepts in social analysis. One major contribution of feminist epistemology has been its insistence 'on being politically engaged, and on being constantly alert to the politics of location and diversities of class, race, culture, sexuality and so on'. Only in more recent years has gender entered academic syllabuses. Amina Mama traces the significant increases in gender studies in Africa, often driven by dedicated feminist scholars and their networks. Although considerable progress has been made, Amina Mama has reason to bemoan the reticence of African intellectuals over issues of gender. Whether their consciousness was nationalist or pan-Africanist, African intellectuals have continued to display a quite remarkable reticence over questions of gender.

Culture and African intellectuals

One task of ideas in both the enslavement and colonization of Africa was to dehumanize the enslaved and the colonized by denying their history and denigrating their achievements and capacities. The colonialists' claims to universalism for their culture and values, and the demotion of

5

other cultures to only particularistic and exotic significance, could not but provoke response and resistance. It is perhaps not surprising that some of the earliest intimations of pan-Africanism invariably included a vindication of the cultures and histories of peoples of African origin. And among the first intellectual 'schools' to emerge in Africa were those of historians; in Ibadan, Dakar and Dar es Salaam, for example. These schools took upon themselves the task of challenging the imperial narrative, one of whose intentions was to obliterate the memory of their pre-colonial existence. For Cheikh Anta Diop one task was to bracket (*mise entre parenthèse*) the colonial experience as simply a moment in the long history of Africa. Ochada argues that this nationalist historiography sought to correct the one-sidedness and racist historiography that served the colonial ideological apparatus. Colonial historiography denied African agency and was essentially an account of the itineraries of explorers, trade merchants, missionaries and colonizers. Dethroning this view and placing Africans centre-stage in the history of their continent was perceived as an urgent task in the construction of an intellectual arsenal for the liberation of the country and the decolonization of the mind. In the process, this analysis fell victim to the sins committed by colonial historiography – the sins of one-sidedness and idealization. The Africa that emerged out of this history was both ahistorical and asocial – ahistorical in the sense that it talked only of a glorious past uninterrupted by conflict and reversal and asocial in the sense that it failed to deal with the social contradictions that drive all social history. Hannington Ochwada insists on the importance of history in forging the new 'renaissance' and reconstituting a new personality not on the basis of an idealized and un-problematized past but on a full understanding of the complex heritage.

Related to the question of history has been that of language, which has arisen both in the context of discussing the role of intellectuals in giving Africa its own modernity and in development. As pointed out by several authors, African nationalism did not uncritically embrace 'modernity' as prescribed by the imperial order. Rather it attempted to realize modernity adapted to the cultural and historical experiences of Africa. Not surprisingly some of Africa's most prominent political actors have sought an ideology and identity that would give the project of modernization an African soul – Nkrumah's 'African Personality', Senghor's 'Negritude', Nyerere's 'African Socialism', Azikiwe's 'irredentism'. Ngugi wa Thiong'o argues that in order for Africa to advance it must rescue African memories from the clutches of the colonial past, whose vestiges still crowd out Africa's own memories and obstruct the vision of the future. So far none of the attempts to infuse modernity with African cultural subjectivities has been satisfactory, how-ever. Ali Mazrui, Ngugi wa Thiong'o and Beban Sammy Chumbow touch upon a recurring preoccupation in African intellectual circles, namely how to reconnect to their societies. How do African intellectuals embed their intellectual activities within African cultures? How does an intellectual class formed in the languages of the erstwhile colonial masters cease being one of 'informed natives' talking to the outside world, bearers of the memory of the colonizers, and become instrumental in turning African cultures into pillars of a self-confident Africa? Related to this has been the question as to what institutions and actors African intellectuals should be close to and how. Mazrui argues that while it is important to maintain a critical distance from the state, cultural embeddedness is important for the vitality and originality of African intellectual creativity. African intellectuals have been viscerally populist, not in the pejorative sense of the word but rather in the sense that their moral reflexes have favoured the weak. Not surprisingly there has been considerable soul-searching about the link to society at large. Linking up to the nation and community and valorization of the populist inclinations of African intellectuals, however, have been encumbered by the weight of colonial languages, which have, at the same time, accounted for the extraversion of African intellectual output, if not in content, at least in its dissemination.

The issue of language is not merely an expression of cultural chauvinism or romanticism. The interest in language is not only because it is a vehicle for regaining Africa's memory but also because the language medium is crucial for harnessing human resources and grounding scientific knowledge in African realities. It is the only way science and technology can become part of the common sense and world-view of the wider African public and underpin the scientific and technological knowledge required for the development of the continent. Chumbow forcefully argues this 'developmentalist' perspective on language. Succinctly stated, the argument he advances is that human resources are the linchpin of any development. In order for human resources to act as 'agents of change', however, they must be transformed, through education, into knowledgeable and skilled actors. Education takes place as a result of effective communication through the medium of language. Hence the importance of the language question to development. Ngugi and Chumbow argue that if African intellectuals are to rise to the challenge, then they will have to address the historical language legacy, which has made African intellectuals outsiders in their own society. There are, of course, many obstacles to this task but, as Chumbow argues, these have been overcome in many cultures in similar circumstances.

Africa and its diaspora

Pan-Africanism has been driven by history, geography, politics and

7

imagination. The concept has had to reconcile the different meanings that each of these influences has left as its stamp on pan-Africanism. These meanings did not always point in the same direction, nor did they always display the same intensity and coherence. And each of these meanings suggests a wide range of options. Africa's diaspora has played a major role in bequeathing Africa a significant part of the concept of African nationalism. It was central in the construction of Africa as an idea, as an object for study, in the establishment of Africans as academics and pan-Africanism as a project. And today Africa's diaspora is a major source of knowledge on Africa. But Africa's diaspora is neither monolithic nor univocal. In terms of diasporas in the United States, Paul Tiyambe Zeleza identifies four streams that have each contributed to the development and understanding of pan-Africanism, each from its own vantage point and historical experience. Within Africa, Mazrui, with his characteristic penchant for conceptual taxonomy, points to the fact that continental pan-Africanism intersects with the pan-Arabism of North Africa and with diasporic pan-Africanism, illustrative of the presence of black pan-Africanism and Afro-African pan-Africanism. One can also imagine a Euro-Africanism that will emerge with the demise of apartheid in South Africa. Although intellectuals have contributed to the shaping of pan-Africanism, the complex and conflicted spatial locations and cultural situations of contributors have contributed to its connotative complexities and ambiguity. The contrasting circumstances have led to differences in perspectives and priorities. Thus while diaspora studies have tended to focus on civilizational and cultural issues, the pan-Africanism on the continent has tended to be more developmentalist and more contemporary.

Today migration and globalization have added to the historic diaspora a new African diaspora. The issue now, as always, is how to creatively engage the African diaspora in the various endeavours that the continent has embarked upon over the years – liberation, nation-building, development, cultural renaissance, integration, etc. Zeleza argues that the mere presence of a diaspora does not indicate whether it is a curse or a blessing. This depends on deliberate and conscious efforts to harness both the commitment and the capacities of the diaspora. It also requires going beyond the sentimental to creating a mechanism through which diasporas can be useful to Africa in facing the main political and material changes. Africa's diaspora problem is partly due to the absence of a clear agenda in Africa itself. For Zeleza, then, the challenge for Africa is 'how to rebuild the historic pan-African project, spawned by the global dispersal and exploitation of African peoples over the centuries, by creatively engaging the African diaspora in the various endeavours that the continent has embarked upon over the years'. Such an engagement will necessitate regularly updated mapping of the diasporic intellectual terrain, and Zeleza proposes a tentative legend for such a map. It will also demand that the diaspora's antennae are receptive to the voices from the continent. Historically, when Africa has embarked on a clear project such as national liberation or the end of apartheid, Africa's diasporas have responded magnificently, even when burdened by their own oppressive conditions.

Zeleza observes that the contemporary academic diaspora in the United States and elsewhere in the North is becoming a force to reckon with in terms of 'knowledge production on Africa'. This has the positive effect of injecting African voices into interpretations. It does, however, also pose the danger that the privileging of the intellectual expressions of diaspora will mute the voices on the continent. This would eventually undermine intellectual focus on Africa everywhere. A detached diaspora would be like a head without a body.

Autonomous intellectual spaces

From the earliest days of independence African intellectuals have clamoured for autonomous spaces for their thinking. And not many such spaces were offered by the various repressive regimes that have reigned in much of Africa since independence. It was partly in response to this restrictive space that pan-African research networks such as CODESRIA emerged to provide spaces for critical reflection and to challenge the colonial discourse, which was still firmly entrenched in the new universities.

As Amina Mama and Mazrui remind us, however, the restrictive use of these spaces was due not only to the repressive apparatus of the state. Academics themselves could compromise the autonomy of the institutions or make the autonomy a source of self-imposed marginality. The mismanagement of such spaces has led to much soul-searching among African academics. Self-censorship, ethnic politics, intolerance and misogyny within such spaces are some of the problems that have been raised. Feminists have played an important role in highlighting the problems within academia itself, where women continue to be under-represented and where patriarchal and misogynistic cultures continue to make African campuses 'deeply difficult and challenging places for women at many levels'.

As the papers in this volume suggest, African intellectuals cannot be accused of self-referencing and navel-gazing. If anything they have been excessively extroverted, and not always aware of their collective output. There is, however, a growing self-consciousness about the circumstances of this output, its production and its relationship with the wider world. This volume is a testimony to this self-consciousness.

9

2 | African intellectuals and nationalism[1]

THANDIKA MKANDAWIRE

Some years ago I wrote about three generations of post-colonial[2] intellectuals. It struck me then that the fate of all three generations has been tied to the triumphs and tribulations of the nationalist projects whose problems have set their intellectual agenda over all these years. Elsewhere I have discussed the 'shifting commitments' of the nationalist movement (Mkandawire 1999). Interesting parallels to these shifts in commitments were the developments taking place among the generations of intellectuals. Periodization is always a treacherous exercise, involving as it does an arbitrary imposition of discrete time markers on what is essentially a continuum. One should also note that periodization may not be exactly the same across all countries.[3] With this caveat in mind I will use periodization only for heuristic utility and for purposes of exposition.

In recent years, both nationalism and its main projects have fallen on hard times – betrayed by some of its heroes, undercut by international institutions and the forces of globalization, reviled and caricatured by academics, and alien to a whole new generation of Africans born after independence. In intellectual circles, nationalism stands accused of a whole range of crimes and misdeeds. And yet in defiance of its death foretold, nationalism in Africa and elsewhere has displayed a remarkably enduring resonance, although in the eyes of some incongruously and regretfully so. Some of the metamorphoses it has undergone, however, have rendered it far removed from the original version that people like Julius Nyerere represented. More recently, it has taken the enormous integrity and courage of a Nelson Mandela to remind us what African nationalism was all about.

The relationship between nationalism and intellectuals or the intelligentsia has been widely debated. More specifically, there has been interest in explaining the fascination of intellectuals with or their adhesion to nationalism. Some have attributed it to self-interest by intellectuals whose path to material or professional ascendancy was blocked by the colonizer. National liberation is thus seen as a way of acceding to positions of power. Other less cynical interpretations attribute it to the skills of intellectuals in articulating in coherent form the aspirations of their countrymen and -women. Still others attribute to the intellectuals a fascination with a fad – nationalism being one of the products of modernization. All this may be true, but it seems to me that, to the extent that most colonized peoples seek decolonization, it would have been strange if intellectuals had not shared this aspiration. There is a strong moral case against colonization and there is, after all, a moral agency in many intellectual endeavours.

The protagonists

Let me start by presenting the two protagonists of my narrative.
The nationalists and their agenda First, the nationalists and nationalism. I will use nationalism as defined by Ernest Gellner as 'primarily the principle which holds that the polity and national unit should hold together' (Gellner 1983: 1). In many ways, the nationalists and their struggles have been occulted partly by their own gross simplification of the nature of the struggle they had been engaged in, partly by the hagiography cultivated by the post-colonial personality cults, and partly by critics who, deeply disappointed by the failures of the post-colonial state, see no virtue in what they once believed in. Because of the failure of the nationalist developmental project and its mystification, there is now a whole literature deconstructing and demystifying nationalist struggles.[4] This is, of course, a useful exercise, but only if it also happens to be well informed, which it rarely is. One feature of this writing is the extent to which the complexity of the problems faced by nationalists and the structural context of their eventual failure are downplayed. And as it is based on hindsight, it is not particularly enlightening.

To understand the case of the nationalists, one has to understand that the central premise of most of them, even when they lacked a 'state project', was that the struggle for independence and nation-building would take place within the confines of the territorial space drawn up by colonialists. 'Pan-Africanism', to which the African nationalists usually adhered, dictated that something be said about the eventual integration of the independent state with other independent African states – but that this could wait. What nationalists sought instead was an aggregation of the various manifestations of anti-colonialism for the liberation of that particular space – united and indivisible. Basil Davidson (1992) has argued that this was the fatal flaw of African nationalism – 'the Black Man's Burden', in his words – the acceptance of colonial borders and the premising of subsequent nation-building and future African integration on these borders. The assumption here is that there were some 'natural' or 'traditional' borders around which new states could be created or over which the edifice of pan-Africanism would be built. A thought experiment involving national independence along the many 'parochial' lines or along the markers established by ancient African empires, however, should immediately point to the limited and unreal-

11

istic alternative constructs that the nationalists had to contend with.[5] The problem is not so much that the nationalists accepted existing colonial borders, but rather that this acceptance gave individual states carte blanche in terms of what they could do to their citizens within these borders. An Idi Amin could go on a murderous rampage in his own country and still chair the OAU.

In any event, having accepted the colonial borders, they had to deal with the concrete fact of 'nations' consisting of many ethnic groups and nationalities. Africa's social pluralism, its division into more than a thousand ethnic groups, has always been a source of concern in terms of modernization, nation-building, development and governance. At times this pluralism has been made central to the analysis, while at other times it has been entirely banished. But it has, like the sword of Damocles, hung over any other social categorization used in social analysis: class, nation or gender, always threatening to render incoherent any analysis based on these categories. The nationalist movement saw recognition of this pluralism as succumbing to the 'divide and rule' tactics of the colonialist and neo-colonialist forces that were bent on denying African independence, or, when they accepted independence, of emptying it of any meaning by nursing the fissiparous potential that social pluralism always harboured. And so nationalism saw itself as up in arms against imperialism and the retrograde forces of tribalism. In the process something else happened: in combating 'tribalism', nationalism denied ethnic identity and considered any political or, worse, economic claims based on these identities as diabolic as imperialism. The nationalists can be excused for their conflation of tribalism and identity for, in many ways, the forces ranged against nationalism tended to abuse identity. The shock of Katanga, in which Africa's worst enemies – imperialism and racism – championed tribalism against the central government and Patrice Lumumba's martyrdom in the name of the independence and national integrity of the Congo, was so profoundly to affect African nationalism's perception of ethnicity and regional claims that 'Tshombes' and 'Katangas' were seen behind every movement challenging the authority of the central government.

In some countries radicalization of the nationalists, through armed struggles, was to banish ethnicity even farther from any serious political consideration. In those states where 'Marxism' became the leading ideology, class analysis simply rode roughshod over any other social cleavages. They were part of 'false consciousness', 'invented' by the colonialist or the petty bourgeoisie. This may have been the case, but 'false consciousness', while subjective in its origins, can assume an objective historical presence that can only be dismissed at one's peril.

The nationalists were cheered on by the 'modernization school' which considered ethnic identities and social pluralism as 'barriers to development'. If nationalist leaders could somehow bedazzle those mired in their tribal world-view with a more cosmopolitan ('nationalist') outlook, modernization would begin. The leaders could, in a Weberian way, use their 'charisma' to symbolize the new nations. The new myths claimed that nurturing such charisma would gradually replace the retrograde and anti-developmental myths of the tribe. Development presupposed a strong state running a coherent nation. Ethnicity was seen as inimical to both. It weakened the state by the conflicts it engendered, and the multiplicity of its claims simply denied the new countries their 'national image'. This image of the nation was essentially 'European', in its mystified forms: one race, one language, one culture. Alternative images of nation-states, multi-ethnic, multi-cultural or multiracial, were never seriously considered, and if considered had been so tarnished by apartheid's claims as to be of no lasting or sympathetic interest.

Economic development and developmentalism A second key element in the nationalist project and, in a sense, a corollary to the 'nation-building' agenda, was 'economic development'. Such a link between nationalism and development was not, of course, exclusive to Africa. The association between nationalism and development, often understood as involving industrialization, has been so close that Ernest Gellner (1983) suggested that the two were virtually inseparable. Indeed, in the African case independence was associated with the 'right to industrialization'. It is important to stress this point, especially in light of the argument that 'development' was externally imposed, which was, to say the least, misinformed and quite frankly insulting to the many African leaders and intellectuals who have sought material progress for their societies. The link between Africa's domination and techno-economic backwardness did not escape the nationalists. The 'founding fathers' of pan-Africanism, such as William Blyden, were keenly aware of the imperatives of 'modernization' if Africa were to escape the domination and humiliation it had suffered at the hands of the West and attain 'self-reliance and independence'.[6] One did not have to have the idea of 'catching up' imposed from outside. 'Guns' and 'steel'[7] had been decisive in Africa's subjugation and guns and steel it had to have.

It is quite clear from nationalist historiography that development – the eradication of the 'unholy trinity of ignorance, poverty and disease' – was a central component of the nationalist agenda. Indeed, one of the major indictments of colonialism was its failure to provide colonies with access to the knowledge and other means that were available for dealing with these issues. It may be true that development was eventually to be sidetracked from its central objectives or captured to fulfil neo-colonial objectives. It may also be true that internal development and external impositions may have led to undesirable 'development models'. In this case, one can talk of 'imposed' or 'failed' models, but the objective of development in the broad sense of structural change, equity and growth was popular and internally anchored.

Starting with the oil shocks of 1973 and 1979, African economies entered a period of crisis and policy initiative that were to produce two 'lost decades'. Already by the end of the 1970s, with the oil crisis and a hostile external environment, the nationalist developmental project was in crisis. In many cases, import substitution based on the national market had come to a premature halt. For a while greater attention was paid to possible collective responses to the crisis through 'collective self-reliance' and calls for a 'New International Economic Order' (themes reminiscent of the spirit of Bandung two decades earlier). The ideal of regional integration was picked up again and solemnly adopted by the heads of state in the form of the Lagos Plan of Action. Individually, however, every country was under pressure to seek assistance from the Bretton Woods institutions (BWIs) and accept the message of the Berg Report. Structural Adjustment Programmes (SAPs) marked a major defeat of the 'developmentalist project' – a defeat from which Africa has yet to recover.

The nation-building project had also run aground. The few nationalists who remained in power had become tyrants who had squandered all the political legitimacy they previously enjoyed. The soldiers who assumed power through military *coups d'état* did not have the slightest clue as to what nation-building might require politically. And in any case, many of them had been catapulted into power through the machinations of their erstwhile colonial masters or the new imperialists. And few of the men in uniform had the slightest idea of the role the nationalists had envisaged for the universities. The scabrous figure of Idi Amin visiting Makerere and pronouncing on its prospects was probably the most nightmarish turn of fortunes of the African universities.

This era of adjustment spawned a group that was hailed as the 'New Leaders of Africa': Yoweri Museveni of Uganda, Paul Kagame of Rwanda, Isaias Afwerki of Eritrea and Meles Zenawi of Ethiopia. They were said to be free of the burden of nationalism which had blamed everything on outsiders. They did not hesitate to admit errors and collaborate with others. (For a celebratory account of these leaders, see Connell and Smyth 1998.) The 'nationalism' of the new leaders was often detached from the pan-African ideal and free of its moral imperatives. The new leaders also did not seem

14

to respect the nationalists' understanding of the inviolability of existing borders, and almost all of them were soon to be embroiled in border conflicts. Furthermore, they seemed more enamoured of being appreciated outside Africa than concerned with building a reputation among their benighted neighbours. To compound matters, 'post-nationalist' leaders have tended to define the nation either in more exclusivistic terms or in adversarial terms. In the former case, the emphasis is on more precise definitions of who are nationals, as in the case of Côte d'Ivoire's President Conan Bedia's insistence on 'Ivoirité' or Zambia's Frederick Chiluba's genealogical definition of a Zambian. The latter shows up in dreams of territorial extension or redefinition of colonial borders, which has been broached by some Tutsi intellectuals. The discreet charm of African nationalism was its vagueness with regard to the nature of its national base and its adhesion to a more open-ended pan-Africanism, which did not allow for crossing each other's borders. The new nationalism took a much more divisive turn. Archie Mafeje's observations in this respect are worth citing at length:

> ... loss of faith in the proto-nationalists of the independence movement has brought forth a new generation of African meta-nationalists who are decidedly anti-imperialist. Having seen the effects of chauvinistic nationalism in situations in which ethnic diversity is the rule, they are hard put to find rationalizations for it by imputing pan-African cultural continuities where none exist, historically and anthropologically. This must be regarded as a very unfortunate relapse on the part of African scholars. It comes at a time when they are called upon to provide *theoretical perspectives* which could help in reconciling African ethnolinguistic diversity with the need for an expansive political and economic hegemony within the continent. (Mafeje 1993: 63–4)

The problem with democratization The relationship between nationalism and democracy was rarely studied, and was always an ambiguous one. It is interesting to note, as Alfred Stepan observes, that two major texts on nationalism, Benedict Anderson's *Imagined Communities* (1983) and Ernest Gellner's *Nations and Nationalism* (1983), do not discuss the question of democracy. In many cases, nationalist movements used the colonial masters' moral and liberal rhetoric to question the legitimacy not only of foreign rule but also of minority rule.

The questions that immediately arose after independence were: How does one govern societies in which ethnic identities are strong and tend to glide easily into tribalism? And what state structure is appropriate for 'development'? The almost universal response in Africa was one-party rule. In its most idealized form, one-party rule would provide a common forum through which all groups would be heard. It eventually tripped up on the inherent contradictions of 'one-party participatory democracy'. The great source of incoherence was the failure to reconcile what were obviously socially pluralistic arrangements in terms of class and ethnicity with political and economic arrangements that were monolithic and highly centralized.

Nationalism was fraught with many contradictions that severely taxed intellectuals who sought to understand or resolve them. On the one hand, it had adopted the liberal language of 'one man, one vote' and the individual right to morally discredit colonialism. On the other hand, its major objective was collective self-determination. There was no logical or political reason why, upon attainment of the latter, the nationalist should respect individual freedom. Nationalism was a 'force for collective freedom but a threat to both human solidarity and individual freedom' (Cocks 1991). And so one of the promises to which the nationalists gave short shrift was democracy. No sooner had they come to power than they found reason to discard the liberal democratic institutions that they had fought for and which had eventually brought them to power. The arguments given included the need for strong government and unity, for both 'nation-building' and development, and the cultural inappropriateness of Western institutions to African conditions. In most cases, African leaders received moral and intellectual support for theories of modernization. In the cold war days there was always a foreign ally that found the authoritarian regime compatible with or even necessary to its geopolitical interests.

Intellectuals and their responses Now a word about intellectuals. I will use the terms intellectuals and intelligentsia interchangeably, but with the Russian view of the intelligentsia as the underlying concept.

Independence led to a remarkable expansion in all levels of education. One problem of writing about African intellectuals is that we still lack what Jean Copans calls a 'sociology of African intellectuals'. This absence of a sociology does not, however, logically lead to his conclusion that there is no 'Homo Academicus Africanus'. The 'silence' of the 1980s, both imposed and self-imposed, may have fortified this perception not only of invisibility but also of non-existence. African intellectuals exist and have become much more self-conscious of their condition, and with the wave of democratization are becoming more visible (Mafeje 1993). In sociological terms African intellectuals have, at least until quite recently, largely been of peasant and working-class origin, which partly explains their visceral 'populism'. Another increasingly prominent feature of African intellectuals is their diasporic position. 'Brain drain', driven by political 'push' at home and economic 'pull' from abroad, has hit Africa hard and, consequently, a significant proportion of African intellectual contributions emanate from outside the continent.

The age of euphoria? The period up to the late 1970s was when the first African 'professoriate' emerged. During this period the relationship between the state and intellectuals was good. For the first generation of post-colonial intellectuals, this was the era of affirmation of the nationalist project and rejection of imperial intellectual domination and neo-colonial machinations. It was a period in which the African intellectuals' response had two elements: *'d'un part, l'engagement, d'autre part, la prise en charge exclusive, de la construction de l'Afrique'* (Gueye 2001: 231).[8] The mood of commitment to the new nationalist challenge is captured in the letter written by the poet David Diop just before his departure to Sekou Touré's Guinea to Alione Diop, the founder of *Présence Africaine*: *'Je pars pour le Guinée au début de la semaine prochaine en compagnie de Abdou Moumouni, Joseph Ki-Zerbo et quatre autres professeurs africains. Comme je l'ai écrit, il est des cas que celui qui se pretend intellectuel ne doît plus se contenter de voeux pieux et de déclarations d'intention mais donner à ses écrits un prolongement concret'*[9] (cited by Babacar Sall in the preface to ibid.: xiv). Zeneworke Tadesse characterizes this period as one of 'euphoria', not only over the national project but also regarding material comforts (Tadesse 1999). In the words of Abdalla Bujra (1994) this 'was a remarkable period of general unity and agreement about both goals and means'. In his turn, Sadiq Rashid has characterized it 'as a period of mutual tolerance and amicable co-operation between the academic community and the policy-making entities' and of 'mutual accommodation and wilful co-operation' when 'views of academicians were solicited by the latter, while the former readily obliged and often took pride in being associated with the honour of contributing to the crafting of national policies and exposure to the limelight as a result thereof' (Rashid 1994).

Development was essentially a statist and elitist project – not in the sense that it deliberately sought inequality and protection of elite interests but rather that it presupposed the pre-eminence of the elites in both its elaboration and implementation. In such a schema, democracy played a secondary role. The real issue, then, was what types of elites controlled the process rather than how they came to power. In more right-wing circles, there was a greater willingness to accept the military because it brought 'law and order' *à la* Samuel Huntington. In radical nationalist circles, the choice was between a 'national' and a 'comprador' bourgeoisie. The ideal movements were national or class-based ones. There was generally a disdain for mass movements driven by ethnic identities or religious particularisms, as these were considered retrograde and divisive.

We should also remember that this was the era of the cold war, which deeply affected the intellectual climate in Africa. The nationalist choice had been 'positive neutralism'. One consequence is that no full-blooded liberal or communist movements emerged in Africa. Early liberal experiments such as *Transition* magazine at Makerere were severely affected by their association with the CIA through its front organization, the Congress for Cultural Freedom. Vanguard Marxist-Leninist parties emerged only in Egypt, Sudan and South Africa. The favoured political stance was the 'mass party'. Much of the criticism of the mass party was focused on the fact that it lacked clear ideologies, was led by the wrong class, did not allow serious debate, and lacked clear channels for mass participation. There was then little attachment to the 'one party' state itself.

African nationalism always contained some notion of cultural reaffirmation and race liberation. This may never have been adequately theorized, although there can be no doubt that leaders such as Kwame Nkrumah, Léopold Senghor and Cheikh Anta Diop did try in their own way. In reaffirming their own identities, they constantly ran the danger of being accused of being racist essentialists, a charge that Kwame Anthony Appiah has tenaciously articulated (Appiah 1992). Significantly, for African intellectuals the cultural correlate to African nationalism was not national cultures or ethnic identities but pan-African ones: Negritude, African personality, consciencism and so on. During the struggle for independence, nationalism sought historical and cultural anchors – or a usable past – for its sustenance. And in the early years of independence, there was a genuine attempt to find new expressions for what was happening, or expected, in post-colonial Africa. African intellectuals shared this quest. Philosophers sought to elaborate African philosophies or what were disparagingly to be called ethnophilosophies. Historians set out to tell Africa's past, not merely to glorify it and its ancient kings and empires as some were wont to do, but also to establish the humanity of the people's Africa – a humanity denied by Hegel's assertion that Africans had no history other than merely a 'blank darkness' (Miller 1985). It is perhaps not surprising that of all the social science disciples, it was history which had its own major 'schools' during this era: those of Ibadan, Dakar and Dar es Salaam being among the best known. They were soon to discover, however, that the 'usable' pasts they had sought to construct for the nationalists could be turned into 'abusable pasts' in the hands of an increasingly self-serving political class which could unscrupulously declare that authoritarian rule corresponded to traditional forms of governance or that multi-party democracy was alien to African culture.

The intellectual correlate to the nationalist quest for political and economic independence was intellectual independence. It was an aspiration that was quite broadly shared in African intellectual circles and across the entire ideological spectrum. The independence sought ranged from the simple right to set our own research agenda or identify problems specific to our circumstances to the fundamental question of the basis on which the West had captured the epistemological ground and how it had come to 'know' us or, as an extreme, to 'invent' us. Polemical texts such as Chinweizu's *The West and the Rest of Us* (Chinweizu 1975) were emblematic of this response. This was part of what Valentin Y. Mudimbe called the 'search for the epistemological foundation of an African discourse' (Mudimbe 1988: 164). It ranged from nativism to a reinterpretation of what was universal in the light of the African experience or culture.

Concern over development or, more prosaically, the eradication of poverty, ignorance and disease, the unholy trinity against which the nationalists' swords were drawn, was widely shared in African intellectual circles. One has only to look at the publications of CODESRIA to see this. The name of CODESRIA's flagship publication is *Africa Development*, and for years every research programme had the word development attached to it: 'Technology and Development', 'Education and Development', 'Women and Development', and so on. The developmentalist impulses stimulating the African intellectuals' activities were not confined to social scientists. Some of the most eloquent statements in defence of the quest for material development were made by African writers who railed against cultural nationalism (such as Negritude) that they thought was backward-looking. In an essay entitled 'Negritude is Crying over Spilt Milk', Taban Lilong (cited in Mnthali 1999: 15) said: 'quite a few [false starts] have been made in Africa. We may be failing in doing certain things, but most of us know the direction we are going – straight into the twenty-first century. And to arrive there we are not going to go the way our grand parents would have gone – on foot and by canoe. We shall fly, we shall go by missiles, we shall go with the white man, we shall go with the yellow man. And we shall go by all means.'[10] Criticizing 'cultural nationalism' for its failure to come to grips with technological developments, Abiola Irele, in a paper provocatively entitled 'In Praise of Alienation' (Irele 1992), discusses what technological transformation will entail. He quotes a Yoruba saying: *'Adaniloro k'oni logbon'* (One who causes you injury also teaches you wisdom) and urges Africans to embrace development even if it entails alienation, a position that would drive many a post-modernist to the armoury, given their view that development is a child of the fatally flawed modernist 'enlightenment' project.

One feature of the African intellectual temperament was a populist streak. Many would probably have accepted the characterization of the intelligentsia made by Samir Amin:

> The intelligentsia (in the periphery) is not defined by the class origin of its members. It is defined by (i) its anticapitalism; (ii) its openness to the universal dimension of the culture of our times and, by this means, its capacity to situate itself in the world, analyse its contradictions, understand the weak links, and so on; and (iii) its simultaneous capacity to remaining in living and close communion with the popular classes, to share their history and cultural expression. (Amin 1990: 136)

The commitment to the under-privileged was accompanied by the view that serious research was good for them. There was a class factor in all this. Pierre van de Berghe observes that in one university in 1960–62, about 61 per cent of the students came from homes in which fathers were either farmers, traders, unskilled workers or artisans; 6.2 per cent from clerical homes; and 22.6 per cent from the homes of semi-professionals. Only 11.2 per cent had fathers who were fully fledged professionals. Paul Tiyambe Zeleza also observes, 'When I attended the University of Malawi in the early 1970s many of my fellow students were from rural and peasant backgrounds, few were from the then minuscule middle class' (Zeleza 2003: 69).

One outstanding feature of the post-independence African state was its reach and its pervasive presence in all walks of life. Its tentacles extended not only to all sectors of the economy but to every nook and cranny of civil society. The ubiquity of the state meant that it was loathed and courted at the same time. This led to insecurity, paranoia, self-censorship, opportunism and even sycophancy among those who sought access to state patronage (Ake 1993; Diouf 1993). With the state looming so large, it is no surprise that this led to statist perceptions of social transformation among African intellectuals by obscuring or overshadowing other social actors – an oversight for which they have been severely criticized (Diouf 1993; Mamdani 1993).

A troubled relationship In order not to exaggerate the sense of harmony during the phase of 'euphoria' and the pre-eminence of nationalism we should recognize the early series of conflict. Already, during the first years of independence, a number of conflicts were arising. This was perhaps inevitable. There was always tension between the intellectual's critical mentality and his/her political affinities, especially among those who insisted on sycophancy and blind faith. In addition, nationalism has always been double-sided. Many of the virtues of nationalism – a sense of community, patriotism, a sense of a shared historical past – are also its dark side – strong communal feeling can easily turn into xenophobia, and the need for unity can generate pressures for conformity that can stifle intellectual work. The mythical dimensions of nationalism may alienate the intellectual's constitution as a critical thinker. This is in no way to suggest that intellectuals were somehow inherently immune to the 'dark side' of nationalism. There are too many cases in history in which some intellectuals have reinforced this dark side of nationalism or where they have legitimized special interests and commitments.

It is important to state that during much of this period African social sciences operated within the paradigm of 'modernization'. There were therefore some serious attempts to rationalize the authority of the nationalists in power in terms of the putative exigencies of modernization – 'strong government', 'charismatic leadership', and so on. The concerns of this approach related to the problems of transition from 'charismatic' to a more rational and more legitimate rule in the Weberian sense (see, for instance, Sylla 1982). There were, of course, African scholars who rejected the linear approach of 'modernization' to development; most of them were attracted to the view that (a) development was not a linear process and nations could achieve growth via paths other than those traversed by the developed countries; and (b) the world system was not neutral or benign with respect to development. To confront a world system that was seen as hostile to development, 'delinking' or 'collective self-reliance' was proposed. There were also considerable controversies as to what social class or institutions would be most appropriate under the circumstances. In general, many radical African intellectuals doubted whether the African political class had the 'political will' to seriously pursue the development of their respective countries. The corruption and self-aggrandizement of the leaders merely lent more support to these doubts.

Critical works, such as those of writers like Frantz Fanon, who talked about the 'pitfalls of national consciousness', were being widely read in African intellectual circles. African scholars had also contributed to the work of Fanon (see, for instance, Hansen 1976; Onwanibe 1983). Fanon strongly criticized bourgeois anti-colonial nationalism, whose goal he saw as 'quite simply ... [to] transfer into native hands ... those unfair advantages which are the legacy of colonialism'. Most tellingly, Fanon argued that the 'mission' of the new elites 'has nothing to do with transforming the nation; it consists, prosaically, of being the transmission line between the nation and a capitalism, rampant though camouflaged, which today puts on the mask of neo-colonialism' (Fanon 1966: 152). A vocal minority of

21

intellectuals argued along these lines and began to distance themselves from the nationalist project. It should be stressed, however, that 'far from representing an abstract repudiation of nationalism as such, Fanon's criticism of bourgeois nationalist ideology is itself delivered from an alternative nationalist standpoint' (Lazarus 1999: 162). Even those who claimed to derive inspiration from Marxism could not entirely do away with nationalism as merely one form of 'false consciousness', with the result that African Marxists were often denigrated by the Western left as, at best, 'radical nationalist'. They often accused the nationalists in power of having 'betrayed' the nationalist cause or being a petty bourgeoisie or comprador class that would never rise to the stature of a 'national bourgeoisie' that might address the 'national question'.

No sooner had the demolition of the short-lived democratic structures been accomplished than a host of theories and justifications for authoritarian rule were advanced. As far as academic freedom was concerned, the sign of things to come was signalled by Kwame Nkrumah in the following words:

> We do not intend to sit idly by and see these institutions which are supported by millions of pounds produced out of the sweat and toil of common people continue to be centres of anti-government activities. We want the university college to cease being an alien institution and to take on the character of a Ghanaian University, loyally serving the interest of the nation and the well-being of our people. If reforms do not come from within, we intend to impose them from outside, and no resort to the cry of academic freedom (for academic freedom does not mean irresponsibility) is going to restrain us from seeing that our university is a healthy university devoted to Ghanaian interest. (Cited in Hagan 1993)

The particular circumstances behind Nkrumah's remarks are discussed by George Hagan (ibid.) and need not detain us. What is ominous here is that, first, Nkrumah was raising an issue that has dogged the state–university relationship ever since – reconciling utilitarian views about universities and the maintenance of standards and the autonomy of universities. This immediately raised the question about the appropriateness of the university models inherited from the metropolitan countries, including their vaunted autonomy. Seseko Mobutu jumped into the fray:

> We need to emancipate the educational system in the Congo from the Western model by going back to the Authenticity while paying due attention to scientific knowledge: I have always thought it inappropriate for us to train our youth as if they were Westerners. It would be more desirable to have an

educational system which shapes the youth according to our requirements. That would make them authentically Congolese. Their ideas, reasoning and actions would be Congolese, and they would see the future in Congolese terms. (Cited in Yeikelo ya Ato and Ntumba 1993: 165)

Non-organic intellectuals

Many African academics were willing to submit themselves to the exigencies of nationalism and the new state, which they viewed as 'the custodian of the development process and the university as an institution that must train human resources for development. It then seemed natural to them that the state play a key role in managing the university' (Mamdani 1993). And yet, noting the general consensus among policy-makers and intellectuals on the basic tasks of the new nations, Abdalla Bujra observed:

Unfortunately however it is not clear whether the knowledge produced by these institutions at the time had any direct or indirect contribution to the modest economic growth of most African countries during the 60s. Furthermore and with hindsight, barring the few brilliant exceptions of scholars such as Samir Amin and Ali Mazrui, there were no sparks nor any form of development in the social sciences in African countries during the period. These institutions were largely transmitters of metropolitan social science in their respective countries. (1994: 125)

Few African leaders, however, sought to cultivate an indigenous 'intellectuariat' that was, in the Gramscian sense, 'organic'.[11] The default position of the African political class was a profound distrust of its country's intellectuals. The kind of rapport that the Indian nationalists sustained with the intellectuals in the post-colonial period, or the links that Jewish intellectuals had with the Israeli state, was rarely seen in Africa.[12] This did not happen on the continent, except perhaps in Algeria, where the intellectuals were organic to the FLN movement and government,[13] and South Africa, where Afrikaner intellectuals were close to the apartheid regime. One consequence is that the African nationalist post-colonial project had no organic intellectuals and the few that sought to assume that role were reduced to acting as apologists. The African governments tended to reduce their relevance to the provision of 'manpower' resources for development and to indigenize the civil service. And so the first wave of the African intelligentsia was absorbed by the state and parastatal bureaucracies. Once indigenization was achieved, most governments had little motivation to continue support for the African university. The earliest collision between the nationalists and intellectuals occurred over the relationship between excellence and the relevance of African universities. Excellence

23

was associated with the universal 'Gold Standard' – which in the African case really meant the standards of universities of the erstwhile colonial power. The nationalists sometimes read this as a 'colonial mentality' or 'elitism'. This conflict was in a sense superficial.

Second, African governments relied heavily on foreign mentors, admirers or sycophants for intellectual inspiration or affirmation. In the post-war period there were 'welfare intellectuals' of post-world-war Europe who were organic and subservient to the creation of the welfare state. Some of these spilled over to the colonies as advisers in the 'colonial and welfare' programmes. The more radical were to stay on as advisers to the nationalist governments, setting the stage for the technical assistant syndrome that has done so much damage to Africa and placed a wedge between African intellectuals and the nationalists. Thus Julius Nyerere had a band of foreign 'Fabian socialists' who had easy access to him, in sharp contrast to Tanzanians, who had difficulties in seeing him. Kenneth Kaunda had as a close intellectual associate John Hatch, who was invited to be the first director of the Institute for Humanism. Kwame Nkrumah surrounded himself with pan-Africanists from Africa's diaspora, such as George Padmore and W. E. B. Dubois. In later years there were European and American 'radicals' who were to appear as peripatetic advisers to a whole range of 'progressive' regimes in Africa.

Third, African leaders had a penchant for assuming the role of philosopher-king and reducing intellectual work to the level of incantation of the thought of the leader. Leaders sought to acquire intellectual hegemony by themselves or through advisers, constructing intellectual frameworks that would guide national debates. Nkrumah with his pan-Africanism and Nkrumaism, Nyerere with his Ujamaa, and Kaunda with his humanism are some of the well-known examples. Even characters adamantly committed to mediocrity and obscurantism promulgated ideologies that were supposed to inform their countries' transformation. Mobutu's 'authenticity' was, alas, not the only one. In many cases most of the ideological schemas propounded by African leaders were highly idiosyncratic and often so incoherent as to be beyond the comprehension of the propagators themselves. Adhesion to them was not only difficult but also hazardous for those sycophants who diligently sought to follow the leader through infinite twists and turns as he sought to bridge the cavernous gap between the rhetoric of national goals and the reality of predatory self-aggrandizement. There were even some intellectuals who tried to be exegetes of nationalist texts and wrote fawningly about whoever was in power, but in most cases these were to be hoisted on the petard of their own opportunism. African states were apparently never in great need of any social category other than that of disposable sycophants, and few African leaders bothered to curry favour with African intellectuals qua intellectuals.

Finally, there was complete misunderstanding of the task that lay ahead. African leaders either overestimated the power and capacity of the 'kingdom' Nkrumah had enjoined them to seek, or underestimated the intellectual and political complexity of the processes of development and nation-building. As Kwame Anthony Appiah notes: 'When the postcolonial rulers inherited the apparatus of colonial rule, they inherited the reins of power; few noticed, at first, they were not attached to a bit' (Appiah 1992: 164). And by all accounts they and the foreign donors continue to underestimate how knowledge-intensive the process has to be.[14]

To make matters worse, few of the debates on development were 'national' in focus, for a number of reasons. First, repression and the self-censorship that went along with it meant that it was safer to talk about such entities as 'centre' and 'periphery' without incurring the wrath of any particular national potentate. Indeed, the anti-imperialism of most governments in Africa meant that such discourse was quite palatable and usable. And to the extent that it blamed outsiders for our failures, it was comforting to the African leaders. Second, a large number of African scholars were 'outsiders' in many ways. They either belonged to racial or ethnic minorities than were systematically excluded from power, or were exiled scholars who could not be expected to influence local politics or insult their host countries. One has only to look at such debates as 'the Kenya Debate' or the 'Dar Debates' to see what I mean. While expatriates debated the efficacy of Ujamaa and villagization and its socialist or petty bourgeois character, Tanzanian scholars largely remained silent, and the few who did participate were preoccupied with a detailed understanding of the social processes in Tanzania, as illustrated by Issa Shivji in his book, *Silent Class Struggles* (1976).[15] Ultimately the ideological denigration of nationalist positions by largely expatriate or refugee scholars undermined an autonomous discussion by a new African left which was still in awe of its expatriate counterparts.[16]

Deafening silence or silent struggle?

Ki-Zerbo has characterized the attitude of the time as one proclaiming 'Silence: Development in Progress'. The apparent silence of the intellectuals prompted Issa Shivji (1993) to declare: 'the present crisis has brought in sharp relief the complete passivity and marginality of African intellectuals in the political and social life of our nations'. He added: 'We as intellectuals have distinguished ourselves by our silence, submission and subservience rather than courage and consistency.'

Nationalism and its rhetoric and proclamation were difficult to contend

25

with. First, in the early years the triumphant nationalists, armed with impeccable testimonies to their personal commitment to the nation (many years in exile or detention), stood on very high moral ground. Indeed, they could, with some justification, claim that they spoke for the nation when they chastised academics for abusing academic freedom by engaging in trivial pursuits that did not address the urgent tasks of nation-building and development. Second, the nationalists had demonstrated their commitment to university education and their genuine belief that universities would produce the manpower required for development by funding the universities lavishly, especially when compared to the parlous funding status of African universities today. Third, African universities were cursed by their parentage, which made them easily suspect in the eyes of the nationalists. Most of the universities were modelled after similar institutions in metropolitan countries and were initially staffed by expatriates. This genesis made them vulnerable to charges that their opposition to the nationalist agenda was a reflection of their alien character or, worse, their 'colonial mentality', which made them a 'veritable breeding ground of unpatriotic and anti-government elements', to use Nkrumah's characterization of University College (cited in Hagan 1993).

Fourth, academics themselves shared the nationalist ideology and aspirations. This meant that African intellectuals had to make hard choices. Since most of them shared the nationalist objectives and were in some way sceptical of the appropriateness of foreign ideas, including liberal democracy, they were at pains to find the democratic or 'popular' kernel in the many variants of the 'one-party' democracy that resulted.[17] In any case, few found the moral case for intellectual freedom in the context where basic freedoms – freedom to live – were severely constrained. The visceral populism of most African intellectuals tended to persuade them to accept, albeit grudgingly, the option that democracy would have to wait. In the 'developmentalist' logic it always appeared immoral to ask for freedom to think and express oneself when people were denied basic rights such as the 'right to food'. Claude Ake posed the question quite sharply:

> ... why should we care about academic freedom in Africa? It is difficult enough to justify the demand for political freedom where limitations of poverty, illiteracy and poor health and the rigour of the daily struggle seem to demand entirely different priorities. It is difficult still to defend the demand for academic freedom which is a very special kind of bourgeois freedom limited to a very small group. Why do we think we are entitled to demand academic freedom and why do we think that our demand deserves to be upheld by the rest of society? (Ake 1993)

There was, of course, no correlation between the silence of academics and the lives of the poor – not in Africa anyway. But such was the force of nationalism and developmentalism that even the prospect that there might indeed be no trade-off between academic freedom and national welfare was discounted.[18]

And if one adds to the overall ideological congruence the material comfort and the bright prospects promised by a rapidly expanding civil service and indigenization programmes, one has all the preconditions for a harmonious state–academe relationship. And indeed there was relative peace between the state and academics. African academics were constantly reminded that they were part of the privileged class and 'bourgeoisie of the diploma' to boot. From time to time there were altercations on campus but these were largely confined to the material well-being of the community and rarely touched upon the larger societal issues of governance. Generalizing from this period, many observers of African politics have sometimes argued that this relative harmony was because the intelligentsia in Africa were themselves the recruiting ground for high state functionaries. Consequently, social analysis on their part would be uncomfortably close to self-analysis. The academic community was therefore conceived as basically collaborationist. This may be true, but it is equally true that academic communities shared ideologies with those in power.

In many cases, the emerging intellectual class found itself in the invidious situation of being pampered while also being muzzled or marginalized. Amin Khan, writing on Algeria, could just as well have been portraying the situation in any African country by the end of the 1970s:

> Until the late 1970s, neither the society nor its elites, the intellectuals in particular, had any driving urge to break free of these general norms. The norms were clearly at loggerheads, by definition, with such essential intellectual values as freedom, the cultivation of critical attitudes, and a readiness to challenge unreasoned orders and assumptions. They were also hostile to the basic conditions of intellectual creativity. But somehow, Algerian intellectuals managed to live with them. Technically qualified people were invariably found slots in the bureaucracy or the economic establishment. Critical thinkers could be kept busy ruminating about new problems facing State and society within the limits of acceptable discourse, or at any rate of what was considered acceptable. All university graduates were sure to get jobs, along with the prestige associated with the executive-class posts set aside for them. As for freedom, well, had not the entire nation just fought for and won that? Those in a position to demand higher standards of liberty in both public and private life were not only few; they

27

were also under a cloud of social suspicions, because after all they too were privileged people. And the concept of freedom as an absolute necessity, the central value of an enterprise on modernity, was never invoked in any social framework. (Khan 1993: 290)

The age of delusion

The second period was that of disenchantment and disillusionment when the intellectuals blamed the leaders for 'betraying the nationalist struggle'. It was also a period of self-organization. First, nationalism had lost much of its lustre. Many of the key nationalist leaders had been thrown out of office, killed or sent into exile, sometimes by colleagues in the nationalist struggle. Others clung to power, but age had began to take its toll on body and soul. During the two decades after independence the mantle of nationalism had been worn by so many dictators that it is difficult to imagine it ever had popular support.

The alienation of African intellectuals deepened in the 1980s. First, the worsening material conditions of the universities simply eroded the basis of the distant but still-cosy relationship between the university and the state. The splendid isolation to which they had been confined was now reduced to squalor as overcrowding and lack of maintenance became pervasive. In response to the more vocal criticisms from academics, the state argued that universities were not doing relevant research, or were undertaking research that was not immediately usable in policy matters. Governments often insisted on eschewing basic research to engage in what was called 'applied research'. In this they were strongly supported by donors, both governmental and non-governmental. In any case, African governments resolved the conflict by simply denying universities excellence and relevance, in which they received the intellectual support of the World Bank, whose 'rates of return' mumbo-jumbo suggested Africa could do without much higher education.

Significantly, this was the period when the brain drain began to assume alarming proportions. Zeleza cites studies which indicate that in the 1980s an average of 23,000 qualified academic staff were emigrating from Africa each year. An estimate in 1995 gave the figure of 50,000 (Zeleza 1998). In his usual provocative manner, Ali Mazrui (1978) tried to give a positive gloss to all this by suggesting that this migration was Africa's revenge, a 'counter-penetration' of the imperial citadel which would subvert Western claims to universalism. Zeleza is more accurate in placing these movements in their proper economic context of labour market processes.

The 1990s also saw the emergence of many movements and social concerns that had been submerged by both the nation-building and the developmentalist project. Women first pointed out their specific role in development and insisted on the recognition of their contributions. Later the 'Women in Development' agenda shifted towards a more gendered approach to social issues. Feminist scholars attacked African scholarship and intellectual endeavours for their blindness to gender issues and declared that the nationalist projects had been fundamentally patriarchal. Even as they criticized the research agenda in Africa, however, they also had to ensure that the specificities of their own concerns were not submerged by the dominant Western feminism – the old issue of the particular and the universal.

By the time of the arrival of the 'second generation' things had begun to turn sour. They became worse with the end of the post-independence euphoria and consensus, and even worse with the arrival of adjustment, when African governments turned their ears elsewhere. There are a number of ways of reacting to the failure to 'develop' – or to the 'impasse', as it has been dubbed.[19] One response was to question the commitment to and the interpretation of development while another was to question the validity of the objective itself and to say that we never wanted 'development' anyway, that it was a Eurocentric, external imposition. The first reaction was aimed at how 'developmentalism' had become an ideology that was abused by African governments, including those for whom development had never been on the agenda. And so by the 1980s a reaction began to emerge. African intellectuals began to critique 'developmentalism' – not because material progress was undesirable but because as an ideology it absolutized economic growth to the exclusion of other values such as culture and human rights (Ake 1979; Shivji 1980). 'Development' had also become an extremely mystificatory objective. As a team of Congolese scholars observed: 'There is no need to expatiate here on the use of the educational system including universities, by ruling regimes as ideological agencies of system maintenance. It is perfectly clear that the educational system in Zaire helps maintain the existing situation by educating people to work in it. In this process the most anomalous realities are veiled under the concepts of development and underdevelopment' (Yeikelo ya Ato and Ntumba 1993: 166).

At the 1986 CODESRIA General Assembly, a decision was taken to drop 'development' again, not because it had ceased to matter but because it tended to overshadow other growing concerns of the African intellectual community, such as human rights, cultural autonomy, gender equality and national cohesion; because it negated or marginalized other values by posing as the ultimate end of all African endeavours and not as a means to some high goals; and because of the totalizing and repressive hold it had on politics and its use by both donors and national governments to justify whatever they were doing. It was an objection to the sign 'Silence: Development in Progress' that African leaders sought to hang at the door to our nations and societies. More specifically in the African context, African intellectuals were responding to the terrible uses to which the notion had been put – to suppress human rights, to compel people into undesirable social arrangements, to ride roughshod over people's identities and cultures, and so on. But development in the sense of addressing the material needs of society was squarely on our agenda. Indeed, the urgency of defending 'development' understood as material progress in an inclusive manner was to be highlighted by the 'adjustment' ideology, which reduced economic policy to debt repayment and the satisfaction of an ideologically driven reification of the market, and relegated issues of economic development, democracy and equity to perfunctory rhetoric.

The criticisms of African intellectuals have been focused on examining what went wrong in achieving what they generally view as desirable.[20] Their theorizing was still committed to material realities and was firmly tethered to the task of liberating Africa not only from the scourge of foreign domination but also from home-bred tyrants and material deprivation. The majority of African intellectuals may have disagreed on the diagnosis and prescriptions, but they agreed that there was a malaise which afflicted Africa and that knowledge would play an important role in the quest for the cure. The abuse of authority, the obvious positive correlation between authoritarianism and poor economic performance, the demystification of nationalism, the growing political protest and the explosion of conflicts that had hitherto been covered up by repression – all these emboldened African academics to begin to speak out and to insist on both academic freedom and democratization.[21] The argument was basically one of 'Bringing Development Back In', but this time with a democratic face and a cultural soul. Their criticism of the governments was that they had abandoned the developmental vision that was so central to nationalism.[22] Considerable energy had been expended on criticizing structural adjustment programmes, largely for their anti-development bias which favoured stabilization and debt repayment, and their negative effects on democratization, either through weakening of the state to deliver substantive gains to the populace or through their curtailment of democratic space by imposing technocratically driven conditionalities.

Sadiq Rashid (1994) summarizes the experience in this period:

> Beginning with the second half of the 1970s and until the present, readiness to solicit and use social science research for policy-making purposes has waned progressively and almost ceased to exist as related to certain areas. Indeed, the amicable relationship and attitude of mutual tolerance

which characterised the interface between academia and bureaucracy in the immediate post-independence era has soured badly and has given way to an increasingly strained relationship of suspicion, mistrust, antagonism and sterile lack of co-operation. A number of reasons have been responsible for this state of affairs. Many governments ... neglected and declined to actively solicit the views and research inputs of national think-tanks, particularly as related to the primary areas of policy setting or policy prescriptions. While a number of social scientists have continued to produce research that was relevant to policy-making purposes, such efforts have often been wilfully ignored. Where research has produced divergent views, it has usually been considered as subversive. Evidence has also indicated that even when solicited by governments, the rate of adoption of recommendations made by social scientists was dismal.

One should also add here that in many ways the research had become progressively even less likely to be usable by existing regimes: Abdalla Bujra's characterization of research in CODESRIA clearly suggests the growing 'unusability' of its research in the eyes of the state.

> CODESRIA's literature was dominated by advocacy of equity in the distribution of national resources, the participation of poorer classes in decision-making and at various levels of economic management, and full democratization of the political process. It also carried out consistent attacks on corruption, bad government and state oppression. Given the advocacy of these ideas by CODESRIA and the environment of government policy and decision-making, it is not surprising that CODESRIA has made little impact on state policies. (Bujra 1994)

The commitment to the under-privileged was accompanied by the belief that serious research was good for them. Or as two Zairian scholars stated:

> One would expect genuine intellectuals to be patriotic thinkers alive to the demands of the crisis situation. We use the word crisis advisedly, giving it the etymological meaning of 'a decisive turning point, a moment of choice'. From that perspective, intellectuals are people who use such key moments to lay bare the logical roots of the crisis devastating society. In the process they [rip] off the tissue of mystificatory official expiations. The surest way to do this is to examine reality from the perspectives of the underprivileged. For it the privileged who need lies and myths to maintain the status quo. The underprivileged need to use truth to tear down the veil of mystification in their struggle against established order. (Yeikelo ya Ato and Ntumba 1993)

The response of CODESRIA and many individuals to their impotence in influencing government policies was to turn towards other potential uses of research, such as 'civil society'. Recourse to 'civil society' has, unfortunately, not been without problems. First, the new society was not so discursive as to need serious intellectual input. In purely professional terms, the type of research demanded by NGOs – the main direct consumers of research in civil society – was the consultancy type. This was often premised on the assumption that poor research was good enough for the poor, and as such has often been found to be intellectually unsatisfactory and demeaning. In addition, key elements of civil society relished the tribulations of African intellectuals. In Senegal the independent press spoke mockingly of *intellectuels en panne* (the breakdown of intellectuals), referring to the unceremonial withdrawal of intellectuals from public debates in the country. To add insult to injury, the 'masses' with whom intellectuals attempted to identify have tended to be indifferent to the latter's fate at the hands of the state. In some cases, such as Algeria, they were downright and murderously hostile.[23] The striking image of the African intellectual, then, is his/her marginality and disenfranchisement, a theme captured in much of African writing.[24]

The decade of extremes: renaissance or resignation?

The third phase was a decade of what Paul Zeleza describes as 'a period of bewildering extremes for Africa' (Zeleza 2003: 101). This was most dramatically illustrated by the fact that the two major news items on Africa in 1994 were the liberation of South Africa and the genocide in Rwanda. Africa's 'wave of democratization' rippled uneasily side by side with the more violent one of murderous rebel movements and the collapse of a number of states. Not surprisingly the repertoire of responses by African intellectuals was wide-ranging, including self-criticism, withdrawal, re-engagement in democratic politics, participation in tribalistic politics and joining the guerrillas.

Growing self-criticism There was a great deal of self-criticism among intellectuals. For some this self-criticism called for a re-engagement with society in the light of lessons learned; some were left unfazed by criticism and simply chose to serve whoever was in power or had money; still others withdrew into a kind of self-preoccupation and navel-gazing. The question of the relevance, appropriateness and meaningfulness of what they were producing touched a nerve among African scholars and was 'a source of considerable soul searching among the social science community' (Bujra 1994). African intellectuals have been under enormous pressure to 'account for themselves' (Mafeje 1993).

The first point of self-criticism was the lack of relevance of the institutions they inhabited or ran. Ali Mazrui has argued that:

The African university was conceived primarily as a transmission belt for Western high culture, rather than a workshop for the transfer of Western high skills. African universities became nurseries for a Westernised black intellectual aristocracy. Graduates of Ibadan, Dakar, Makerere acquired Western social tastes more readily than Western organization skills. Those graduates became steeped in Western consumption patterns rather than Western productive techniques. We became wordsmiths – and often despised blacksmiths! (Mazrui 1993: 119)

In a similar vein Mahmood Mamdani has articulated this concern thus:

In our single minded pursuit to create centres of learning and research of international standing, we had nurtured researchers and educators who had little capacity to work in surrounding communities but who could move to any institution in any industrialised country and serve any privileged community around the globe with comparative ease. In our failure to contextualise standards and excellence to the needs of our own people, to ground the very process and agenda of learning and research in our conditions, we ended up creating an intelligentsia with little stamina for the very process of development whose vanguard we claimed to be. Like birds who cross oceans when the weather turns adverse, we had little depth and grounding, but maximum reach and mobility. So that, when the going got rough, we got going across borders. (Mamdani 1993: 1,795)

As to the question of relevance, my own view is that if our research was 'irrelevant', it was not in terms of the simplistic 'basic' and 'applied' research dichotomy. It was, rather, at two other levels. One was the oppositional stance of most African intellectuals and their unwillingness to be 'usable' by some of the unsavoury regimes that littered the African continent. One simply did not want to be relevant to a Mobutu[25] or Banda. 'Relevance' would have been as good a case as any of 'adverse organicity'. Those of a more revolutionary temperament simply did not see any point in advising regimes that were doomed by history or by imminent revolution. In addition, repression bred alienation which, combined with Africans' visceral populism, in turn bred an oppositional stance towards government.

The second related to the quality of intellectual works themselves. Abiola Irele stated:

The moral indolence is matched by an intellectual indolence. Outside a few circles of writers and intellectuals, generally of radical persuasion – pools of light in a vast conceptual darkness – there is no sustained thought in

33

this country, no coherent intellectual, cultural, moral connection with any scheme of ideas, Western or African. The Israelites in exile singing of their unhappy lot likened the sky above them to a sheet of bronze over their heads. Matthew Arnold, in his *Culture and Anarchy*, made use of this biblical image to characterise the intellectual climate of Victorian England. Here, I am afraid the intellectual sky above us is made of gross material: it is not even bronze but wooden. (Irele 1992: 212)

A more serious problem was whether the basic research really addressed the key issues and whether, when it borrowed concepts, it was sufficiently sensitive to the specificities of our own conditions. Here I have my doubts.

Related to the question of quality was the idea of the originality of African intellectual endeavours. The analysis of Africa was dominated by others whose purposes in studying Africans were driven by their own concerns. Africans consequently ended up studying themselves as if they studied the 'other' – only in their case the 'other' was themselves.[26] Part of the self-criticism among African intellectuals has focused on this 'extroversion' and the fact that they had been too attentive to the intellectual fads of the West. Paulin Hountondji and Kwesi Prah accused African scholarship of mimetism of the worst kind (Hountondji 1992; Prah 1998). Kwesi Prah argues:

> For us who ... have the benefit of middle age and hindsight, we recognise that we have in our formation been subjected to successive intellectual fashions born in the west. The intellectual fads have affected successive generations of African intellectuals and shaped their thinking on Africa and the world, but have hardly provided viable inspirational or ideological sources for transformation which translate into the betterment of the quality of life of African humanity. (Prah 1998: 160)

A related criticism was something that was tantamount to treason. African intellectuals were accused of being no more than the 'informed native guide, the *comprador* in cultural commodities'. They were accused of being the 'Trojan Horse' of Western culture, 'a relay of cultural imperialism' (Verhaegen 1995), disseminating ideas that undermined or denigrated their own cultures. Thus Kwame Anthony Appiah (1992: 240) suggests that:

> Post-coloniality is the condition of what we may ungenerously call a *comprador* intelligentsia: of a relatively small, western-style, western-trained group of writers and thinkers, who mediate the trade in cultural commodities of world capitalism at the periphery. In the West they are known through the Africa they offer; their compatriots know them both through the West they present to Africa and through an Africa they have invented for the world, for each other and for Africa.

Another criticism has been of how 'state-centric' African intellectuals have been, i.e. their tendency to view the state as the motivational force of social change and development or to define themselves only in relationship to the state. Although such state-centricism can result in 'entryism', the view that one can influence the state by assuming some functions within it, this need not be the case.[27] Mamdani argues that 'one does not need be inside the state to articulate a statist conception' (1993: 254). Writing on Senegalese intellectuals vis-à-vis the state, Aminata Diaw (1993) accuses them of continuing to define themselves only in relation to the state or the political parties opposed to it. They have thus failed to create and manage the instruments of a genuine autonomy that might have ensured a participatory involvement with society commensurate with its stature. The absence of independent publishing or distribution endowed with financial resources from non-governmental sources, and the lack of research outfits with independent financial backing, also contributed to the atomization of the intelligentsia.

It is a fact that whether as duly invited luminaries or as rowdy gate-crashers, the country's intellectuals have been known to invade the political scene as idols or ideologues, technocrats or experts, critics or censors. They have always needed opposition to or collaboration with the regime as reference points and yardsticks for their own performance (Mamdani 1993: 318).

For some this raised serious questions about the integrity of African intellectuals and their relationship with the state. John Ihonvbere and Timothy Shaw (1998) capture this self-criticism:

> ... one tradition which has emerged in Nigeria is that there has always been a distinction between scholars' performances at the university service and when in government. While in the former, the Nigerian intellectuals have been known for their radical politics and relative forthrightness, honesty and insistence on accountability and justice. As part of the corporatist strategy, however, the government has increasingly picked on militant and vociferous intellectuals and appointed them to important political positions which is where such qualities previously associated with them evaporate. It is therefore appropriate, in some respects, to place the blame for the crisis of the Nigerian society on a section of the intellectual 'class'.

Jibrin Ibrahim raged against Nigerian political scientists for their sycophantic role and for serving as advisers to the military regime in its machinations against the democratization of Nigeria:

> Virtually all the antidemocratic measures were devised and implemented by leading members of the political science establishment recruited from

Nigerian universities. For all practical purposes, political scientists played the role of a competent technocracy that was a willing accomplice of the military in subverting the democratic struggles and aspirations of the people. Each blockage of democratic space, each device for defeating democratic forces, and every refusal to keep the schedule of power transfer to elected candidates, was vigorously defended by a coterie of political science professors working for the military dictatorship. (1997: 114)

In that they certainly bear responsibility for their stewardship of Babanginda's kleptocratic and anti-democratic politics, they have not lived up to the reputation they had previously built of responsible and respected professors of political science. Those professors of political science who designed a transition programme aimed at frustrating the democratic aspirations of Nigerian people, enabling President Ibrahim Babanginda to perpetuate his tyrannical and corrupt rule for eight years, have clearly betrayed the deontology that guides their discipline. They have consciously and actively schemed against the evolution of the good state and good governance in their country. They have used their skills to thwart popular demands for a genuine democratic pluralism in the country. The Nigerian people have suffered enormously under the policies that they have formulated and they bear responsibility for that (ibid.: 123).

A recent pillorying of the African intellectual comes from the right:

Throughout Africa's post-colonial history, the opportunism, unflappable sycophancy and trenchant collaboration have allowed tyranny to become entrenched. Doe, Mobutu, Mengistu and other military dictators legitimised their regimes by buying off and co-opting Africa's academics for a pittance ... Do Africa's intellectuals learn? Never ... Therefore whatever happens to Africa's intellectuals – whether at the hands of the military despots or their own people – shed no tears for them. Never. (Ayittey 1996: 35)[28]

And finally, it was suggested that, given their dependence on foreign funding, African intellectual work could not be expected to serve African interests. The late Bade Onimode stated this position most forcefully:

The imperialist funding of social science teaching, research and staff development in the Third World also imposes the same ideological and imperialist orientation and surveillance on peripheral social science scholarship. The issue here is more: 'who pays the piper, calls the tune'. This is how valuable energies of Third World scholars are diverted into the pursuit of false problems, the mystification of the realities of their countries, and the whims and caprices of imperialist foundations and other research grant donors. True enough, the recipient institutions and scholars should be able to define their own academic priorities, but the problems are that some of the foreign grants are project-tied 'aid' (in reality subsidies for donor countries' exports), while the pro-imperialist orientation of peripheral social scientists ensures that their most irrelevant and obscurantist projects may be funded from abroad in the symbiotic relationship between comprador scholars and imperialist donors. This is how the system of imperialist intermediary in the larger neocolonial economy and society is reproduced in the intellectual sphere. (Onimode 1988: 36)

And still others have decried the distance and oppositional stance of African intellectuals. Archie Mafeje has suggested that the failure to join the political class may have something 'to do with the self-image of African scholars in contrast to their Latin American counterparts, some of whom are part of the "political class"'. Unfortunately he does not elaborate this point, although one can interpret him as saying that if one has strong views about a policy issue, then one should get into the political act.[29]

There are also those who have criticized African scholarship for its obsession with development. In the more solipsistic renditions of all this, the reality of poverty and underdevelopment are occulted so that the validity of debates on development is determined entirely at the level of discourse, with some boldly proclaiming that in Africa, we have, unbeknownst to ourselves, entered a post-developmentalist era, where we can now frolic in our myriad identities and hybridity, without the nagging narratives of poverty, ignorance and disease.[30] This view was given credence by the prosperity of the advanced capitalist countries. Critics of Western materialism sometimes suggested that economic development would simply bring down doom on Africans. Comfortably ensconced in the material accoutrements of modernity, these preachers seem to suggest that other mortal souls would simply go under were they to attain anything close to their material lifestyles. They would somehow lose the virtues 'of simplicity and conviviality, of noble forms of poverty, of the wisdom of relying on each other, and of the arts of suffering' (Rahnema 1997: x).

Others of a more nihilistic inclination attacked African scholars for having been engaged in the process of nation-building and development. In a number of cases, intellectuals now inveigh against the stultifying nationalist ideology. In extreme cases, they go as far as rejecting the nation-building and development project. In these 'second thoughts' on nationalism, some have sought to co-opt Fanon to the project. But Fanon's critique of 'bourgeois nationalism' is itself delivered from an alternative nationalist standpoint. Fanon's criticism of nationalism never degenerated into the kind of ontological pessimism akin to the Afropessimism of the 1990s.

37

Others criticized African scholarship for its combativeness and for its 'victimology'. This position was articulated most eloquently by Achilles Mbembe. Mbembe took what Paul Ricoeur has called 'the hermeneutics of suspicion' – the idea that every grand theory and noble sentiment hides a base motive – to extremes. Convinced that the African intellectual project is exclusively one of self-pity, he read any narrative of protest along these lines. His casual mode of allusion to the writings of others allows him the possibility of never describing in enough detail what individual scholars have actually said. Mbembe is not bothered by any distinction between 'genesis' and 'validity', and so he relies heavily on *ad hominem* arguments, the clanking of theoretical armour and an obscurantism that is de rigueur.[31]

Indeed, the call was for the defenestration of anything that might be considered nationalistic or populist. Those who saw themselves as cosmopolitan accused African scholars of provincialism and nativism, insisting, as Benedict Anderson suggested they might, on 'the near-pathological character of nationalism, its roots in fear and hatred of the Other, and its affinities with racism'. The arguments that Africa's recent past and current dependence might have anything to do with the present conditions were met with the kind of eye-rolling impatience with which committed postmodernists treat people who still fail to understand that history has come to an end and so has struggle. Africans were urged to stop harping about the past and forge ahead towards a brave new world which is well within their grasp if they only let go of their anti-imperialism, their critiques of the endless external impositions on Africa, and so on. In trying to demonstrate that any protest from the victim was simply evidence of 'victimism', some easily moved to the extreme of justifying victimization itself. For some of these writers, being African bordered on an ontological tragedy that condemned Africans to whining and self-pity. Any invocation of their identity was simply reification of their origins, being and locality – a nativism of the worst kind – and any call for joint action was racist and exclusivistic.

My response to this is that while this self-criticism is a healthy antidote to any complacency we may have been lulled into, some of it borders on self-flagellation. Understandable though some of the anger and frustration may be, it does considerable injustice to the record of African intellectuals. First, it generalizes too much. Second, I doubt that African intellectuals have been that silent. I tend to agree with Mafeje's assertion that 'by any standard African intellectuals have not been that silent, submissive or subservient: if anything, the likelihood is that they talked too much too soon'.[32] One should also bear in mind that, as national intellectual spaces were squeezed by the state, African intellectuals actively sought to create new regional or continental spaces through which they could find a voice.

Given the extremely meagre resources and limited political spaces, African intellectuals have been quite productive. It is true that many of their insights were ignored or repackaged and resold as foreign technical assistance. But if the rulers did not pay attention, the blame cannot entirely be placed on the intellectuals. And over the years they have persistently raised questions about national sovereignty, development, the legitimacy of power, equity and democratization. Indeed, in many cases they have been the only ones who have kept all these issues on the agenda. The frustrating experience in Africa is that African governments often paid dearly for advice from foreigners that was common knowledge in African intellectual circles. Just look at the fortune being made by 'good governance' experts.

I also doubt that African intellectuals have been as aloof and detached as is often suggested. The variegated range of dictators that tormented Africa simply left no room for the growth of intellectuals occupying public space.[33] Many spaces that were open (at least theoretically) to intellectuals elsewhere were either erased, infested or occupied, sometimes physically, so that no 'ivory towers' or 'Olympian detachment' or 'self-imposed' marginalization was a meaningful option. Such were the constraints that in most cases the choice was between exile, sullen self-effacement and invisibility, or sycophantic and fawning adulation of power. There were, however, many who heroically chose the option of standing up and fighting, and often ended up in jail or dead.

To be sure, there are cases of resignation and escapism into 'fashionable nonsense' to borrow Alan Sokal and Jean Brichmont's characterization of some of the postmodernist writing (Sokal and Brichmont 1998). This posture was given intellectual respectability by the Foucaultian tragic view that we are all slaves of an all-pervasive structure of power which can sustain only a limited range of meaningful action. This view authorized disengagement and moral irresponsibility. Those who chose this path contented themselves with simply condemning the activism that has been quite strong in African intellectual circles. For some this requires a rejection of the validity of social analysis itself. Instead of social and historical analysis, we were now bombarded by new high-concept abstractiveness which often concealed an essentially vacuous social analysis – social poetry riding on a series of untestable hypotheses sustained by a cascade of false paradoxes. If an earlier generation of African scholars was stifled by the obsession with the nationalist project, or by the revolutionary oppositional stance that refused to propose anything before everything else had been challenged, the new generation of African intellectuals runs the risk of operating under the paralysing auspices of 'post-colonial' pessimism, which suggests that, everything being contingent, there are no more grounds for action. Fortunately these kinds of intellectuals are few, but unfortunately, as often happens, the ideas and moods informed by a passing fad in the 'centre' have found much more zealous adherents in the periphery.

Of those who seem to suggest we have passed through 'development' and entered 'post-developmentalism' without our knowing it, I can say only that their views, when imported into the contexts of extreme material deprivation, sound like a cruel joke. We must remember that for those in developed countries, rejection of material progress and prosperity (most of which is never more than rhetorical) is a matter of choice and discretion. It is more like choosing to fast. In Africa, it would be at best making virtue out of necessity, or like trying to find the moral equivalence of starvation and fasting.[34] Although fasting and starvation may involve similar nutritional processes (eating less) yielding identical biological outcomes (loss of weight), they are entirely different social processes.

The turning away from the material side of life towards verbal and symbolic politics was accompanied by a disdainful abstractness and lofty obscurity that masqueraded as social science. From the heights of high bourgeois living and the surfeit of the new affluence, it is easy to be contemptuous of such modest demands as better schools and health. Against the pronouncements of a post-history of bliss in which the multiplicity of identities and fluidity of class and national identities flourished, African intellectuals had to relate to a world rooted in the conflict of states and peoples. This was the period of structural adjustment programmes (SAPs), unrestrained violation of human rights, famines and AIDS. It would be rather awkward, if not morally reprehensible, to find oneself with little or nothing to say about such fundamental issues.

Reading some of the recent descriptions of the development débâcle, you could be forgiven for believing that the whole thing was a 'discourse' that took place in Northern capitals or aid missions with some spillover to an African intelligentsia who drew inspiration and ideas uncritically. In most cases this has involved well-meaning paternalism, which invariably fails to take African agency in the development saga seriously, or is a reflection of the ignorance of how 'development' entered our respective national agendas. However well intentioned some of the forewarnings of the dangers of prosperity and consumerism, and of the 'Faustian bargain' that development entails, they often ring hollow as nostalgic paeans to a past and living conditions that none of these 'advocates of post-developmentalism' would seek for themselves. Given Africa's history, much of the current 'anti-developmental' discourse is tantamount to a call for unilateral disarmament, and as such it remains suspect.

All this advice to let go of the past may be sensible. 'But', to quote

Martin Hopenhayn (2002), 'the form in which forgetting tends to be invoked these days in the wake of its invitation to plasticity and liberty, reeks of the consecration of injustice.' It also distracts attention from many unresolved issues in Africa – poverty, violations of human rights, growing inequality and foreign domination. Fortunately African intellectuals have been too immersed in the real-life situation of the post-colony to allow themselves the self-inflicted angst of postmodernism. Many would probably ask the same questions as Ato Quayson:

> What, for instance, is the use of discursive analysis of the language of the IMF's economic recovery packages when this does not address the terrible economic and social disjunctures produced in developing countries by the application of IMF policies and those of other international monetary agencies? ... What, to follow E. San Juan's anguished queries of post-colonial critics, is the use of undermining discourses of power when we never encounter any specific scenario of injustice, domination or actual resistance from which we may gather intimations of the passage through the 'post-colonial' order? What to put it bluntly and even simplistically do academic post-colonial studies contribute to the experience of post-colonialism in the world today? (Cited in Quayson 2000: 8)

Taken seriously, the nihilistic posture informing this criticism would have undermined the strong humanistic concerns that have sustained African scholarship all these years. I am, however, consoled by the knowledge that most African social scientists still possess enough sense to see that poverty is far from being an endangered species and still roams Africa unchallenged by the vast human knowledge, social skills and experience of its populations. I am inclined to share Abiola Irele's impassioned call for the revitalization of our intellectual endeavours and a recommitment to what he calls the 'modernity project':

> But it is time to shove off dejection and all the other disabling emotions, and begin to work diligently to put our house in order. We must look around us and take to heart the sneers, the put-downs, the insults, the condescension and the contempt of our detractors, respond to them as spurs to renewed commitment to the welfare of our continent. The signs are there that the tide may be turning for the better in Africa. Despite the vicissitudes it has gone through, the partial successes and the frustrations it has known, the democratisation movement that has been making its way through the continent since the early nineties attests to a new impulse for reform. This suggests a groundswell moving Africa towards a new internal order. It is essential that this new order be marked by a reprise of the modernity project. (Irele 2000)

41

To conclude, the problem with the relationship between intellectuals and the state was not so much that of corruption or aloofness or even irrelevance but of an unrequited love for the 'Prince' – the state – which African intellectuals generally felt constituted the major instrument for development and nation-building. Much of the distance between the African intellectual and the politician did not come about by choice. The instinctive position of African intellectuals was in a sense to be 'organic' to the national movement and to submit their intellectual values to the nationalist project. If they were naïve at all, it was in the belief that they would directly or even individually influence policy without any mediation or support from social movements.

Protest and self-organization We noted that for much of the post-independence period, African intellectuals had acquiesced in the nationalist project and had in many cases failed to insist on the importance of intellectual freedom. By the end of the 1980s, African scholars' organizations began to speak openly against the suppression of academic freedom – a process that culminated in the Kampala Declaration on Academic Freedom that was adopted at a major conference organized by CODESRIA in 1990. Significantly, the decision to organize the conference was reached before the wave of democratization in many countries. It is also significant that the question of democracy was back on the intellectual agenda. Some argued for democracy in essentially instrumentalist terms, suggesting that it would lead to better performance; others argued that democracy was intrinsically good and should be defended on these grounds. There were questions about the meaning of democracy, the adequacy of liberal democracy to the African situation and crisis, and the relationship of democracy to the economic liberalism that was being imposed on African economies.[35] There was a return by many intellectuals to politics either through more active participation in political parties or through other advocacy movements.

By the 1990s, there was a major shift in the conditions and responses of the intellectuals. First, there was the growing 'compradorization' of the intellectual enterprise which came with the greater compradorization of the economy.[36] Nationalist developmentalist strategies had been finally defeated as economies were privatized, opened and generally conditioned by policy initiatives from outside the continent. Compradorization of the intellectual exercise was the result of the dramatic rise of the consultancy industry and the contract research it spawned. There was now a new wave of African professions closely linked with the need for greater control of development by the aid establishment and its insatiable quest for feasibility studies, evaluations and 'rapid assessment' results. Professionalization of intellectual life was thus due not to the munificence of African states but to the contracts from foreign governments and NGOs (Bangura 1994; Mkandawire 1998). African governments could access their own intellectuals only through donor-contracted reports. This should not be interpreted as suggesting that African intellectuals were close to the foreign 'prince'. Donors themselves usually exhibited ill-disguised contempt for local intellectuals, whom they saw as either mercenary or as people who criticized them but offered no alternatives, or were part of the rent-seeking or clientelist cliques that had benefited from past policies, which meant that their opposition to 'reform' was self-serving. With such a view of local capacities, donors were to embark on the unending task of 'capacity-building' aimed at producing a cadre well versed in whatever donors thought was necessary knowledge.

African intellectuals are today much freer than they have ever been since independence. The sullen silence of the 1980s was broken by the emergence of the movement for democratization. This also marked a growing self-consciousness of intellectuals as a social group, with rights and responsibilities. Academics themselves had been quick to clamour for academic freedom.[37] Once again, we see African intellectuals adopting a self-consciously public position on national issues. But they work under incredible conditions. They are probably much less 'organic' to the current project of reintegrating African economies through structural adjustment, dependent as it is on global technocrats. African intellectuals have emerged from the débâcle of authoritarian rule much less tarnished by involvement with the oppressor than, say, the Japanese intellectuals were with the fascist regime. They thus have the opportunity of moving away from a focus on the state to engage other social actors who have been unleashed by both the political and the economic liberalization. In a sense our 'irrelevance' saved our skins since we emerged from the débâcle of the 1980s with our hands relatively clean, a fact demonstrated by the role given to intellectuals in national conventions and other democratic happenings of the 1990s.

The new cartography of African intellectual endeavours is such that a distressingly large number of African intellectuals form part of a diaspora. Many still maintain deep emotional and intellectual commitments to Africa. There are, however, no structures within Africa to exploit their conscious or obvious desire to be useful. Mamdani has commented on the extremely important contribution of Africa's Creoles and diaspora to pan-Africanism and African intellectual work in general (Mamdani 1999). The argument seems to be that their alien status has given them unique insight and driven their pan-Africanism. There is another side to this status, however: it may also have created a distance that distorted what

43

they saw, or prevented them from seeing certain things. The result could easily be frustration, or the narcissism and self-defensiveness that come with nostalgia and in the sadder cases of self-deprecation. This sociological character of African intellectuals – exile, racial and ethnic minority – could also lead to tone-deafness to various localisms, including nationalism. In addition, the privileging of the intellectual expressions of the diaspora could mute the voices in the periphery and render them neutral by simply positing them as part of the hybridity. We still need to know more about the implications of the cartography.[38]

The new agenda?

Bringing democracy back in By the mid-1980s, there was a trend towards a greater focus on the problems of democratization. A number of factors accounted for this. The first was the deepening economic crisis and the imposition by the BWIs of an adjustment process which was not only inequitable but that was widely perceived as non-developmental. The model of adjustment was also politically associated with authoritarian rule. A second fact was the realization in African intellectual circles that what was wrong with African economies was not 'market distortions', as the folks from Washington tended to argue, but state–society relations or 'governance'.[39] The World Bank's problem with the African-inspired debate on governance was that it did not leave much room for the bank. Its insistence on the importance of local initiatives, political accountability to citizens and the reconciliation of African traditions and institutions with 'modern' traditions and institutions are not exactly the types of issue the World Bank can relate to in a quantifiable and practical manner. It is significant that the World Bank's concern with governance was influenced by African scholars. From this concern with state–society relations and resistance to foreign domination arose the interest in democratization – a concern signalled by the activities of two of the major social science networks in Africa: CODESRIA and the Third World Forum. Both embarked on research or instituted social movements for democracy, which suggested that the forces for democratization would be internal. It is significant that this upsurge of interest in democratization took place at the time when Africanist research was mired in an Afropessimism that essentially saw no internal sources of change within Africa.

Development once again Through all the twists and turns, development still remains on the agenda and is part of African debates on democracy. Anyang' Nyongo's defence of democracy (1988) was on the grounds that it would lead to better governance and more development. Even those who objected to this instrumentalization of democracy admitted that it would be worthwhile exploring the possibilities of a process in which democracy and development were not only synergetic but also mutually constitutive. Increasingly, there were attempts to explore 'democratic developmental states', especially in the light of the failure of new democracies to escape the deflationary vice of the BWIs (Ake 1996; Mkandawire 1995). There were, of course, those who rejected the whole idea of 'development'. Much of this rejection was informed by postmodernism and has reached Africa largely via African scholars in the diaspora and South African (mostly white) scholars. Francophone African scholars have also played a leading role here, partly because economics has rarely dominated the discourse on development in their circles, as it has in anglophone intellectual circles. Some elements of the ecological critique have also entered African discourse, questioning the replicability of the Western model, especially with respect to environmental sustainability. This has not had much resonance in African intellectual circles, however, in which concerns with intra-temporal distribution issues (North–South issues) overwhelmingly exceed the inter-temporal, inter-generational concerns that dominate Western discourse on the environment.

Nation-building once again One of the paradoxes of recent years is that theories of dependence lost their intellectual supremacy at precisely the time when African economies were entering a phase of greater foreign control than ever before since their independence. 'Conditionalities' basically dictated African economic policy; the debt noose was being drawn tighter for economies whose growth was now anaemic. There were more 'experts' in Africa than there had ever been under colonial rule. 'Anti-imperialism' had lost its purchase, especially among the 'third generation', who had experienced Africa's decline under African rule. They were simply not going to buy the 'foreign domination' argument. And in any case the heroic epoch was too far in the past to have any resonance among this generation. Furthermore, the obviously egregious mismanagement of national affairs meant that there was considerable room for domestic reform, even in the face of a hostile external environment.

Lessons from the so-called 'failed states' of Sierra Leone, Liberia and Somalia are important reminders that the nation-building project was and still is a vital one for Africa, and that it is, therefore, something on which African scholarship must still expend resources. It is by critically revisiting issues of nation-building, pan-Africanism, development and democracy that we will be able to address the main issues that devastate the lives of so many of us – poverty, wars, repression. Obviously the premises and

45

reasons for revisiting these issues need not be the same as those of the 'founding fathers'.

In more recent years, there has been a call for an 'African renaissance'. As Mamdani has argued, there can be no renaissance without an intelligentsia to drive it. Such an African renaissance requires an Africa-focused intelligentsia. This will also demand a major rethink by both the political actors and the intelligentsia of the relationship between them.

Conclusion

The nationalist modernity project is inherently fraught with dilemmas that require careful and constant attention. The critical intellectual task is not to simply state this rather banal fact but to engage society in acknowledging and addressing (without necessarily eliminating) such dilemmas. The dilemmas include those of individual or local rights and national sovereignty; the conflict between the particularism of nationalism and the universalism of its aspirations; the thin line between unity and uniformity; and cultural homogeneity and provincialism; the trade-offs in the development process. Every case of nation-building has had to address these questions.

We have a moral obligation to ourselves and to humanity to put our house in order and to think ourselves out of our current predicament. The construction of a democratic, developmental and socially inclusive social order has become a moral imperative and a question of survival in Africa. This is a project that will tax our collective moral, material and physical strength.

Like all communities of intellectuals, African intellectuals will not always be able to resist the contingent and transitory call of passing fads, material detractions and mystification. I believe that the African intellectual must continue to be, in the words of Wole Soyinka, an 'author of the language that tries to speak truth to power'. One can only hope that this time around both state and society will realize that an unfettered intellectual class is an emancipatory force that can be put to good use.

Notes

1 This is a significantly revised version of a lecture I gave in Australia. A day before the death of Julius Nyerere I received a reminder from the organizers of this conference to submit the topic of my keynote address. I settled on this topic because I thought I could use the sad occasion of the death of this extremely decent African nationalist to reflect on the turbulent link between African nationalism, African intellectuals and the academic community. Nyerere was also interesting as a prop to my lecture because he was one of the few African nationalists who straddled the two worlds of thought and action,

not only by providing leadership to nationalist movements but also by articulating both their ideologies and their visions. The other leaders in the same category would be Léopold Senghor and Kwame Nkrumah.

2 Throughout this text I use post-colonial only in its purely chronological sense, without suggesting any socio-philosophical condition, let alone psychological mood.

3 It is interesting to note that, for example, 'post-independence' intellectuals would be defined differently in a country such as Ethiopia. See, for instance, the periodization of intellectuals in twentieth-century Ethiopia (Zewede 1994).

4 One should point out that although the new critics seem to act as if they are really on to something new, the exposure of nationalists as the new emperor without clothes is, of course, not new. By the 1960s our writers had already embarked on the demolition job; for example, see Chinua Achebe's *Man of the People*, or Ayi Kwei Armah's *The Beautiful Ones are not Yet Born*. See also Mnthali (1988).

5 Ali Mazrui ('Decaying Parts of Africa Need Benign Colonization', *International Herald Tribune*, Paris, 1994), provoked a storm when he suggested that recolonization would provide a solution. His choice of words was unfortunate and his schemes rather hare-brained. Pushed to explain himself, he backtracked and argued that what he was promoting was a kind of 'Pax Africana', an idea that goes at least as far back as Nkrumah, in which Africans could set up arrangements for common security. The issue was a distinction between 'state security' and 'human security'.

6 William Byden, cited in Mudimbe (1988).

7 I borrow these two expressions from the title of Jared Diamond's book (1997).

8 'On the one hand commitment to and on the other taking exclusive charge of, the construction of Africa'.

9 'I leave for Guinea at the beginning of next week in the company of Abdou Moumouni, Joseph Ki-Zerbo and four other African professors. As I have written earlier, those who aspire to be intellectuals should not be content with pious wishes and declarations of intent, but give to their writing a concrete end.'

10 This prompted the Malawian writer, Felix Mnthali, to wonder 'whether the Africans on the spaceships would go as shuttle commanders, first engineers, mere cooks or glorified messengers' (Mnthali n.d.).

11 Léopold Senghor tried after the 1968 student revolt. The state launched a programme of intellectual recruitment to recover the lost space. The Nation and Development Club, open to people outside the ruling party, was set up. Mamdou Diouf notes that in the view of the new generation of ruling party intellectuals, 'the key failing of the post-colonial compromise was its reliance on "the politics of mere politicians". Their proffered solution was the creation of a new legitimacy on the basis of technocratic nationalism.'

12 See, for instance, the account in Sand (1997).

13 Algerian intellectuals have paid a heavy price for the divisions along francophone and arabophone lines and for the inclusion of the one and the exclusion of the other.

14 Claude Ake's observation on the importance of knowledge in the development process is apt: 'Development requires changes on a revolutionary scale; it is in every sense a heroic enterprise calling for consummate confidence. It is not for people who do not know who they are and where they are coming from, for such people are unlikely to know where they are going' (1996: 16).

15 One reason could have been fear of voicing criticism, but it would also have been due to the sense of helplessness as one's village was being experimented upon and one's intellectual mentors cheered the exercise or criticized it for not being radical enough and failing to 'capture' the peasantry. What was one to say when, after all the disruption and the forced villagization, someone argued that the peasants were still 'uncaptured'? I do not deny here that some indigenous 'modernizers' with Stalinist inclinations may have seen all this as the price to pay for the process. Rather, I am suggesting that for many Tanzanian scholars the process was too close to home for comfort.

16 One remarkable fact is that while African scholars distanced themselves from the state and were encouraged to do so by their foreign colleagues or mentors, quite a number of the latter were themselves advisers or counsellors to neo-colonial powers. While deploring nationalism in African scholarship, these scholars were Gaullist in their perception of the world. To be sure, the Africanists were confronted with an intellectual incomprehension on the part of the state officials dealing with Africa, who apparently had no use for Africanist studies. Jean Copans' account of the role of the Africanists who accepted the role of 'conseiller de prince' is quite illuminating in this sense, although he conveniently avoids examining the implications of this position. To be sure, there was some soul-searching, especially in the United States, where the CIA was quite active and had surreptitiously funded cultural and intellectual activities in Africa – the case of Transition being the most notorious.

17 Jibril Ibrahim was to cause an outcry when he suggested that African intellectual 'icons' had not shown much enthusiasm for democracy. As Archie Mafeje clearly suggested, the issue was not 'democracy' per se but the capacity of liberal democracy to deliver on such issues as distribution and equity (Mafeje 1993).

18 The strength of the position comes out sharply in the responses to my claim that democracy has intrinsic value and that support for it need not be confined to its instrumentalist facilitation of economic development, as Peter Anyang Nyongo had suggested.

19 There has been a considerable amount of soul-searching on the 'impasse' of development. Much of this is written from the perspectives of the 'development industry' and aid establishment abroad. African thinking and intellectual moods are rarely considered in such debates. For some of the interesting readings on this see Booth (1994), Munck (1986) and Schuurman (1993). Some have, of course, gone so far as to declare development studies 'dead', and have proceeded to a 'post-development' phase. See for instance Rahnema (1997) and Sachs (1992).

20 This they have done by looking for both internal and external reasons for the failure. Contrary to the caricature of the African discourse, it has never

been exclusively internalist in its critique. African writers began complaining about problems of corruption, waste and mismanagement long before it became fashionable in the donor community to talk about these things.

21 The single most important manifestation was the symposium on Academic Freedom organized by CODESRIA in Kampala in 1990. One important outcome of the conference was the 'Kampala Declaration on Intellectual Freedom and Social Responsibility'.

22 Claude Ake, who had earlier accused African leaders of 'developmentalism', ended up arguing that 'the problem is not so much that development has failed as that it was never really on the agenda' (Ake 1996). It was a position Archie Mafeje (1997) believes can be challenged for being an 'overstatement'.

23 See especially el Kenz's account (1996) of the 'baffling' and devastating realization by Algerian intellectuals that not only were they not organic to the state but that the people they had considered friends had now turned into mortal enemies; and of the cultural hegemonic struggles into which intellectuals have been often violently drawn.

24 See Mnthali (1988). He concludes his article by noting that the characters to whom various African writers assign the role of intellectuals 'have common traits which have made their role in Africa somewhat marginal'. He then adds, 'Perhaps this marginality has contributed to Africa's crisis. Perhaps' (p. 31).

25 V. V. Mudimbe is reported to have fled Zaire after having refused a seat on the central committee of Mobutu's ruling party.

26 It is interesting to compare this with how the Japanese have 'read' the West. As an example, among Japanese economists Marx, Schumpeter, List and Keynes were viewed as outstanding theoreticians of change in the West. The Japanese read these texts with a decidedly 'nationalist' twist. If concentration of capital were crucial to imperialism, then concentration of capital in Japan would be crucial both for blocking the colonization of Japan and eventually for its own imperial ambitions. If capitalism could generate class conflict, then 'nationalism' had to be used to undermine class conflict. These texts appeared to make it clear that national competitiveness could not be assured by free markets. These might lead to an efficient but colonized nation, which could not resist the thrust of the monopolies from abroad. One consequence of this was that Japanese industrial policy encouraged the Zaibatsus as a way not only of organizing industrial activities but also as a means of enhancing Japanese competitiveness. If competition could be both destructive and constructive, it was necessary to reduce the former qualities and encourage the latter by avoiding 'excessive competition' (Gao 1997). Of course this reading also suggested the intimate relationship between intellectuals and the Establishment.

27 In a rather enigmatic comment Archie Mafeje seemed puzzled by Claude Ake's not seeking some post in intra-African organizations, given his strong views on the Lagos Plan of Action.

28 Ayittey has been closely associated with some of the most rabidly right-wing think tanks in the United States and is likely to be hostile to African intellectuals for their largely progressive and humanistic positions.

29 Mafeje makes this comment in a review of Claude Ake's book (Ake

49

1996). He states: 'Claude Ake narrates the unfolding drama, blackmail, capitulation, and the ultimate defeat of the impecunious Africans with such intensity, unrelenting persistence, and dark anger that one wonders why he never made a bid for high office in the relevant intra-African political structures. Has the failure anything to do with the self-image of African scholars in contrast to their Latin American counterparts, some of whom are part of the "political class"?' (Mafeje 1997: 82).

30 This is not idle speculation. One observer of a CODESRIA symposium on globalization noted: 'It was also surprising that the symposium did not engage some of the most pressing problems facing the continent, such as the numerous wars, the alarming increase in poverty, ethnic conflicts, the problems posed by Islamic fundamentalism, the continued pervasiveness of undemocratic regimes, the growing prevalence of homophobia and xenophobia. Questions about relevance and utility of Africa social science can only properly be answered if the real problems confronting Africa become focal points of analysis.' One shares Takaki's concerns that a political economy of development will be sacrificed to 'scholarly representations of other scholarly representations of original representations – feasts of intellectual delights detached from the reality of poverty, racism, greed, theft, chicanery and exploitation'. R. Takaki (1995) 'Culture Wars in the United States: Closing Reflections on the Century of the Colour Line', in J. N. Pieterse and B. Pakesh (eds), *The Decolonisation of the Imagination: Culture, Knowledge and Power*, London: Zed Books.

31 Mbembe's analysis was too choked with rancour to achieve its lofty ambitions, whatever these were.

32 Mafeje attributes their lack of inhibition or reserve to the fact that they were part of the dominant African elite. There, 'at the beginning they felt no need to be submissive or subservient to anybody'. Such a state did not, of course, last long.

33 For problems of academic freedom in Africa see Africa Watch (1991), CODESRIA (1996), Diouf and Mamdani (1983) and Mkandawire (1996).

34 Or as Dennis Ekpo forcefully argued (1995), 'nothing stops the African from viewing the celebrated postmodern condition ... as nothing but the hypocritical self-flattering cry of overfed and spoilt children of hypercapitalism. So what has hungry Africa got to do with the post-material disgust ... of the bored and the overfed?'

35 For a good review of the literature, see Buijtenhuijs and Thiriot (1995).

36 Francis Njubi, a keen observer of Africa's intellectual diaspora, has written trenchantly on this new breed of 'intellectual compradors' (2002): 'Members of the comprador class use their national origins, colour and education to serve as spokesmen and intellectual henchmen for organizations such as the World Bank and International Monetary Fund. They serve as the sweetener that makes it easier for African countries to swallow the bitter pills of illegitimate debt and structural adjustment. Although some of them work directly for the international financial institutions, most continue to teach at colleges and universities in the West while serving as "consultants" to international financial institutions. They receive lucrative contracts for research and development

that serve a dual purpose: putting a human (black) face on international capital while forcing client states to accept draconian conditions that amount to debt peonage.'

37 See, for instance, the papers in Diouf and Mamdani (1983), and especially the Kampala Declaration on Academic Freedom, which is reproduced as an appendix in the book.

38 Work is beginning on Africa's intellectual diaspora but much of it remains rather tentative. See, for instance, Gueye (2001), Njubi (2002) and Zeleza (1998).

39 Among the Africans at the World Bank were Mamadou Dia and Dunstan Wai. Among contributors to the background documents were Claude Ake, George Ayittey, Makhtar Diouf and Balghia Badri. The World Bank acknowledged their contributions thus: 'The World Bank's Long-Term Perspectives Study (LTPS) on Sub-Saharan Africa introduced an additional dimension when it explicitly considered noneconomic issues in its analysis of the continent's present crisis and prospects for growth into the next century. Consideration of these aspects was very much a result of the collaborative approach adopted early in the preparation of this report. In the process, it became clear that any assessment of the region's performance in the past and directions for the future would have to be informed by issues that cut across various disciplines to include history, culture, politics, and the very ethos of Africa. By listening to the report's African and other collaborators, it was evident that a report with a scope such as that of the LTPS could no longer evade these issues. These collaborators greatly strengthened that ability of the LTPS to address, if not authoritatively, at least in a well-informed manner, the deep-seated concerns that ultimately shape and direct the course of economic growth and development. The ten papers presented in this third volume of the LTPS Background Papers contain some of those invaluable contributions' (Ahmed 1990: 1).

References

Africa Watch (1991) *Academic Freedom and Human Rights Abuses in Africa*, New York: Human Rights Watch

Ahmed, Z. (1990) 'Introduction', in *The Long-term Perspective Study of Sub-Saharan Africa: Institutional and Sociopolitical Issues*, Washington, DC: World Bank

Ake, C. (1979) 'Ideology and Objective Conditions', in J. Barkan and J. Okumu (eds), *Politics and Public Policy in Kenya and Tanzania*, Nairobi: Heinemann, pp. 117–28

— (1993) 'Academic Freedom and Material Base', in M. Diouf and M. Mamdani (eds), *Academic Freedom in Africa*, Dakar: CODESRIA

— (1996) *Democracy and Development in Africa*, Washington, DC: The Brookings Institution

Amin, S. (1990) 'The Social Movements in the Periphery: An End to National Liberation?', in S. Amin, G. Arrighi and E. Wallerstein (eds), *Transforming Revolution: Social Movement and the World-System*, New York: Monthly Review Press

Anderson, B. (1983) *Imagined Communities*, London: Verso

Anyang' Nyongo, P. (1988) 'Political Instability and the Prospects for Democracy in Africa', *Africa Development*, VIII: 1

Appiah, K. A. (1992) *My Father's House: Africa in the Philosophy of Culture*, London: Methuen

Ayittey, G. (1996) 'No Tears for Africa's Intellectuals', *New African*

Bangura, Y. (1994) 'Intellectuals, Economic Reform and Social Change: Constraints and Opportunities in the Formations of a Nigerian Technocracy', Dakar: CODESRIA

Booth, D. (ed.) (1994) *Rethinking Social Development: Theory, Research and Practice*, London: Longman

Buijtenhuijs, R. and C. Thiriot (1995) *Democratisation in Sub-Saharan Africa, 1992–1995: A Review of the Literature*, Leiden: African Studies Centre

Bujra, A. (1994) 'Whither Social Institutions in Africa? A Prognosis', *Africa Development*, XIX(1): 119–66

Chinweizu, O. J. (1975) *The West and the Rest of Us: White Predators, Black Slavers and the African Elite*, New York: Vintage Books

Cocks, J. (1991) 'Passion and Paradox: Intellectuals Confront the National Question', Princeton, NJ: Princeton University Press

CODESRIA (ed.) (1996) *The State of Academic Freedom in Africa*, Dakar: CODESRIA

Connell, D. and F. Smyth (1998) 'Africa's New Bloc', *Foreign Affairs*, March/April, pp. 80–94

Davidson, B. (1992) 'The Black Man's Burden', London: James Currey

Diamond, J. (1997) *Guns, Germs, and Steel*, New York: Norton

Diaw, A. (1993) 'Democracy of the Literati', in M. Diop (ed.), *Senegal: Essays in Statecraft*, Dakar: CODESRIA, pp. 221–68

Diouf, M. (1993) 'Intellectuals and the State in Senegal: The Search for a Paradigm', in M. Diouf and M. Mamdani (eds), *Academic Freedom in Africa*, Dakar: CODESRIA, pp. 212–46

Diouf, M. and M. Mamdani (eds) (1983) *Academic Freedom in Africa*, Dakar: CODESRIA

Ekpo, D. (1995) 'Towards a Post-Africanism', *Textual Practice*, 9(1)

El Kenz, A. (1996) 'Algeria from Development Hope to Identity Violence', in CODESRIA (ed.), *The State of Academic Freedom in Africa*, Dakar: CODESRIA, pp. 45–55

Fanon, F. (1966) *The Wretched of the Earth*, New York: Grove Press

Gao, B. (1997) *Economic Ideology and Japanese Industrial Policy: Developmentalism from 1931 to 1965*, Cambridge University Press

Gellner, E. (1983) *Nations and Nationalism*, Oxford University Press

Gueye, A. (2001) *Les intellectuals africains en France*, Paris: L'Harmattan

Hagan, G. (1993) 'Academic Freedom and National Responsibility in an African State', in M. Diouf and M. Mamdani (eds), *Academic Freedom in Africa*, Dakar: CODESRIA

Hansen, E. (1976) *Frantz Fanon: Social and Political Thought*, Columbus, OH: Ohio State University

Hopenhayn, M. (2002) *No Apocalypse, No Integration: Modernism and Postmodernism in Latin America*, Durham, NC: Duke University Press

Hountondji, P. (1992) 'Recapturing', in E. Mudimbe (ed.), *The Surreptitious Speech: Présence Africaine and the Politics of Otherness 1947–1987*, University of Chicago Press, pp. 238–42

Ibrahim, J. (1997) 'Political Scientists and the Subversion of Democracy in Nigeria', in G. Nzongola-Ntalaja and M. C. Lee (eds), *The State and Democracy in Africa*, Harare: AAPS Books, pp. 114–24

Ihonvbere, J. and T. Shaw (1998) *Illusions of Power: Nigeria in Transition*, Trenton, NJ: Africa World Press

Irele, A. (1992) 'In Praise of Alienation', in V. Y. Mudimbe (ed.), *The Surreptitious Speech: Présence Africaine and the Politics of Otherness – 1947–1987*, University of Chicago Press, pp. 201–24

— (2000) 'The Political Kingdom: Toward Reconstruction in Africa', <www.africahome.com/community/africanist/categories/scholar/ecopolitics/EpEAZAupAZdEYAxAwf.shtml>

Khan, A. (1993) 'Algerian Intellectuals: Between Identity and Modernity', in M. Diouf and M. Mamdani (eds), *Academic Freedom in Africa*, Dakar: CODESRIA

Lazarus, N. (1999) 'Disavowing Decolonisation: Fanon, Nationalism, and the Question of Representation in Postcolonial Theory', in A. Alessandrini (ed.), *Frantz Fanon: Critical Perspectives*, London: Routledge, pp. 161–94

Mafeje, A. (1993) 'On "Icons" and African Perspectives on Democracy: A Commentary on Jibrin Ibrahim's Views', *CODESRIA Bulletin*, 2: 18–21

— (1997) 'Democracy and Development: A Tribute to Claude Ake', *African Journal of International Affairs*, 1(1): 78–92

Mamdani, M. (ed.) (1993) *The Intelligentsia, the State and Social Movements in Africa*, Dakar: CODESRIA

— (1999) 'There Can be no African Renaissance without an African-focused Intelligentsia', in M. W. Makgoba (ed.), *African Renaissance: The New Struggle*, Cape Town: Mafube Publishing

Mazrui, A. (1978) *Political Values and Educated Class in Africa*, London: Heinemann

— (1993) 'The Impact of Global Changes on Academic Freedom in Africa: a Preliminary Assessment', in M. Diouf and M. Mamdani (eds), *Academic Freedom in Africa*, Dakar: CODESRIA

Miller, C. (1985) *Blank Darkness: Africanist Discourse in French*, University of Chicago Press

Mkandawire, T. (1995) 'Beyond Crisis: Towards Democratic Development States', 8th CODESRIA General Assembly held at Dakar, 26 June–2 July

— (1996) 'The State, Human Rights and Academic Freedom', in John D. Turner (ed.), *The State and the School: An International Perspective*, London: Palmer Press

— (1998) 'The Social Sciences in Africa: Breaking Local Barriers and Negoti-ating International Presence, the M. K. O. Abiola Distinguished Lecture Presented to the 1996 African Studies Association Annual Meeting', *African Studies Review*, 40(2): 15–36

— (1999) 'Shifting Commitments and National Cohesion in African Countries', in L. Wohlegemuth, S. Gibson, S. Klasen and E. Rothchild (eds), *Common Security and Civil Society in Africa*, Uppsala: Nordiska Afrikainstitutet, pp. 14–41

Mnthali, F. (1988) 'Change and the Intelligentsia in African Literature: A Study in Marginality', *Africa Development*, XIII(3): 5–32

— (1999) 'The Challenge of Culture in the Twenty-First Century', Inaugural Lecture, University of Botswana, Gaborone

Mudimbe, V. Y. 1988. *The Invention of Africa: Gnosis, Philosophy, and the Order of Knowledge*, London: James Currey

Munck, R. (1986) *The Difficult Dialogue: Marxism and Nationalism*, London

New York Review of Books (2001) 'The Lure of Syracuse', XLVIII(14)

Njubi, F. N. (2002) 'Migration, Identity and the Politics of African Intellectuals in the North', 10th CODESRIA General Assembly held at Kampala, Uganda

Onimode, B. (1988) *A Political Economy of the African Crisis*, London: Zed Books

Onwanibe, R. C. (1983) *A Critique of Revolutionary Humanism: Frantz Fanon*, St Louis, MO: W. H. Green

Prah, K. K. (1998) *Beyond the Colour Line: Pan-Africanist Disputations: Selected Sketches, Letters, Papers, and Reviews*, Trenton, NJ: Africa World Press

Quayson, A. (2000) *Postcolonialism: Theory, Practice and Process*, Oxford: Polity Press.

Rahnema, M. (1997) 'Introduction', in M. Rahnema and V. Bawtree (eds), *The Post-development Reader*, London: Zed Books

Rahnema, M. and V. Bawtree (eds) (1997) *The Post-development Reader*, London: Zed Books

Rashid, S. (1994) 'Social Sciences and Policy-making in Africa: A Critical Review', *Africa Development*, XIX(1): 91–118

Sachs, W. (ed.) (1992) *The Development Dictionary: A Guide to Knowledge and Power*, London: Zed Books

Sakaki, R. (1995) 'Culture Wars in the United States: Closing Reflections on the Century of the Colour Line', in J. N. Pieterse and B. Pakesh (eds), *The Decolonisation of the Imagination: Culture, Knowledge and Power*, London: Zed Books

Sand, S. (1997) 'Between the Word and the Land: Intellectuals and the State in Israel', in J. Jennings and A. Kemp-Welch (eds), *Intellectuals in Politics: From the Dreyfus Affair to Salman Rushdie*, London: Routledge

Schuurman, F. (ed.) (1993) *Beyond the Impasse: New Directions in Development Theory*, London: Zed Books

Shivji, I. (1976) *Class Struggles in Tanzania*, London: Heinemann

— (1980) 'The State in the Dominated Social Formations of Africa: Some Theo-retical Issues', *International Social Science Journal*, XXXII(4): 730–42

— (1993) *Intellectuals at the Hill: Essays and Talks 1969-1993*, Dar es Salaam: Dar es Salaam University Press

Sokal, A. and J. Brichmont (1998) *Fashionable Nonsense: Postmodern Intellectual Abuse of Science*, New York: Picador

Sylla, L. (1982) 'Black Africa: A Generation after Independence', *Daedelus: Journal of the American Academy of Arts and Sciences*, III(2): 11–28

Tadesse, Z. (1999) 'From Euphoria to Gloom? Navigating the Murky Waters of African Academic Institutes', in W. Martin and M. West (eds), *Out of One, Many Africas: Reconstructing the Study and Meaning of Africa*, Urbana, IL: University of Illinois Press

Verhaegen, B. (1995) 'The African University: Evaluation and Perspectives', in E. Mudimbe (ed.), *The Surreptitious Speech: Présence Africaine and the Politics of Otherness – 1947–1987*, University of Chicago Press

Wa Thiong'o, N. (1986) *Decolonising the Mind: The Politics of Language in African Literature*, Nairobi: Heinemann Kenya

Yeikelo ya Ato, B. and Ntumba L. (1993) 'Ideology and Utopia', in K. Mbaya (ed.), *Zaire: What Destiny?*, Dakar: CODESRIA

Zeleza, P. T. (1998) 'African Labour and Intellectual Migration to the North: Building New Transatlantic Bridges', symposium on African and African-American Intellectuals, Santiago, CA: University of California

— (2003) *Rethinking Africa's Globalisation: The Intellectual Challenge*, Trenton, NJ: African World Press

Zewede, B. (1994) 'The Intellectual and the State in Twentieth Century Ethiopia', papers of the 12th International Conference of Ethopian Studies held at Michigan State University

3 | Pan-Africanism and the intellectuals: rise, decline and revival

ALI A. MAZRUI

The origins of modern intellectualism and the origins of pan-Africanism are intertwined. We can imagine intellectualism without pan-Africanism, but we cannot envisage pan-Africanism without the intellectualization of the African condition. It is not a historical accident that the founding fathers of the pan-Africanist movement were disproportionately intellectuals – W. E. B. Dubois, Kwame Nkrumah, George Padmore, Léopold Senghor and others.

V. I. Lenin believed that without intellectuals and the bourgeois intelligentsia there would have been no socialism: 'The theory of socialism ... grew out of the philosophic, historical, and economic theories elaborated by educated representatives of the property classes, by *intellectuals*. By their social status, the founders of modern scientific socialism, Marx and Engels, themselves belonged to the bourgeois intelligentsia.'[1] Lenin was suggesting that in the realm of ideas economic forces may not be enough. There is an underlying intellectual determinism as well. The peasants and the proletariat may have the power to pull down the old order. But it takes intellectuals and educated minds to conceive and construct an alternative social paradigm.

I have borrowed this Leninist idea of intellectual determinism from the domain of the origins of socialism to investigate the origins of pan-Africanism. Just as Lenin was convinced that socialism without the intellectuals was a dead duck, I propose to demonstrate that pan-Africanism without the intellectuals was similarly doomed.

Pan-Africanism and the intelligentsia

But what is an intellectual? I prefer the definition I advanced over thirty years ago when I debated with Akena Adoko, Uganda's head of intelligence, on 'The Role of African Intellectuals in the African Revolution'. In the 1969 debate in the town hall in Kampala, I defined an intellectual as 'a person who has the capacity to be fascinated by ideas and has acquired the skill to handle many of them effectively'.

W. E. B. Dubois was the most towering intellectual of the black diaspora in the twentieth century. He was a man of great ideas and great ideological aspirations. He has to be included among the founding fathers of modern pan-Africanism. He led the movement following Sylvester Williams's first Pan-African conference in London in the year 1900. The most historic of the congresses led by W. E. B. Dubois was the Pan-African Congress held in Manchester, England, in 1945.

These congresses attracted black nationalists of different social backgrounds, but the organizers and speakers were always disproportionately intellectuals. The Manchester conference included at least two future heads of state – Kwame Nkrumah of the Gold Coast and Jomo Kenyatta of Kenya. Also at Manchester were George Padmore of Trinidad and Dudley Thompson of Jamaica, as well as W. E. B. Dubois of the United States.

But as a system of ideas, does pan-Africanism really need as much intellectual sophistication as modern socialism? Karl Kautsky (1854–1938) believed that 'modern socialist consciousness can arise only on the basis of profound scientific knowledge'. With Lenin's concurrence, Kautsky argued that proletarian class struggle was not the mother of socialist consciousness: 'the vehicle of science is not the proletariat, but *the bourgeois intelligentsia* [Kautsky's emphasis]: it was in the minds of individual members of this stratum that modern socialism originated; it was they who communicated it to the more intellectually developed proletarians who, in their turn, introduced it into the class struggle when conditions allowed it to be done'.[2]

In *depth* pan-Africanism as a system of ideas did not aspire to be as 'scientific' as Marxism and modern socialism. But in *breadth* pan-Africanism covered a wider agenda – concerned not only with political economy, but also with African culture, aesthetics, poetry and philosophy. In 1947 Alioune Diop, a Senegalese intellectual in Paris, founded *Présence Africaine*, which became a major vehicle of cultural pan-Africanism. In 1957 Diop called for a world conference of black writers and intellectuals. The conference gave birth to the Société africaine de culture (SAC) and to its branch in the United States, the American Society of African Culture.

It was also in Paris that black intellectuals invented the pan-African concept of Negritude, a celebration of African identity and uniqueness. The Martinique intellectual Aimé Césaire is often credited with having coined the term 'negritude', but the most famous proponent of this pan-African cultural philosophy subsequently became Léopold Sédar Senghor, founder-president of independent Senegal.

Senghor's pan-Africanism was basically in the realm of ideas and aesthetics rather than in that of political activism. He wrote poetry, promoted African music and opera, and hosted pan-African cultural festivals, but he was not a flag-waving activist in pursuit of the unification of Africa.

Also more an intellectual celebrant than a pan-African activist was Senghor's compatriot, Cheikh Anta Diop, who authored various works about Africa's contribution to world civilization. Diop has become an icon among pan-Africanists, both in Africa and the wider diaspora.

More activist in his pan-Africanism was Kwame Nkrumah of Ghana. He became the champion of the most ambitious form of pan-Africanism – the quest for the regional integration of the whole of the African continent. In 1958 Nkrumah hosted in Accra, Ghana, the All Africa Peoples' Conference (a people-to-people mobilization). He subsequently hosted the first conference of African states. He even attempted a regional unification of three African states – Ghana, Guinea and Mali – which turned out to be more an experiment than an achievement.

This was the golden age of high pan-African ambitions and towering intellectual aspirations in Africa. Great minds articulated Africa's great dreams. Both pan-Africanism and African intellectualism were flying high. Kwame Nkrumah adopted for Africa what William Wordsworth had once said of the French Revolution: 'Bliss was it in that dawn to be alive, / but to be young was very heaven!'.

Then what happened? The Organization of African Unity was indeed created in 1963, but there was already a scaling down of Kwame Nkrumah's ambition of massive continental integration. Pan-Africanism was indeed still alive, but the process of slippage had begun. Africans were becoming less idealistic and more pragmatic as cautious post-coloniality replaced the vigour of anti-colonialism.

Within African countries domestic forces were unfolding which were lethal to both the spirit of pan-Africanism and the ideals of intellectualism. This can be illustrated by trends in eastern Africa, where the author of this paper was directly involved as an intellectual and a scholar. How did East Africa fare between the fortunes of pan-Africanism and the fluctuations of intellectualism?

Erosion of solidarity, decline of intellectualism

Over the last forty years East Africa has experienced the rise and decline of African intellectuals. What is intellectualism? *It is an engagement in the realm of ideas, rational discourse and independent enquiry.* Post-colonial African university campuses were once the vanguard of intellectualism. When I was an academic at the University of East Africa in the early years of independence, my colleagues consisted substantially of people who were capable of being fascinated by ideas. Every week there was a range of extra-curricular events on campus. Public lectures at the Makerere campus in Uganda or at the University of Nairobi were often heavily attended.

In the case of my own evening lectures at both Makerere and Nairobi, students sometimes gave up their suppers in order to get a seat at one of my presentations. The main halls were packed to overflowing. At that time the University of East Africa was a pan-African institution with a campus in each of three different countries – Uganda, Kenya and Tanzania.

As head of state Kenya had the nation's first black social anthropologist, Jomo Kenyatta – author of *Facing Mount Kenya*. Uganda had as head of government a person who had changed his name because of his admiration for the author of the great English poem *Paradise Lost*. Obote became Milton Obote. These were badges of intellectual status.

The most intellectual of East Africa's heads of state at the time was Julius K. Nyerere of Tanzania – a true philosopher, president and original thinker. He philosophized about society and socialism, and translated two of Shakespeare's plays – *Julius Caesar* and *The Merchant of Venice* – into Kiswahili. The Swahili translations were published by Oxford University Press – beginning in 1963, the year of Kenya's independence. Nyerere was also a major leader in the efforts to liberate southern Africa from white minority rule and a leader in the experiment of regional integration in East Africa.

East Africa had vivacious and scintillating intellectual magazines – such as *Transition*, based in Kampala, and *East Africa Journal*, based in Nairobi. Contributors to these magazines were intellectuals from the campuses, from wider civil society and from the governing class. The late Tom Mboya of Kenya, one of the most brilliant East Africans of his time, wrote for them from time to time.

These were the days when it was possible for me, a Kenyan, to be engaged in a public disagreement with the head of state of Uganda, Milton Obote. It was also possible for a public debate to occur in the town hall of Kampala between a Kenyan professor of political science (myself) and the head of intelligence in Uganda's security system (Mr Akena Adoko). Mr Adoko was at the time the second-most powerful civilian in Uganda after the head of state. These were intellectual debates conducted under the umbrella of pan-African tolerance.

The campuses vibrated with debates about fundamental issues of the day – nationalism, socialism, democracy and the party system, and the role of intellectuals in what was widely designated as 'the African revolution'. Since then, *who has killed intellectualism in East Africa?*

In Uganda part of the answer is obvious. A military coup occurred in January 1971 which brought Idi Amin into power. Eight years of brutal dictatorship followed. No less a person than the vice-chancellor of Makerere – Frank Kalimuzo – was abducted in broad daylight from the campus and never heard of again. A similar fate befell the judicially courageous chief justice of Uganda, Benedicto Kiwanuka. The scintillating intellectual voices of Uganda either fell silent or went into exile. Before long I too packed my bags and left my beloved Makerere.

The decline of intellectualism and the decline of pan-Africanism unfolded almost simultaneously. The regional university of East Africa disintegrated into three national institutions. The East African community as a whole was under stress.

Who killed intellectualism in Kenya? The killers included rising authoritarianism in government and declining academic freedom on the campuses. The very fact that the University of Nairobi was unable to hire me when I resigned from Makerere was a measure of the impact of political authoritarianism on the university's freedom of choice. These were the mid-1970s when Kenyatta was still in power. The fate of intellectualism became worse during the years of President Daniel arap Moi.

If the first two killers of intellectualism in Kenya were rising political authoritarianism and declining academic freedom, the third killer was the cold war between Western powers and the Soviet bloc. The government of Kenya was co-opted into the Western camp, sometimes at the expense of Kenya's own citizens. Being socialist or left-wing as an intellectual became a political hazard. All sorts of laws and edicts emerged about subversive literature. Possessing the works of Mao Zedong of the People's Republic of China was a crime in Kenya, and people actually went to jail for it. My own nephew, Dr Alamin M. Mazrui of Kenyatta University, was detained without charge by the Moi regime for more than a year for being a left-wing Kenyan academic in the company of such other left-wingers as Ngugi wa Thiong'o and Micere Mugo.

Intellectual opposition to capitalism in Kenya became increasingly a punishable offence. Lives of socialists were sometimes in danger, as in the case of the relatively powerless Pinto, who was assassinated. Moderately left-wing political leaders such as Oginga Odinga were ostracized. All these were forces fatal to intellectualism in Kenya.

Who killed intellectualism in Tanzania? In Tanzania intellectualism was slow to die. It was partially protected by the fact that the head of state – Julius Nyerere – was himself a superb intellectual ruler. He was not only fascinated by ideas, but also stimulated by debates.

But two factors in Tanzania played paradoxical roles – the ideology of Ujamaa (Tanzania's version of socialism) and Nyerere's one-party system. On the one hand, Ujamaa and the justification of the one-party state stimulated a considerable amount of intellectual rationalization and conceptualization. On the other hand, there was no escaping the fact that one-partyism was a discriminatory system of government, and the enthusiasm for socialism in Tanzania intimidated those who were against it. I visited the campus of the University of Dar es Salaam many times in the 1960s and 1970s and witnessed some of the consequences of ideological intimidation in the name of socialism.

What this means is that while in Kenya intellectualism died partly because of the cold war's opposition to socialism, in Tanzania intellectualism died partly because of excessive local enthusiasm *for* socialism.

On the other hand, it was a measure of pan-African tolerance that I was respected more as an intellectual by Milton Obote in Uganda and Julius Nyerere in Tanzania than I was by my own heads of state – whether Mzee Kenyatta or Daniel arap Moi – in Kenya. Even Idi Amin, when he was in power in Uganda, wanted to send me to apartheid South Africa as living proof that Africans could *think*. Idi Amin wanted me to become Exhibit A among black intellectuals to convince racists in South Africa that black people were human beings capable of rational thought. It was Amin's vision of how to use intellectuals in pan-African liberation. Fortunately, I was able to convince Amin not to humour racists with such a theatrical display.

But apart from ensuring a climate of academic freedom and the free flourishing of intellectualism, what does society have to do to develop a university before intellectuals and scholars become capable of helping to develop society? Clearly resources are crucial. The society has to be ready to invest sufficient resources in intellectual pursuits to ensure a high quality of intellectual recruitment and an ability to retain staff in relevant institutions.

Resources will also be needed for high-quality curriculum development and high-quality research and general development. Students and staff are human beings whose motivation and sense of commitment need to be sustained by a system of rewards and recognition. Grades for students should be a true measure of achievement; so should staff promotions. Promotions without performance should come to an end if the spirit of intellectual ambition is to be restored.

But no university or research organization can be a first-class institution of learned enquiry if the training schools that feed into it are all mediocre. In order to fully develop a university, society also has to develop the educational ladder as a whole. Quality of education at the primary and secondary levels needs to be sustained if the final candidates for possible admission to the universities are to be of a high standard. The capacity to be curious and fascinated by ideas has to start early in the educational process. The spirit of intellectualism has to be nourished from primary school onward, but it can die at university level if mediocrity prevails.

In relation to the wider world, a university has three crucial relationships. A university has to be *politically distant* from the state; second, a university has also to be *culturally close* to society; and third, a university has to be intellectually linked to wider scholarly and scientific values in the world of learning.

Can a university be funded by the state and still maintain political distance? It has been done in other societies; there is no reason why it cannot happen in Africa as well. British universities still depend heavily on the state, even when they have large endowments. This is a common pattern in Europe. In the United States, government-funded universities are supported mainly at the state rather than the federal level. Nevertheless, the federal government contributes billions to higher education generally without compromising academic freedom.

In Kenya, President Mwai Kibaki's administration may have started the process of depoliticizing the public universities by a new atmosphere of academic autonomy. The president's decision to hand over the chancellorships of the six public universities to ordinary Kenyans is an important symbol of decentralization and depoliticization.

In addition to political distance from the state, each university needs to be culturally close to society. This is a much tougher proposition in Africa, especially since African university systems are colonial in origin and disproportionately European in tradition. African universities are among the major instruments and vehicles of cultural Westernization on the continent.

There is a contradiction between the university's duty to be culturally close to its society and its ambition to be intellectually linked to the wider world of scholarship and science. In this connection it is worth bearing in mind important differences between the Westernization of Africa and the modernization of Japan after the Meiji Restoration of 1868. Japan's original modernization involved considerable selectivity on the part of the Japanese themselves. The whole purpose of selective Japanese Westernization was to protect Japan against the West, rather than merely to submit to Western cultural attractions. The emphasis in Japan was therefore on the technical and technological techniques of the West, rather than on literary and verbal culture. The Japanese slogan 'Western technique, Japanese spirit' of the time captured this ambition to borrow technology from the West while deliberately protecting a substantial part of Japanese culture. In a sense, Japan's technological Westernization was designed to reduce the danger of other forms of cultural dependency.

The nature of Westernization in Africa has been very different. Far from emphasizing Western productive technology and downplaying Western lifestyles and verbal culture, Africa has reversed the Japanese order of emphasis. Among the factors that have facilitated this reversal has been the role of the African university as a vehicle of Western influence on African culture. If African universities had borrowed a leaf from the Japanese book of cultural selection, and initially concentrated on what is indisputably the West's real area of leadership and marginal advantage (science and technology), the resultant African dependency might have been of a different kind. It is not too late, however. The process of encouraging intellectuals in Africa can still attempt to combine indigenous authenticity with universal rationalism. There is still hope not only for the reactivation of intellectualism in Africa's orientation but also for a reinvigoration of pan-Africanism.

Towards a new intellectual revival

As the twenty-first century approached, new developments began to help an intellectual revival in Africa. First and foremost were the pro-democracy movements which burst out from Lusaka to Lagos, from Algiers to Accra. Not all the movements were successful in their own countries, but they contributed greatly to a new era of pluralism and transparency. In over twenty countries opposition parties were legalized; in others the military returned to the barracks. Newspapers started publishing voices of dissent, and private radio stations flourished in countries such as Ghana.

A supportive contributor to intellectual revival was the end of the cold war. For as long as the cold war had lasted Western donor countries often supported African dictators such as Mobutu Sese Seko and Daniel arap Moi, as long as the rulers were clearly anti-communist. With the end of the cold war Western donor countries started supporting pro-democracy forces and anti-corruption policies.

A third factor behind the intellectual revival is the clear demonstration that long-established incumbent regimes can actually be overthrown in free elections at the polls. Central Africa had earlier set the pace with the defeat of Kenneth Kaunda in Zambia and Hastings Banda in Malawi. In Ghana Jerry Rawlings stepped down in response to term limits, but he could not save his political party either. It was defeated at the polls. In Kenya a similar thing happened – as Daniel arap Moi stepped down, and the Kenya African National Union was defeated after nearly forty years in power. Even earlier the ruling party of Senegal was trounced after four decades in power. And President Abdou Diouf was defeated after reigning for twenty years. The incoming president, Abdoulaye Wade, tried to inaugurate a new political era in Senegal.

A fourth factor behind Africa's intellectual revival is the rapid collapse of political apartheid in South Africa. Notwithstanding the resilient survival of economic apartheid, South Africa had become the most open society on the African continent, endowed with the most liberal constitution on Planet Earth.

Pan-African academic and research organizations have provided linkages between the first phase of post-colonial intellectualism and this new revival. Such pan-African scholarly institutions include the Council for the Development of Social Science Research (CODESRIA), based in Dakar, Senegal, and the African Association of Political Science, based in southern Africa. Newer pan-African scholarly organizations which have been active in research, publishing and organizing conferences include Abdalla Bujra's post-CODESRIA organization, the Development Policy Management Forum (DPMF).

CODESRIA has provided its own avenues of debate such as the *Codesria Bulletin* and has also supported sister organizations such as the Association of African Historians in publishing *Afrika Zamani: A Journal of African History* in English and French.

During difficult years the Department of Philosophy at the University of Zambia has attempted to maintain an international African journal of philosophy, *Quest: Philosophical Discussions*. South Africa has experienced the mushrooming of a great diversity of magazines, journals, books and electronic programmes as part of this intellectual revival. President Thabo Mbeki's reinvention of the concept of an 'African Renaissance' has also provided a stimulus for related themes of intellectual discourse.

This second intellectual upsurge in Africa does not have the towering 'philosopher kings' of the first phase – thinkers such as Kwame Nkrumah, Léopold Senghor, Augustinho Neto, Gamal Abdel Nasser and Julius K. Nyerere. But the decentralization of this new intellectual revival may itself be a virtue.

If these are the tendencies that are making a new intellectual revival possible in Africa, what are the forces that are favouring the revival of pan-Africanism? It is to this second part of the equation that we must now turn.

Pan-Africanism: sub-Saharan and trans-Saharan

There are in fact different levels of pan-Africanism, varying in degrees of sustainability. *Sub-Saharan pan-Africanism* is a quest for the unification of black people in Africa below the Sahara. There are two possible versions of sub-Saharan pan-Africanism. The *subcontinental* version would seek the union of black states while excluding Arab Africa. As an idea this has been floated from time to time, but it does not seem to have much political support. More triumphant has been *trans-Saharan pan-Africanism*, which formed the Afro-Arab basis of the Organization of African Unity. Another version of sub-Saharan pan-Africanism, however, is *subregional* rather than subcontinental. The sub-regional variety has produced organizations such as the Economic Community of West African States (ECOWAS), which in recent years has been more activist as a peacekeeping force than as a vanguard for economic change. The Southern African Development Community (SADC) has also received a new lease of life since South Africa became a full member in the post-apartheid era. Uganda, Kenya and Tanzania have been trying to revive the East African Community since it collapsed in the 1970s. But by far the most ambitious idea floated in the new era of intellectual speculation is whether the whole of Africa and the whole of the Arab world are two regions in the process of merging into one. Out of this speculative discourse has emerged the concept of *Afrabia*.

Two tendencies have stimulated new thinking about African–Arab relations. One tendency is basically negative but potentially unifying – the war on terrorism. The new international terrorism may have its roots in injustices perpetrated against such Arab people as Palestinians and Iraqis, but the primary theatre of contestation is blurring the distinction between the Middle East and the African continent. For twelve Americans to be killed in Nairobi in August 1998, over two hundred Kenyans died in a terrorist act at the United States embassy. In 2002 a suicide bomber in Mombasa, Kenya, attacked the Israeli-owned and Israeli-patronized Paradise Hotel. Three times as many Kenyans as Israelis died.

African countries such as Uganda, South Africa, Tanzania and Kenya have been under American pressure to pass anti-terrorist legislation – partly intended to control their own Muslim populations and partly targeted at potential al-Qaeda infiltrators. Uganda and Tanzania and others have already capitulated to American pressure.

Independently of the war on terror, Islam as a cultural and political force has also been deepening relationships between Africa and the Middle East. Intellectual revival is expressed not only in the Western idiom. It is also expressed in the idiom of African cultures and African Islam. The heated political debates about the shariah (Islamic law) in Nigeria constitute part of the trend of cultural integration between Africa and the Middle East.

The new legitimization of Muammar Qaddafi as a viable African leader has contributed to the birth of no less a new institution than the African Union. In my own face-to-face conversations with the Libyan leader I have sometimes been startled by how much more pan-Africanist than pan-Arabist he has recently become. At least for the time being Qaddafi is out-Africanizing the legacy of Gamal Abdel Nasser.

The fourth force that may be merging Africa with the Middle East is political economy. Africa's oil producers need a joint partnership with the bigger oil producers of the Middle East. In the area of aid and trade between Africa and the Middle East, the volumes may have gone down since the 1980s. But most indications seem to promise a future expansion of economic relations between Africa and the Middle East. In the Gulf countries of the United Arab Emirates and the sultanate of Oman the concept of Afrabia is beginning to be examined at higher and higher echelons. Let us look more closely at this concept in the light of the revival of both intellectual discourse and new approaches to pan-Africanism.

Who are the Afrabians?

It was initially trans-Saharan pan-Africanism which gave birth to the idea of Afrabia. The first post-colonial waves of pan-Africanists like Nkrumah believed that the Sahara was a bridge rather than a divide. The concept of Afrabia now connotes not only an interaction between Africanity and Arab identity; it is also seen as a process of fusion between the two. While the principle of Afrabia recognizes that Africa and the Arab world are overlapping categories, it goes on to prophesy that these two regions are in the historic process of becoming one.

But who are the Afrabians? There are in reality at least four categories. *Cultural Afrabians* are those whose culture and way of life have been deeply Arabized, but falling short of their being linguistically Arabs. Most Somali, Hausa and some Waswahili are cultural Afrabians in this sense. Their mother tongue is not Arabic, but much of the rest of their culture bears the stamp of Arab and Islamic impact.

Ideological Afrabians are those who intellectually believe in solidarity between Arabs and Africans, or at least between Arab Africa and black Africa. Historically such ideological Afrabian leaders have included Kwame Nkrumah, the founder president of Ghana; Gamal Abdel Nasser, arguably the greatest Egyptian of the twentieth century; and Sékou Touré, the founding father of post-colonial Guinea (Conakry). Such leaders refused to recognize the Sahara Desert as a divide, and insisted on visualizing it as a historic bridge.

Geographical Afrabians are those Arabs and Berbers whose countries are members of both the African Union and the Arab League. Some of these countries are overwhelmingly Arab, such as Egypt and Tunisia, while others are only marginally Arab, such as Mauritania, Somalia and the Comoro Islands.

As for *genealogical Afrabians*, these are those who are biologically descended from both Arabs and black Africans. In North Africa these include

Anwar Sadat, the president of Egypt who concluded a peace treaty with Israel and was assassinated in 1982 as a consequence. Anwar Sadat's mother was black. He was politically criticized for many things, but almost never for being racially mixed.

Genealogical Afrabians in sub-Saharan Africa include Salim Ahmed Salim, the longest-serving secretary-general of the Organization of African Unity. Genealogical Afrabians also include the Mazrui clan scattered across coastal Kenya and coastal Tanzania. It should be noted that northern Sudanese qualify as Afrabians in terms of both geographical and genealogical criteria.

These four sub-categories of Afrabians provide some of the evidence that Africa and the Arab world are two geographical regions that are in the slow historic process of becoming one. But what about the relationship between Africa and its diaspora abroad? This is neither *sub-Saharan* pan-Africanism nor *trans-Saharan* pan-Africanism.

What we are confronting now is the oldest form of the modern ideology of black solidarity – *transatlantic* pan-Africanism. Let us now turn more decisively to the diasporization of the African experience.

Globalizing the dual diaspora

A major factor has been the *dualization* of the African diaspora. There has been the new migration of Africans to the Middle East, Europe, the Americas, Australia and elsewhere – the new Bantu migration on a global scale. In a sense this process has been creating two African diasporas – the new *diaspora of colonialism* alongside the older *diaspora of enslavement*.

The diaspora of enslavement consists of survivors of the Middle Passage and their descendants. The diaspora of colonialism consists of the survivors of the partition of Africa in exile and their descendants: the casualties of the displacement caused either directly by colonialism or by the aftermath of colonial and post-colonial disruptions.[3]

European influences were a 'given'. Thomas Jefferson and the founding fathers looked to such European thinkers as John Locke and Montesquieu. Euro-Americans liked to think of themselves as heirs to Greece and Rome. But where was the American personality?[4]

Frederick Jackson Turner (1861–1932) provided one answer – the significance of the *frontier* in American history. He argued that the American character was decisively shaped by the conditions of the frontier, which evoked such qualities as 'coarseness and strength ... acuteness and inquisitiveness, that practical turn of mind ... restless, nervous energy ... that buoyancy and exuberance which comes with freedom ... '[5] He argued that what was uniquely American in its institutions was not the *Mayflower*, but boundless land, and the spirit of taming the rugged frontier. But Frederick Jackson Turner forgot one thing – what was uniquely American was also the black presence alongside the frontier. This is the presence which nurtured American capitalism in its infancy and nurtured American democracy in its maturation.

In its infancy, American capitalism needed black labour. This is the link between America and the imperative of labour. In its maturation in the twentieth century American democracy needed the civil rights movement and deracialization to realize its original concept that 'all men are created equal'. It was blacks who held American democracy accountable to its own ultimate ideals. The echoes were heard all over Africa in the new Afro-World Wide Web. The Afro-Atlantic paradigm was at work again. The civil rights movement fed into the feminist movement. Young capitalism often needed young black labour; but more mature US democracy needed more mature black stimulation. The World Wide Web has forged US links. The African presence in America has also deeply influenced music, literature, food culture, sports and the performing arts.

The distinction between the diaspora of enslavement and the diaspora of colonialism gets more complicated with the distinction between (a) *African Americans* (Americans is the noun and African the adjective) and (b) *American Africans* (Africans is the noun). The great majority of African Americans are a product of the diaspora of enslavement. The term 'African Americans' can be either hemispheric (meaning all descendants of enslavement in the Americas) or national (meaning all descendants of enslavement in the United States).

American Africans (or Americo-Africans), on the other hand, are products of the diaspora of colonization. They are usually first- or second-generation immigrants from Africa to the Americas. They may be citizens or permanent residents of Western-hemisphere countries.[6]

What is distinctive about American Africans is that their mother tongue is still an African language. (In the case of Americo-Liberians, they may still speak Liberian English.) Second, American Africans usually still have immediate blood relatives in Africa. Third, they are likely still to be attached to the food culture of their African ancestry. Fourth, American Africans are still likely to bear African family names, although this is by no means universal, especially among Lusophone Africans, Liberians and Sierra Leoneans.

On the whole African Americans tend to be more race conscious in their political orientation than American Africans. On the other hand, American Africans may still be more fundamentally 'tribal' when the chips are down.

When does an American African family evolve into an African American family? When it loses its ancestral language. The umbilical cord is language. The children of Professor Nkiru Nzegwu of Binghamton University are still American Africans (hemispherically) because the children still speak fluent Igbo. On the other hand, my children are now more African Americans – their linguistic umbilical cord has been cut.

But when American Africans become African Americans, it does not mean that other ties with Africa are cut. Relatives in Africa still abound. Concern for Africa is often still intact. And the Internet is now providing a new network of Afro-Atlanticism, a new language.

Let me repeat that in the case of African Americans the noun is 'Americans'. What kind of Americans? *African* Americans. In the case of American Africans, the noun is 'Africans', the adjective is American. What kind of Africans? *American* Africans!

Between African Americans and American Africans

We must focus not just on relations between African Americans and Africans but also on those between African Americans and *Africa* as a continent. Do African Americans empathize with Africa? If so, how much? Indeed, it is worth examining relations within the United States between American Africans and African Americans. There are areas of solidarity in these relations; and there are areas of tension.

When Amadou Diallo from Guinea was killed by four white policemen in New York City pouring forty-one bullets into him, it sent shock waves through the Big Apple, not just among immigrant Africans but also among African Americans, Latinos and other disadvantaged groups. Being fellow victims of white racism and police brutality is an area of solidarity.

And yet many African Americans feel that Africans generally are not sufficiently concerned with race because of vastly different historical experiences. *Among African Americans many give race 60 per cent relevance in their lives while Africans give it only 35 per cent relevance.* This difference in racial preoccupation can be a cause of stress.

The majority of Africans (or American Africans) and African Americans support affirmative action. This is an area of solidarity. But who precisely gets the jobs or the educational opportunities?

In reality the greatest beneficiaries are probably white women, but there is sometimes rivalry between African Americans and American Africans over jobs, business opportunities and other scarce resources. This area of professional and occupational competition can be a source of stress. Intellectual jobs are particularly prone to this kind of rivalry.

Until recently the great majority of Africans in the United States were college graduates or members of the intelligentsia in the process of acquiring college degrees. Many Africans who came to the USA came for educational purposes or acquired their visas and green cards on the basis of special qualifications. The majority of African Americans, on the other hand, did not have college degrees. This introduced a partial *class factor* between the two groups. It was like a divide between a black intelligentsia and a black proletariat.

This class factor is being eroded for two reasons. There are more Africans in the United States who do not have a college degree and are not seeking one. Second, there are many more African Americans who are exceptionally well trained and educated.[7] So this difference between African Americans and American Africans is evening out.

Many African American heroes are also African heroes. These include the late Martin Luther King, Jr, the boxer Muhammad Ali, the basketball player Michael Jordan, the novelist Toni Morrison, and many African American singers. This is an area of solidarity. Even controversial Louis Farrakhan has millions of African admirers. On the other hand, African heroes are seldom well known in black America, apart from Nelson Mandela. Only the staunchest pan-Africanists among African Americans have ever heard of Kwame Nkrumah, Sékou Touré, Julius Nyerere or Wole Soyinka. African global celebrities are disproportionately intellectuals. African American lack of familiarity with African heroes is not really a cause of stress. It just represents a missed opportunity for further solidarity.

Expanding globalization may restore the balance. In any case African American heroes receive much more global publicity because they are citizens of a superpower. It has therefore been easier for Africans in Africa to know about them than for African Americans in the United States to hear of Julius Nyerere or Kofi Annan.

Globalization has also witnessed the rise of Africans to positions of leadership in global organizations. But here it may be worth distinguishing between *Africans of the soil* and *Africans of the blood*. Boutros Boutros-Ghali, the first African secretary-general of the United Nations, was an African of the soil. Kofi Annan, the second African secretary-general, is an African of the blood. North Africans such as Boutros-Ghali belong to the African continent (the soil) but not to the black race (the blood). On the other hand, African Americans are Africans of the blood (the black race) but not of the soil (the African continent). Sub-Saharan Africans such as Kofi Annan are in reality both Africans of the soil (the continent) and of the blood (the race). Globalization has given Africans of the soil and of the blood new opportunities for leadership at the global level itself. Africans of the soil are often also Afrabians.

Even before the two African secretaries-general of the United Nations,

Africa had already produced a black director-general for UNESCO (the United Nations Educational, Scientific and Cultural Organization) in Paris. He was Amadou Mahtar M'Bow, an African of the blood from Senegal. He was a cultural Afrabian. His openly pro-Third World policies infuriated the United States, which finally withdrew from UNESCO in 1985 followed by its compliant ally, the United Kingdom. The United Kingdom returned to UNESCO in 1997 after the sweeping victory of the Labour Party in the elections. The United States is now following suit.

With regard to the United Nations itself, Africa is the only region of the world apart from Europe to have produced more than one secretary-general for the world body in the twentieth century. Europe has produced three secretaries-general, Africa two, and the other regions of the world have produced either one each or none so far. Annan is an Afrabian ideologically. Boutros-Ghali was Afrabian culturally and geographically.

In 1994 the International Court of Justice at The Hague elected an African of the soil for its president – Mohammed Bejaouni of Algeria. Since the 1990s the World Bank has had two African vice-presidents – Callisto Madivo, an African of the blood from Zimbabwe, and Ismail Serageldin, an African of the soil from Egypt. In 1999, Serageldin was also a serious candidate to become the first UNESCO director-general of the new millennium. Madivo was Afrabian ideologically, while Serageldin was Afrabian geographically.

The Commonwealth (what used to be called the British Commonwealth) has fifty-four members. Its secretariat is at Marlborough House in London. Throughout the 1990s the Commonwealth had Chief Eleazar Emeka Anyouku as its secretary-general. The chief is an African of the blood from Nigeria. The largest member of the Commonwealth in terms of population is India; the most industrialized include Canada, Great Britain and Australia; and the largest black member of the Commonwealth is of course Nigeria.

Globalization has also permitted the emergence of black and African moral leadership on a world scale. It began with the Nobel Prize-winners for peace. These have been disproportionately intellectuals and over the years have included Ralph Bunche (1950), Albert Luthuli (1960), Martin Luther King, Jr (1964), Anwar Sadat (1978), Desmond Tutu (1984), Nelson Mandela (1994), and F. W. de Klerk (1994).

Ralph Bunche and Martin Luther King, Jr, were of course African Americans and therefore Africans of the blood in our sense, but not of the soil. Anwar Sadat and F. W. de Klerk were Africans of the soil but not of the blood. Albert Luthuli, Desmond Tutu and Nelson Mandela were Africans of both the soil and the blood. All three were South Africans, as was F. W. de Klerk.

But we should note that F. W. de Klerk is an 'African of the soil' by adoption rather than by indigenous roots in the continent. Most North Africans, on the other hand, are indigenous to the continent, although there has been considerable racial mixture with immigrants over the centuries.

As the twentieth century was coming to a close, Nelson Mandela achieved a unique status. He became the first truly universal black moral leader in the world in his own lifetime. Martin Luther King, Jr achieved universal status after his death. When Dr King was alive half of mainstream America rejected him and regarded him as a troublemaker. Mandela was fortunate to have achieved universal moral admiration without having to undergo assassination beforehand. No other black man in history has pulled off such a 'pre-humous' accomplishment (as distinct from a post-humous one). In the recognition of Mandela the human race may have taken one more step forward in the search for universalized ethical sensibilities. It just so happens that Mandela is also Afrabian ideologically.

Globalization has also forged new links between Islam and global Africa, and provided opportunities for African Muslims to play a bigger role in both the global *ummah* and among countries in global Africa.

When Mahtar M'Bow was the director-general of UNESCO he was the highest-ranking Muslim of any race in the United Nations system. Professor M'Bow was an African of the blood from Senegal, as indicated. He was Afrabian genealogically and culturally.

Ismail Serageldin, as one of the vice-presidents of the World Bank in the 1990s, had been one of the highest-ranking Muslims in the International Bank for Reconstruction and Development. Serageldin was, as noted, an African of the soil from Egypt, and was of course Afrabian.

Another African Muslim of the soil became head of the World Court at The Hague when Justice Mohammed Bejaouni of Algeria was elected president of the International Court of Justice in 1994. He was a geographical and cultural Afrabian.

The Organization of Petroleum Exporting Countries (OPEC) – with its headquarters in Vienna, Austria – has four African members. These are Nigeria and Gabon (Africans of the blood) and Algeria and Libya (Africans of the soil). From time to time these African countries have provided secretaries-general and other OPEC leaders, often Muslim and Afrabian.

And of course the Organization of African Unity, the most important continent-wide organization in Africa, had a Muslim and Afrabian secretary-general throughout the 1990s and into the new millennium. Salim Ahmed Salim was an African of the blood from Tanzania.

There are 1.2 billion Muslims in the world – but the only continent which has a Muslim majority is Africa. The total population of Africa is over 800 million, of whom over half are now Muslim. The merger between Africa and the Middle East gathers momentum.

Nigeria has more Muslims than any Arab country. When Nigeria is combined with Ethiopia, Egypt and Congo (Kinshasa) – the four most populous African countries – the Muslim population is over 200 million. Africa and the Middle East continue to converge while the struggle unfolds.

Conclusion

We have sought to demonstrate in this paper that the origins of pan-Africanism and the origins of modern black intellectualism are interlinked. The architects of modern pan-Africanism were primarily intellectuals, beginning with the intelligentsia of the black diaspora.

Africa's independence witnessed a flowering of both intellectual activity and pan-African euphoria on the continent. But among the casualties of the post-colonial decay in Africa have been this intellectual vibrancy and pan-African fervour. The decline was compounded by the brain drain from Africa, and by the falling standards at major institutions of higher learning and research on the continent. Eloquent voices of dissent either went silent or found their way to more receptive lands.

The pro-democracy movements of the late 1980s and the 1990s, combined with the end of the cold war, helped to re-create conditions of transparency and open society in large parts of Africa. Black intellectualism received a new lease of life. It was aided by pan-African scholarly institutions such as CODESRIA, by friendly donors and charitable foundations, and by such United Nations agencies as UNESCO. Southern Africans started identifying an African renaissance as political apartheid collapsed.

This paper has also addressed three levels of pan-Africanism – sub-Saharan, trans-Saharan and transatlantic. Experiments in regional integration such as ECOWAS and SADC were trying to find new roles in a turbulent subcontinent.

Trans-Saharan pan-Africanism brought black Africa and Arab Africa into a new if fragile partnership. This level of pan-Africanism gave birth to the Organization of African Unity (1963–2002), followed by the African Union (from 2002).

But more fundamentally trans-Saharan relations have historically been creating conditions in which Africa and the Arab world can slowly merge into a single regional system. The concept of Afrabia is asserting its relevance. This paper has identified cultural, ideological, geographic and genealogical Afrabians.

But Africanity does not end on the shores of the African continent. Across the oceans Africa has a diaspora of enslavement, born out of the ravages of the slave trade, and a diaspora of colonization, caused by the disruptions of the imperial experience. Transatlantic pan-Africanism has now produced not only African Americans (survivors of the Middle Passage), but also American Africans (refugees from the anguish of post-coloniality).

The black presence in the Americas and the Caribbean has helped redefine the human condition from Bahia in Brazil to Birmingham, Alabama; from black Toronto to Afro-Trinidad. An Africa on a global scale is in the making. Its consciousness requires an intellectual vanguard. Its unification may one day become the ultimate triumph of the pan-African struggle.

> Winds of the world give answer,
> They are whimpering to and fro,
> And who would know of Africa
> Who only Africa know?

Appendix

Changing the guard in Africa's regional integration: from the OAU to the AU [summary of presentation at the annual meeting of the African Studies Association of the United States, held in Boston, Massachusetts, 30 October–1 November 2003].

After World War I the League of Nations came into being in 1919. It was succeeded in 1945 by the United Nations Organization after World War II.

In 1960 more than fifteen African countries became members of the United Nations. Three years later all of them, plus other newly independent African countries, along with the older African states, met in Addis Ababa in Ethiopia to form the Organization of African Unity (the OAU).

But just as the League of Nations gave way to the United Nations after a quarter of a century, the Organization of African Unity gave way to a new African Union (AU) after nearly forty years. The OAU gave way to the AU at a summit meeting of African heads of state in Durban, South Africa, in 2002.

What the OAU helped Africa to accomplish and the AU now has to build upon were the following:

I. OAU Maintain the inviolability of the colonial boundaries of African states in the conviction that redrawing them would cause more problems than it would solve.

OAU on the side of the Nigeria rather than Biafra.

OAU on the side of the Sudan rather than Anyanya.

OAU on the side of Ethiopia rather than the separation of Eritrea or the Ogadem.

AU While colonial borders must not be challenged at the sub-state level, they may be changed at the supra-state level.

Regional integration would be enlargement of political scale:

Continental Common Market;

Continental Economic Union;

Continental Single Currency and Monetary Union;

Continental Parliament and Court of Human Rights;

Continental Banking System.

II. OAU Commitment to decolonization, the struggle against apartheid and the crusade against white minority governments.

The OAU's basic platform was of Africa's *disengagement* from its former colonial masters.

AU The AU has virtually adopted NEPAD (the New Partnership for Africa's Development) as its inaugural agenda. This is a strategy of Africa's economic *re-engagement* with its former colonial powers – in contrast to the OAU strategy of Africa's political disengagement from its former colonial powers.

III. OAU The OAU was an organization to moderate tensions between African states – rather than be involved in tensions within African states. On tensions within African states, the OAU was almost inevitably on the side of the government of the day.

In its final decade of existence the OAU was more ready to engage in helping to mediate among domestic contenders, but Salim Ahmed Salim as secretary-general could at best be a moral influence in domestic tensions rather than a peace-enforcer.

AU Considering having an African Security Council with readiness to be more involved in solving African conflicts, both intra-state and inter-state. AU's South Africa led peacekeepers in Burundi.

Some of us have presumed to recommend that on the issue of security the African Union should have a vanguard peacemaking group of states, the equivalent of the UN Security Council's Permanent Members:

South Africa to represent southern Africa

Nigeria to represent West Africa

Egypt to represent North Africa

Ethiopia to represent eastern Africa? Or should it be a smaller state such as Uganda or Kenya?

Central Africa: if the Democratic Republic of Congo survives, this should be the permanent member on the African Union's Security Council.

IV. OAU The OAU was an almost exclusively *political* organization – leaving the bulk of problems of economic development in Africa to the United Nations Economic Commission for Africa in Addis Ababa, Ethiopia.

The OAU had neither the relevant expertise nor the resources to be engaged in issues and strategies of Africa's economic development.

AU The AU has a more interdisciplinary vision of Africa's future: political integration, economic integration, monetary union, parliamentary aspirations, shared judicial ambitions.

Muammar Qaddafi's language policy for Africa – English, French, Arabic plus the most relevant African language of each country. Should the AU be a vanguard of *cultural* integration?

V. OAU Born out of the dreams of a West African leader (Kwame Nkrumah) and the pragmatic wisdom of an eastern African monarch (Emperor Haile Selassie). Nkrumah had helped to sustain the enthusiasm for African unity. Haile Selassie provided the practical headquarters for institutionalized pan-Africanism.

AU Born out of a possible rivalry between a South African leader (Thabo Mbeki) and a North African leader (Muammar Qaddafi). Nelson Mandela had regarded Qaddafi as one of the great allies in the struggle against apartheid. Refused to criticize Qaddafi in a major TV interview with Ted Koppel. Qaddafi as ally of Mandela and rival of Mbeki. Both have ideas about the OAU as a future mechanism of cultural integration.

Mbeki has his mission of the African Renaissance: skill revolution, gender revolution and value revolution.

Qaddafi's vision of a multilingual Africa: French, Arabic, English, and the most relevant indigenous language of each country.

' … a man's reach should exceed his grasp, / Or what's a heaven for?'

Notes and references

1 V. I. Lenin, *What is to be Done?*. See Lenin, *Selected Works*, vol. I (Moscow: Foreign Languages Publishing House), p. 149.

2 Cited by Lenin in ibid., p. 156.

3 There is a plethora of writing on the African diasporas. See, for instance,

Darlene Clark Hine and Jacqueline McLeod (eds), *Crossing Boundaries: Comparative History of Black People in Diaspora* (Bloomington: Indiana University Press, 1999); E. L. Bute, *The Black Handbook: The People, History and Politics of Africa and the African Diaspora* (London and Washington, DC: Cassell, 1997); Joseph E. Harris, *The African Diaspora* (College Station, TX: Texas A & M University Press, 1996); and Michael L. Coniff, *Africans in the Americas: A History of the Black Diaspora* (New York: St Martin's Press, 1994).

4 Isidore Okpewho, 'Introduction', in Isidore Okpewho, Carol B. Davies and Ali A. Mazrui (eds), *The African Diaspora: African Origins and New Identities* (Bloomington: Indiana University Press, 1999), p. xiii.

5 Frederick Turner, *The Frontier in American History* (New York, Chicago, San Francisco, Toronto, London: Holt, Rinehart & Winston), p. 37.

6 On recent African immigrants to the United States, see Kofi A. Apraku, *African Emigrés in the United States: A Missing Link in Africa's Social and Political Development* (New York, Westport, CT, and London: Praeger, 1991); and April Gordon, 'The New Diaspora: African Immigration to the United States', *Journal of Third World Studies*, 15 (spring 1998), pp. 79–103.

7 According to Census Bureau statistics, the number of blacks with associates, bachelors, masters and doctoral degrees has been steadily rising since the 1980s; see Table no. 308, *Statistical Abstract of the United States, 1997* (Washington, DC: Bureau of the Census), p. 194.

4 | African intellectuals, nationalism and pan-Africanism: a testimony

JOSEPH KI-ZERBO

Dear colleagues,

I thank you for having invited me here as a witness to yesterday and today, inasmuch as the duty to remember can be a springboard to the future. Every age, of course, has its tasks, yet history consists of breaks and continuities. It may therefore be useful to quickly glance at the challenges that nationalism and pan-Africanism have persistently posed to African intellectuals over the past decades.

One may also consider that Africa's 'non-development' originates in the generally negative and externally supported conflict between the state, nationalism and pan-Africanism.

Introduction

In the interaction between the state, nationalism and pan-Africanism, intellectuals play a significant and even decisive role through reflection and action, theory and practice. Now what is the cause of the negative interaction? How can one explain the phenomenon whereby the cost of accumulation of wealth and development elsewhere remains the cost of Africa's stagnation and its inability to take off? How come human cost elsewhere becomes human sacrifice here? A re-examination of these problems with the hindsight of my personal experience could shed a glimmer of light on the said problems. Since I have chosen to be both an intellectual and a politically committed man, however, or rather a man deeply concerned with political affairs (a choice that is not all that atypical), it is important that I explain my position on the relationship between the intellectual and politics.

It is easy to establish a dichotomy, with a neat stroke of the theoretical sword, between the political class, on the one hand, and civil society, on the other. The reality is more complex than that, however. In truth, who is an intellectual? Who practises or does not practise politics?

The title 'intellectual' is generously distributed in Africa and jealously guarded. Strictly speaking, producers of scientific, literary or artistic works could be considered as intellectuals. An exceptional police officer can very well meet this requirement. In a broad sense, however, everyone who earns a living mainly from intellectual activities could be viewed as an intellectual. In this light, every type of society and every period or mode of production has its intellectuals. The scribes of ancient Egypt, the *oulemas* and doctors of medieval Timbuktu, dozens of whose names are mentioned at the beginning of *Tarikh es Sudan*, workers in the court of Emperor Ashanti in the eighteenth century, advisers to the king of Burundi who were responsible for interpreting dreams (which is the real function of certain government journalists today), *griots* (praise singers), traditional doctors and psychiatrists, bronze-smiths, sculptors and masked dancers (who are not ordinary dancers!) are all intellectuals.

Every man is, in a sense, an intellectual or an intellectual worker; there is a certain communion between physical work and intellectual work, *Homo faber* and *Homo sapiens*. Under such conditions, can one talk of a group, a class or a caste of African intellectuals?

Yes and no, for intellectuals, in the narrow sense of the word, do not play a specific univocal role in production or the power structure. They can be government workers, servants of the ruling class, workers of the superstructure of ideas, ideologies, symbols and emotions. But they can also be spearheads of the most destructive counter-forces, viruses or retroviruses against the most firmly established political systems. Like the *griot*, they can successively destroy and edify, magnify or drag one and the same person through the mud. The *griot* occasionally even refers to himself as *soungourouba* (free girl). Intellectuals, without necessarily being a mercantile, mercenary and venal lot, can be classified as nomads, like a stock of knowledge listed on the stock exchange.

By definition, in the domain of ideas and spiritual hegemony, the intellectual is indeterminate, independent, critical, called upon to change, to overtake and to bypass others. This is the source of his grandeur and misery, and one of the reasons why he is an alligator at ease in every river or ill at ease outside the river.

When some intellectuals say that they do not dabble in politics, this does not mean that they do not have political ideas, that they do not vote, that they have nothing to say on educational or economic policy, that they are indifferent to the constitution of their country, to laws or decrees, including those governing promotion in their careers, or that they have nothing to do with the safety of persons, nor with university immunities that guarantee their autonomy.

In short, in the narrow sense, there is the family of intellectuals, which is a hybrid, heterogeneous group, and in the broader sense, the collective intellectual (in the general sense of the word). Of course, there is unending interaction (actions and reactions) between these two poles. Politics comes into play between the two poles, or rather between these bipartisan poles, as an initiator, a catalyst, or a snuffer of the mind, depending on the circumstances. According to Hegel, the goal of reason's itinerary in history is the state, that is to say political reason. Marx, by contrast, is of the view that the political superstructure is the reflection of material and social contradictions at various stages of history. Politics obtains in both cases, and it is up to men and women, including intellectuals, to give it meaning.

Invariably, state politics seeks to achieve specific objectives such as conquering, managing and controlling the state through mechanisms in which citizens and, therefore, intellectuals are also called on to participate. One also understands that intellectuals are more allergic to or immune to politics in the narrow sense of the word. This is normal inasmuch as they are the spearhead of civil society, and independence or, at least, autonomy is the decisive yardstick of civil society, as concerns any real or potential power.

Professional intellectuals are fully aware, however, that thought is not an innocent exercise. The problem is not commitment or lack of commitment. Be that as it may, one is committed albeit indirectly to the status quo, which is consolidated by one's very neutrality. But can one afford to be neutral in an African state where de facto monopartism reigns supreme? Can one be a passive observer before unfolding unipolar thought, be it endogenous or exogenous? Can the intellectual encamp like a hardened nomad in an oasis, while all around him are raging genocides, mass movements of refugees, tortures and mutilations, random destruction of the environment and bio-diversity, hostage-taking of the young generation as cannon fodder for warlords, the decimation of whole populations by pandemics, the stranglehold of the republican army, the giving away and eradication of age-old cultures and distinct knowledge?

The intellectual is steeped in his society, immersed in the aggressive ongoing globalization process. He cannot flee from one form of globalization to seek refuge in another. And what is more, he cannot lay claim to total independence from the system, for he is an indispensable cog in the wheel. Many intellectuals are almost more useful to the government in power than activists or apparatchiks, for the latter, who are legally registered and visible, have to be paid, whereas the objective, implicit and anonymous support of anti-political intellectuals is free of charge! This does not mean that intellectuals have to be members of political parties, much less opposition parties. They should develop an active neutrality, however, a positive autonomy, as opposed to one that is inert, amorphous and mute. They would thus earn Péguy's famous peremptory rating of certain intellectuals: 'They have clean hands, but the unfortunate thing is that they have no hands!' This means that African intellectuals have to be at the forefront of responsible citizenship.

For the handful of us university students in the late 1950s, however, the nationalist option was not really a matter of choice; it was structurally programmed as a dialectic and antagonistic break with the realities, interests and values of the colonial nation-state whose intellectuals, drawn from the colonial school, had precisely to contribute to their permanent maintenance in power. Among intellectuals, the nationalist option – not to be mistaken for aggressive and hegemonic nationalism – was initially a refusal, a rebellion and a phenomenon of rejection that, by definition, assumed a precedence and priority that outweighed those of a myth or a postulate. It was the catechism of students at the time, expressed in Kwame Nkrumah's famous 'Seek ye first the political kingdom', which I echoed in an editorial of our journal, *Tam-Tam*, in 1952: *'On demande des Nationalistes!'* (the people demand nationalists!). The conflicting geo-strategic interests of the superpowers; the cold war that fanned the armed conflicts of the liberation struggle; the 'dirty wars' in which the 'Wretched of the Earth' sacrificed themselves mutually under their common master's iron rule, in which Western 'democracies' allied with the apartheid regime and Mobutu against the spectre of Moscow, and distinguished African intellectuals such as Amilcar Cabral and Frantz Fanon, *inter alia*, resorted to guerrilla warfare and ended up paying the ultimate price – a sign that the discourse of intellectuals does not boil down to verbal discourse only – this was more or less the fate suffered by intellectuals of that era. I attended the funeral of Amilcar Cabral in Conakry and saw with my own eyes the impact of the lethal bullet on his head.

Between that opportune moment, the practically unanimous state of grace of the rejection of the colonial system and the decisive historic moment of the construction of an alternative liberal and liberating system lay the dark and deadly period when intellectuals were at one another's throats, thereby derailing or at least impeding the liberation movement. This process is not yet over. It started, as it were, with the hijacking of collaborative intellectuals endowed with the official powers of newly won independence, whereas such sycophants and zombies were being manipulated to derail the struggle for independence. I witnessed first-hand the meteoric rise of a fierce opponent of independence who was virtually catapulted to the highest office, whereas a few months before he had countered the arguments raised in our manifesto, 'Let us liberate Africa!', by asserting: 'Are you students mad? You demand independence whereas economically we have nothing; we cannot even manufacture a needle!' I retorted, 'Do you realize that after sixty years of colonialism, economically we have nothing and you want us to stagnate in this situation?' This debate was futile, anyway.

Now, the most insidious trap awaiting nationalist intellectuals is the appeal for their professional skills, which they cannot deny their fatherland, whatever the reason. Several intellectuals, mostly nationalists, were yoked to the power structure as the most eminent experts in their respective fields and, exclusively in that capacity, they were trapped. How could they have turned a deaf ear to such an offer which satisfied an aspiration, a secret yearning, the apparently uncompromising realization of self? 'Silence! We are developing!'

How many generations of executive officers have thus been politically sterilized! How many newly liberated countries have watched their nationalist executives siphoned off and swallowed up by the state technical apparatus! How many executive officials, initially 'highly skilled and motivated', gradually lose their enthusiasm and expertise! Under the auspices of the nation or the United Nations ... For, apparently, expertise has no colour. The deficit and inflation are neither left-wing nor right-wing ... they say. Is it proper, in building the state dependent on Structural Adjustment Programmes, to compromise the independence of the nation? Yet far too many intellectuals have suffered or died in the savage claws of the supposedly neutral tropical Leviathan that is keen to snuff out the debate once and for all. Rule of law or rule by the right? Class state, clan state, ethnic state, patrimonial oligarchy? ... The clan of African intellectuals 'has reasons that defy reason', reasons that defy nationhood. And yet the ethnic group is the potential seat and unmistakable bedrock of the African heritage. It can also become the African nation's genocide mass grave. This is the pathetic crossroads where African intellectuals find themselves today – between civil society, to which they naturally belong, and the nation-state. Perhaps we should start with some semantic clean-up and fine-tuning, however. Where is the state? Where is the nation?

Nationalism

There was a time when some African peoples, in keeping with Hegel's thought (the state as the ultimate reflection of reason's itinerary in history?), were disqualified because they had not attained the higher stage of state societies. They were labelled as 'segmented', 'acephalic' societies. The World Bank, however, now demands the 'lesser state', the 'non-state'. The functions of the state inherited specifically during the colonial era are coercion, repression, window-dressing or, better still, veneering of the state apparatus, as opposed to the principle, the software, the spirit that justifies the institution – that is, the submission of all without exception to impersonal power. The rule of law is an objective system which keeps its distance and the minimum neutrality in relation to all citizens and groups considered as equals. This calls for the application of the principle of horizontal separation and sharing of powers between the legislature, the judiciary and the executive, as opposed to a situation whereby the latter holds the monopoly of power and identifies (as Louis XIV did) with the state, which is the general trend in Africa.

Given its vertical nature, power in Africa often resembles the two-faced god (Janus) in Roman mythology – with one liberal, democratic, polished, refined and orthodox face looking to the outside world, and another, concealed, surly, implacable, not to say savage, looking towards the interior. The state is the inevitable channel of foreign aid to the people. Some states and even clan regimes live extravagantly and thrive on this lie, this semantic alibi.

And the nation? By a legal falsehood which borders on the taboo, the African state is considered as a nation-state in the sense given it in nineteenth-century Europe. This meaning is already being called into question, and even viewed as outdated in the Europe of the Maastricht Treaty and Schengen Agreement. Who can mark boundaries between nations or indeed nationalities in Africa? With such boundaries marked along lines of local African languages, African peoples, these pre-nations are fragmented into two, four, seven or ten existing states. The official languages, which are mostly foreign, do not reflect the configuration of African nations. There are too many so-called national foreign languages, in spite of the existence of major trans-ethnic languages which, barring Arabic, Kiswahili, Shango, etc., do not play any official role. Is it too early for the African nation, which has not received its baptism of fire through major trials and tribulations or major founding communions? Or is it really too late? As a matter of fact, the globalization of market technologies, new information technologies, attitudes and corporations without borders, rightly called multinationals, makes the composition of a micro-nation in Africa in the third millennium an absurd contradiction. It is not only a contradiction; it is utterly meaningless. Where in the occasionally explosive mixture of diverse allegiances do we situate the feeling of belonging which every human being needs in order to be a person, and which every community needs for visibility and recognition? The only solution is for nations to transcend themselves through integration and decentralization, and not through impossible ethnic-based democracy. This means that the pan-Africanist option remains as inevitable today as it was in the past.[1]

Pan-Africanism

Kwame Nkrumah, supported by a few distinguished intellectuals, solemnly proclaimed: 'The independence of Ghana is meaningless, unless the whole of Africa is liberated; unless Africa is united. Africa must unite!'

I was a humble witness to, and an actor in, that race against time, that exciting, momentous sprint in which Africa searched for its identity while the colonialists sought to thwart its efforts through the divide-and-rule policy and dismantled the federations that they themselves had established. Pan-Africanist euphoria peaked in the years that immediately preceded or followed the accession to *de jure* independence. While Cheikh Anta Diop vehemently inveighed against 'dwarf states', while Léopold Sédar Senghor denounced the 'partitioning' of the continent, while the FEANF (Fédération des étudiants d'Afrique noire en France) highlighted African events in incendiary writings and powerful demonstrations, and while the Parti Africain de l'Indépendance (African Independence Party) was being formed, we launched the manifesto of the African Movement for National Liberation: 'Let us liberate Africa!', in which we opted for immediate independence, the United States of Africa and a socialism that had to be premised on local realities, interests and values. That document, which gave precedence to the pan-Africanist ideal, called for the 'no' vote in the referendum of 28 September 1958 in which the people had to choose between two options: the Franco-African community or independence. The French government, however, had decided that vote-counting during that referendum would be organized at the level of territories instead of federations. The day of the referendum marked the historic break between nationalism and pan-Africanism in a phoney dilemma that had no real stakes, and which threw the French-speaking African intelligentsia into total disarray: would the premature so-called vote for independence, which fell within the inadequate framework of the micro-national territory, not break, *ipso facto*ß the bonds of unity and ultimately compromise independence itself? In presenting the people with that false choice between unity within a colonial system and independence in divided ranks, the colonialists clouded the issue, shooting two birds with one stone, particularly by dividing African intellectuals into two opposing camps: those advocating the pre-eminence and/or the priority of independence, on the one hand, and those in favour of unity first and foremost, on the other; the colonialists, of course, knew that both camps were bound to lose. For several decades, most of us were torn between the two poles of that contradiction, which was a complete fabrication, trying to piece together what was left of a broken dream and to limit the damage. I allude to this in my diary for the second half of 1958.

In July and August, I toured Upper Volta and Dahomey to campaign for independence. During my transit through Ghana, I was able, in two days, to meet Kwame Nkrumah in his office in Christiansburg, thanks to Georges Padmore, who had arranged the visit.

For a young lecturer like myself, that meeting with the prophet of pan-Africanism, which lasted about an hour, was one of the high points of my life. During the meeting, Kwame Nkrumah listened attentively to my presentation on our manifesto and expressed his views on relations between our countries and our continent, before introducing me to his ministers, clad in traditional robes. I felt as if I had earned my passport as a pan-African citizen and emerged as an initiated neophyte from the forest of masks.

In late 1958, we lost the political battle of the referendum: the independence option was massively rejected by all countries except Guinea, where the 'no' victory vote gave the country an impetus that would ultimately lead to the independence of the other countries.

The immediate result of the 'no' vote was the withdrawal of all French technical assistance. Sékou Touré sent an SOS to managerial staff throughout Africa and the Caribbean, appealing to them to come and take over from the French. After negotiations, a few dozen executive workers decided to return to Guinea, abandoning their careers, with the conviction that the dialectic between independence and unity was the only way to salvation. This was the idea I defended before the Political Bureau of the PDG (Parti Démocratique de Guinée – Democratic Party of Guinea), when my colleagues honoured me by appointing me as their spokesperson to explain the purpose of our expeditionary force of pan-African nationalists. The particularly warm welcome we received at the National Assembly from the Guinean people is also one of the high points of my life.

In late 1958, the African Peoples' Conference in Accra, which brought together representatives of political movements and civil society to restore order to the ideas and ranks of pan-African nationalists, was a turning point in the commitment of intellectuals, particularly in the liberation struggle (whether armed or not), alliances, etc. I sat next to Patrice Eméry Lumumba, and I can say that we immediately identified with one another. The conference was also attended by trade unionists such as Abdoulaye Diallo of Ugtan and Tom Mboya (two brilliant leaders). There were delegations of young men and women. Nnamdi Azikiwe and Awolowo, with their retinue of ardent supporters, were also in attendance. Frantz Fanon, who also attended the conference, burst into tears while relating Algeria's tragic martyrdom. In fact, the armed struggle was a recurrent theme during the intellectual discussions. What we were discussing was being put into practice by freedom fighters in the outskirts of Accra, in Algeria, Dar es Salaam, etc. Ahmed

Ben Bella expressed in graphic terms the strategic concept of pan-African nationalism by exclaiming in Addis Ababa in 1963: 'We have talked of a development bank. Why have we not talked of a blood bank? A blood bank to assist those fighting in Angola and everywhere in Africa. Thus, to free the peoples who are still under colonial domination, we all accept to die a little or entirely, so that African unity may not be an empty slogan.'

During the hundreds of meetings held shortly before or after independence, dozens of subjects were studied and researched in an in-depth manner at national, bilateral, multilateral and UN levels, thus yielding a treasure trove of knowledge that deserves methodic and systematic revisiting: congresses for intellectuals, pan-African festivals, colloquia organized by the Economic Commission for Africa, UNESCO, UNIDO, WHO and other specialized agencies of the United Nations, international conferences of ONA or the AAU (Association of African Universities), etc., helped to build a body of knowledge, a rich data bank which is still very relevant today.

There is no shortage of research subjects in the fields of education, African personality, 'sustainable development', the environment, science and technology, conflicts, borders, food security, desertification, democracy, the WTO, etc.

The research approach is at times strictly disciplinary and specialized, to the extent of questioning the epistemological and methodological foundations of science, as was the case with history and philosophy, and as should be much more the case in medicine, demography, public and private law, economics, architecture, regional development, etc. I have written about this: the inter-African approach is an imperative of science. In the social sciences, no discipline can claim to produce excellent scientific results in Africa without taking into account the inter-African dimension, not only because of research costs, but also because desertification, winds and clouds, aerosols, epidemics and epizootic diseases and music and dance forms know no boundaries. In short, the geographical, historical, linguistic, religious, natural and medical sciences, etc., must be studied from an inter-African perspective.

To understand the economy of a country, one has to observe processes under way in neighbouring countries. To trace the evolution of a given people, the historian has to pass through two, three, five or perhaps ten states. In geology or physical geography, river or lacustrine basins can only be understood when they are studied across a large number of countries.

In brief, there is no micro-national science.[2]

Elsewhere, the inter-disciplinary, trans-disciplinary or systemic approach adopted for the study of transverse subjects, as CODESRIA has stressed on several occasions, sheds light on African realities in a more comprehensive manner, as was absolutely required in the case of apartheid, which I had the opportunity to experience cursorily in Rhodesia.

The dimension relating to the diaspora was extremely dynamic, powerful and effective in the nationalist and pan-African movement: pan-Africanist ideas were disseminated in London, in the Caribbean, in *Présence Africaine*, at the WINNEBA Centre for Political Studies (Ghana), in Jamaica and the United States, through the universal message of ideologies and the African American arts. At the Conference on the African Encyclopedia, which I had the honour of chairing, I met W. E. B. Dubois and subsequently attended the state funeral organized by Kwame Nkrumah to pay homage to that great pan-Africanist.

At the 2001 World Conference against Racism in Durban, African American intellectuals played a decisive role, as they had done here and there in the past, with a view to compelling the international community to recognize the slave trade as a crime against humanity.

In brief, the OAU, a provisional and fragile pan-African organization, has achieved only partial independence – partial independence because right up to the turn of the century, former French Prime Minister R. Balladur could still write in his *Mémoires*: 'I decided to devalue the CFA Franc.' Similarly, the OAU has achieved only partial unity because it committed the original sin of maintaining colonial borders, supposedly to prevent conflicts. Yet these same borders are in flames. They are structurally prone to conflict. They make every African a foreigner to at least 80 per cent of the other Africans. African borders are instruments of vivisection of peoples and have, since their establishment, caused untold human sacrifice in the form of fratricidal holocausts, merely out of respect for boundary lines already marked in blood by the colonial conquest; such arbitrary and, at times, imaginary parallel and longitudinal lines are too mathematical to be human. They are often insane, outrageous, divisive and senseless because they underdevelop the people torn apart. I dare hypothesize, not to say postulate, that the OAU's generally mediocre performance stems from the fact that the struggle for African nationalism was delinked from the struggle for pan-Africanism, and the majority of African intellectuals accepted and supported this fatal split. In fact, in making the transition from nationalism, whose separation from pan-Africanism was smooth albeit fatal, to constructive nationalism (nation-building), a major historical and decisive process set in: globalization, which renders more obsolete than ever Kwame Nkrumah's peremptory statement: 'Ghana's independence is meaningless, unless the whole of Africa is liberated; unless Africa is united.' One can even say that such still-born independence deconstructs unity and vice versa.

In other words, Africa must stand on its own feet (independence and unity), if it is to stop being what it is today – lame, bedridden and in a coma. African intellectuals, instead of contributing to the production of theoretical discourse and a parody of development at a structural dead end, must decode, unmask, condemn and refute this in favour of alternative globalization and regionalization that needs to be invented through the discovery, if not of a new New World, at least of another Africa which we ourselves and the world need.

The role of intellectuals in generating the binomial driving force of the African Renaissance

In our opinion, this role will entail adopting the identity option, which consists in knowing oneself (*Yeredon*) and, first of all, building oneself up, forging a personality – that is, a role in the world of today. This calls for active resistance against the neo-liberal globalization ideology imposed by the international financial institutions which were recently criticized by Nobel Prize economics laureate Joseph Stiglitz, former chief economist at the World Bank, who finds that they run counter to the Keynesian expansionist approach in matters of employment, effective demand and state intervention. He writes: 'Today globalisation does not work. It does not work for the poor of the world. It does not work for the environment. It does not work for the stability of the world economy.[3] [...] If there is discontent with globalisation, it is because, clearly, it has placed not just the economy above all else, but also a particular vision of the economy – that of market fanaticism – above all others.'[4] He does not hesitate to talk of 'world injustice' and the 'hypocrisy of the advanced industrialized countries' in matters of state intervention, environmental and social costs, aid, net capital flows, etc.

Now, if there is a social group that should play the role of immune defences to prevent Africa from sinking into the AIDS of structural underdevelopment, it is surely, first and foremost, the intellectuals who are sons of this continent. To take just one example, we will cite the work of Mohamed Larbi Bouguerra: *La Recherche contre le Tiers Monde*.[5]

The mere constraint of abiding by the axioms of the Chicago School, which advocates absolute respect for macroeconomic indicators and aggregates – even if the human costs were to be regarded as collateral or secondary effects – should automatically give African intellectuals two reasons for rejecting such axioms: first, we have shifted from econometrics to econolatrics (worship of economics); and second, our countries have been exploited for selfish ends, manipulated, as they are, like guinea pigs in a fundamentalist ideological experiment.

Let us, however, avoid two fatal pitfalls here. First, we must not, in our own turn, blame all our own performance shortfalls and our complicities on others by painting everyone else black: the North, the West, the East. The axis of evil or good has nothing to do with cardinal points.

Besides, we should remember that the specific solution to this negative balance of power does not lie in bemoaning our lot, inveighing against others or withdrawing into micro-nationalism, but in transforming the unequal terms of trade through pan-Africanist nationalism or nationalist pan-Africanism.

More important, and better than the two sides of the same medal, is the dual nature of the commitment of the African intellectual, who is driven by a sense of dialectical cross-fertilization, given that nationalism without pan-Africanism is meaningless and pan-Africanism without a liberation dimension is also an absurdity.

The micro-national level suffers from two fundamental and structural shortcomings. First, there is the incapacity to drive development to a level and magnitude that can generate a ripple effect or synergy, especially in matters of industrialization and value added (economies of scale). Besides, the dictates of the SAPs do not necessarily rule out cases of denial of justice. It is quite the contrary when the state itself is privatized and subjected to patrimonial, clannish or ethnic management.[6] By subtle subterfuge tribalism is used as a pretext to reject indispensable reforms; 'multiparty democracy plays into the hands of ethnic groups'.

Even religion is also turned to account in this new breed of *kultur-kampf.*

One wonders whether the artificial nature of the nation-state, a fragile state founded on dismembered peoples, with no civil society, no memory and no goals, is not the source of the collective and schizophrenic existential disarray that is poles apart from the nation as a fundamental principle of cohesion.

The untreated traumas stifled for decades or centuries can develop psychotic complexes in the subconscious or the unconscious, which explain the subsequent monstrous and fratricidal explosions. Thanks to the social sciences, we can contribute to the treatment of this type of syndrome, preferably in a prophylactic manner.

In the face of the exploitation of real or artificial ethnic identities for selfish ends, we have to foster a new African, nay – an African neo-personality that espouses the ethnic group and jettisons ethnicism.

In point of fact, even if ethnic group, in the real sense of the term, is the hub of Africa's cultural identity, the combination of the predatory greed of traffickers and the existence of a poor and illiterate youth create fertile ground for the emergence of militias rooted in para-ethnic micro-identities – the veritable metastasis of an evil that is not peculiar to Africa.

The strategic goal of African intellectuals should, therefore, be to forge a new nationalism wherein pan-Africanism will be an integral part, serving as a driving force and giving it meaning.

This calls for a new objective status for knowledge, for all forms of knowledge, including ours. Such authentic knowledge gives intellectuals the legitimacy and credibility to assume leadership of the African Renaissance.[7] Such knowledge is self-driven, not cited or recited.

The challenge is for each community that has this bounden duty to forge new syntheses, a new community that is consistent and compatible with external and internal, specific and universal realities. The universal dimension should not be an imposition of some specifics; neither should it be the sum total of all the specifics. Rather, it should be a fruitful and harmonious blend of the best and the most precious aspects of all the specifics, culminating in unity at the summit of the human pyramid.

The idea is not to produce, by coercing the weak cultures of the world, a high-yield cultural hybrid, a stereotyped cultural GMO, but rather to strengthen the capacities of each culture and to place it in a state of dynamic procreation.

Exclusion must be excluded, for exclusion is barbarism. It is only at this price that cultural diversity will become the 'last frontier' separating us from the new 'New World' – not the new world of some distant era but that of tomorrow.

African intellectuals must refuse and reject all forms of internal and external subordination, arbitrary limitation and exclusion. They must reject the restrictive status quo with its conflict-prone structure: that is, strive for genuine modernity wherein everyone is true to himself or herself and all positive interaction is possible.

In this regard, the African heritage, in all forms, has to be built or rebuilt; even if it cannot be pieced together physically, at least its sources and resources can be tapped through the New Information and Communication Technologies (NICT).

This should be like a monument to Africa's historic places and historic achievements – a reminder of the low ebb as well, for we must eschew retrospective romanticism. It is only the complete history (past, present and future) which will vindicate us.

Drawing from the resources of the electronic web, African intellectuals have to be both teachers and researchers, both disseminators of knowledge and mutually supportive depositories of data. Internally driven growth is not only production but social reproduction as well.

Thus, the New African Nation for intellectuals is not a rigid territorial entity, conveniently defined and confined, but a place and a setting without borders and without shores, open and ecumenical; with the proviso that unfair trade with partners shall be abolished. The diaspora is part and parcel of this new concept of the African nation. Such a concept calls for imagination, method, foresight and organization, as experimentally successfully achieved in many structures and organizations: CODESRIA, the AAU (Association of African Universities), CAMES (Higher Education Council for Africa and Madagascar), disciplinary structures such as the AAH (Association of African Historians), etc. Leadership within civil society – 'hegemony' in the Gramscian sense of the word – comes with that price tag.

It is only at the level of the sub-region, at least, that such a project can be financed, for example through sponsorships, with greater emphasis laid on the productive investment aspect of research in social sciences. Research in history, even the history unfolding before our very eyes, and archaeology is very costly but it also generates considerable revenue. Mr Romano Prodi, president of the European Commission, in his address to the National Assembly in Ouagadougou, referred to Africa as the cradle of humanity and, potentially, the future of the same humanity. Yet when President Idriss Deby went to Montpellier to visit Toumai, the oldest *australopithecus* discovered in Chad, the media talked much less of our common ancestor than of the ceremony at which the president was inaugurating a crude oil exploitation project some weeks later.

Let us not gloss over any area. Oil is all well and good, but it can also be very harmful. We must not forget, however, to place at the centre of our identity the reminiscence that we gave birth to man and to history, as well as the memory of the generations that worked – sometimes making the ultimate sacrifice – to build the African Union, whose first commission president is also an intellectual – Alpha Oumar Konare.

In point of fact, we have multiple identities, multiple citizenships as well, beginning with the village grass roots. But if we do not want our children to be condemned to selling mobile telephone cards, second-hand clothing and disposable hankies at the crossroads of our cities, we must have, somewhere in Africa, a strong geo-cultural and economic nerve centre, with African intellectuals serving as prototypes and vectors.

African intellectuals must help the people to develop a more balanced and healthier view of property, of money, sometimes defined as the 'common denominator', which has wraught untold havoc on states and nations. Without being idealistic, the 'common denominator' or 'measure for all' as a reference point and ultimate goal is man himself. Africans say: 'Money is good but man is better because he answers when he is called.' The content of this answer is another matter. It is also said that 'The old man is worth more than his price'; which takes us to the post-economic realm (metaeconomics?), the importance of which is made evident by the human casualties of the heatwave in Europe in the summer of 2003. Intellectuals should assist in analysing the African social solidarity that mobilizes, on a daily basis, tens, hundreds, millions of Africans. Culture has to be 'infrastructured' to produce the contemporary version that conforms to the famous principle: 'Not everything is available on the market'; in any case, not in the same quantities. Soil, health, basic education, potable water cannot be left to the discretion of the 'invisible hand' of the market.

The values platform often coincides with that of political options. Without being partisan, and precisely as a member of civil society, the intellectual can help to civilize politics, so much so that we become 'masters of our destiny and captains of our soul', to borrow from Nelson Mandela.

In this respect as well, the pan-African platform and structures are necessary – nay sufficient – conditions for better protection of human rights, development and democracy for the benefit of intellectuals and their fellow citizens.

To conclude, I would like to point out that specialists in the social sciences, artists and film-makers do not make good use of the intellectual and emotional shock potential of myths, folk tales and cosmogonies, which are a veritable cornucopia. From the West, let us cite Prometheus (who also exists in Africa), Oedipus, Ariadne's thread, etc.

To draw an analogy between the African continent and Osiris, I would say we have to rebuild the African Osiris. It was the brother of Osiris, the wicked Seth, who murdered him, dismembered him, and went on to scatter the limbs so that he should never be pieced together and revived.

But it was his sister, Isis, sister-cum-spouse, supreme mistress of the occult and quintessential science, who found, gathered and rearranged the limbs, thereby making his renaissance and resurrection possible.

I think there is an obvious analogy here with the case of Africa, which has been dismembered several times over and which now needs to be assembled. Intellectuals can play the role of Isis.

In another African folk tale about the creation of the universe it is said that after creating the whole universe God asked himself the question: 'For whom will the sun shine?' And that is how he created the human being: so that the sun may have meaning ...

Meaning: this takes us back to the role of the intellectual who creates meaning. It takes us back to Kwame Nkrumah's prophetic warning: 'Ghana's independence is meaningless, unless the whole of Africa is liberated.'

Yes, we have to piece together the African Osiris, so that the African nation, African nationalism, may have meaning.

I thank you all.

Notes

1 Yves Aimaizo, *L'Afrique est-elle incapable de s'unir?* (Paris: L'Harmattan, 2002).

2 J. Ki-Zerbo, *La Natte des autres, pour un développement endogène en Afrique* (Paris: CODESRIA, 1984), pp. 3ff.

3 Joseph Stiglitz, *La Désillusion* (Paris : Fayart, 2003), p. 279.

4 Ibid., p. 286.

5 Mohamed Larbi Bouguerra, *La Recherche contre le Tiers Monde* (Paris: PUF, 1993).

6 Odile Goerg, 'Catégorisations et representation des espaces et des populations ou comment échapper au retour des clichés', *Afrika Zamani*, 7 and 8, 1999–2000, pp. 91ff.

7 C. A. Diop, *Towards the African Renaissance: Essays on Culture and Development* (New Jersey: Red Sea Press, 1996).

5 | Gender studies for Africa's transformation[1]

AMINA MAMA

This chapter discusses the institutional and intellectual contribution and potential of gender and women's studies (GWS) as a transformative agent in African contexts. The increased engagement with gender studies is analysed in the context of the political, institutional and social challenges of the contemporary era, and the growth in the number of African women entering higher education. Gender and women's studies is viewed as an innovative trans-disciplinary field deriving its impetus from the work of feminist academics. In African academic institutions it responds to the particular challenges facing African intellectuals and activists who are women, and the experiences of African women's movements. The institutional spread of this field is discussed, as are the changing strategic directions of two key sites, with a view to highlighting the challenges and the potential of feminist intellectual work. Throughout, feminist intellectual work is conceptualized as offering valuable methodological and analytical approaches that facilitate the development of critical intellectual capacities. These are defined as being capacities that draw on cutting-edge critical theory, which are critical of the global status quo, and which are essential in ensuring that Africans can proactively address the myriad challenges facing the development and transformation of the region as we enter the twenty-first century.

The present generation of African scholars are post-colonial intellectuals in the sense of having been schooled in contradictions. On the one hand we were born and educated in environments shimmering with all the promise and optimism of newly independent nations, while on the other hand we have borne witness to a series of unforeseen catastrophes – deteriorating economic circumstances, failing institutions, civil wars and dictatorships – as our societies have remained mired in all the challenges of underdevelopment and dependency. Those who have become professional academics have for the most part spent their professional lives located in public institutions established with the substantial public investment and enthusiasm that followed the end of colonial occupation. The decline of higher education institutions, however, has seen many of Africa's thinkers leading rather peripatetic careers which traverse continents and nations, diverse political contexts, and various academic disciplines. For reasons

of history, African intellectual identities are likely to be multiply constituted and deeply cosmopolitan, located in an epistemological world that
is likely to owe as much to Africa's diverse social movements, civil society
formations and independent research networks as to the universities. The
current global configurations of power challenge post-colonial intellectuals
all over the world, but at the same time provide African thinkers with valuable vantage points from which to conduct critical analysis and reflection.
It might be said that perspectives on global developments are at their
sharpest where the manifestations of globalization reach their negative
extremes. On the African continent, globalization – or at least the dominant forces executing the global development agenda – currently threaten
the hard-won political and policy gains made by popular movements for
social justice, perhaps especially women's movements, since the advent
of nation-statehood.

The global context – in which military and corporate financial interests seem to overrule social justice agendas – frames the importance of
radical intellectual work today. In African contexts, the intensification of
contradictions between policy and practice, between the rhetoric of rights
and the reality of neo-liberal economic strategies, informs and energizes
many kinds of counter-hegemonic intellectual activity. The persistence
of gender injustice and inequality in all major post-colonial political and
social institutions, including Africa's particularly beleaguered campuses,
also stimulates critical reflection among the growing pool of educated
women in Africa in and beyond the academy. Whatever the case, there
has been a deepening interest in feminist-inspired intellectual work, and
this is reflected in the remarkable proliferation in the number of sites
engaging in gender and women's studies in many parts of Africa during
recent decades. The contradictory conditions under which this interest has
grown, however, also present their own challenges and constraints.

The following analysis identifies four conditions that can be seen to
have fuelled the development of gender and women's studies in African
contexts. The first of these is the development of political consciousness
inspired by women's political engagement both during colonial rule and
since independence. This has led to a greater awareness and acceptance of
the emancipation of women as an integral and necessary facet of African
liberation and development in general. Second, the internationalization
of feminism, and the resulting manifestation of gender discourses – however tempered – within international agencies and national governments,
can be seen to have stimulated intellectual, activist and policy interests
in involving women in modernization, and this has been reflected in
development policies. That this has tended to reflect integrationist and

instrumentalist approaches to 'the woman question' is self-evident with the benefit of hindsight. Third, gender studies have benefited from the gradual but steady growth in the overall numbers of women gaining access to higher education, and their related exposure to diverse intellectual resources and influences. Fourth, the political, historical and economic conditions of African intellectual development have inevitably generated much critical engagement with Western intellectual legacies, notably the exclusionary legacies of Western ivory tower universities, the disciplinary organization of knowledge, and the methodologies for the production of knowledge. These have never seemed to make intellectual, organizational or financial sense to scholars confronted with the enormous challenges facing underdeveloped societies, and the demand for a socially responsive and responsible intelligentsia. These popular pressures have given rise to interest in socially engaged and trans-disciplinary intellectual directions on several fronts, one of which is gender studies (see CODESRIA 2001; Gulbenkian Commission 1996).[2]

Feminism and development

Feminism is taken here to refer quite simply to the political and intellectual movement for the liberation of women. As it has arisen in diverse contexts, feminism can be traced to many disparate trajectories, some reflecting highly localized responses to particular conditions, while others are decidedly trans-national in their reach and importance.

In African contexts, it is now well established that women were actively involved in the early-to-mid-twentieth century anti-colonial and nationalist struggles that led up to independence and the establishment of modern nation-states. The ensuing period has seen women's activism continuing, but now being directed at the state structures that women helped to craft. The attainment of nation-statehood has made it incumbent on women to pursue their integration into public life, and much energy has been devoted to lobbying for legal and policy reforms, and demanding women's equal representation in the hierarchies of power and fairer access to resources.

The political premise of this state-focused mode of activism is one that reflects great faith in all the political and public sector institutions that women, like men, had fought and worked to establish, and later often found employment within. In other words, women, as devotees and citizens of the new nations, deserved a fair share of public resources and access to opportunities, as well as to modern legal rights and protections. As a result of both local and international activism, women have indeed achieved significant political, legal and policy reforms, and governments have been pushed to set up national structures responsible for 'women's affairs'.

The efficacy of these legal and policy reforms and government structures ostensibly instituted to address the articulated interests of women has varied, but by and large has been limited in ways that continue to provoke critical debate (Third World Network 2002; AGI/AGENDA 1999).

Whatever the case, their efficacy has been further compromised in the context of the retraction of the public sector within which all such gains are located. The fact is that neo-liberal economic doctrines are depleting the provision of public services and support systems in ways that are having a highly deleterious impact on the lives of ordinary citizens across Africa, a growing majority of whom are already living in debilitating conditions. That these negative consequences are compounded by the dynamics of gender inequality is a fact that bears repeating because the conditions facing ordinary African women continue to be so harsh.

Now that the state has been rolled back (and in some instances has collapsed entirely), feminist analysts who once focused on the challenges posed by the bureaucratization of feminism within government and UN institutions are directing their attention at the devastating impact of globalization (Mohanty 2002). The poorly defined and even more poorly understood logic of 'market forces' appears to be steadily supplanting even the limited benevolence and protection of states that, despite decades of feminism and gender activism, have by and large failed to transcend their own partiarchal premises.

In other words, feminism has made complicated inroads in the world of global development, and the gains and setbacks are the product of complex negotiations within and across the hierarchics of power that constitute and drive the development industry. Each apparent advance has generated its own challenges and risks; each manoeuvre has been greeted with new manoeuvres. As we enter the 'knowledge society', a key concern must be the global inequalities played out in the arena of knowledge production, in which I include feminist knowledge production. If the interaction between feminist movements and development has generated the gender industry, then feminist interventions in African intellectual life can be said to have generated gender and women's studies, in the manner explored below.

Intellectual development in Africa

African peoples' enthusiasm for intellectual development has been expressed in many ways, but most obviously in popular support for the establishment of over six hundred universities since independence. Ordinary people on the poorest continent embrace higher education (HE) as a key means to upward mobility, a route out of the debilitating deprivations of poverty and into the mainstream of national or even international life.

As has been widely observed, most new nations began with a flag, an army, a civil service and the proud establishment of at least one national university.

> Widespread university education is essentially a post-colonial phenom-enon ... only eighteen out of the forty-eight countries of sub-Saharan Africa had universities or colleges before 1960. With the approach of political independence or immediately thereafter, many African countries regarded the establishment of local universities as a major pillar of the post-colonial national development project. The new universities were to help the new nations build up their capacity to manage and develop their resources, alleviate the poverty of the majority of their people, and close the gap between them and the developed world. (Sawyerr 2002: 2)

Gross enrolment rates in African universities increased dramatically during the 1970s, from an estimated 181,000 in 1975 to over 600,000 in 1980. After a plateau in the 1980s, the figures more than doubled to over 1.75 million in 1995, and are still growing fast in most places. Despite this substantial growth, the African region still has the lowest tertiary enrolment rates in the world, with a gross enrolment rate of only 5 per cent. This has not prevented the sector from being targeted for financial reforms likely to constrain growth and public access, and to subject institutional development to elusive market forces likely to compromise social justice and equity agendas (ibid.; Zeleza 2003: ch. 2).

It is also worth noting that, contrary to the rhetoric of their detrac-tors, African universities differ from Western 'ivory tower' ideals in being profoundly modern and modernizing institutions. Despite the more recent obeisance to globalization of some institutions, most university mission statements are not so much 'universal' as regional and nationalist in their visions and goals, and the social responsibility of African intellectuals to their societies is assumed. Academics, while not always loved by politicians, have nevertheless been given key responsibilities in African nations, some taking up ministerial or even presidential positions during the early dec-ades, and many more appointed to high-level public office since. Even military dictators found it expedient to co-opt academics by recruiting whole cadres of personnel from the universities and the intellectual left, as the examples of both Ghana and Nigeria demonstrate very well.

Over time, as nation-states themselves became more inward looking and neo-colonial, so too did the universities servicing them. Even some of the more radical states that claimed to be revolutionary or Marxist un-leashed campaigns of terror against the intelligentsia. Authoritarian and military rulers dramatically diminished intellectual freedom even while they established new institutions. At the same time, economic decline and the imposition of international economic doctrines constrained the availability of public funding, and the quality of intellectual life deteriorated, becoming increasingly constrained, competitive and fragmented.

With hindsight it is easy to see that the 'national' orientation of universities remained unproblematized, and insensitive to the fact that African nations are deeply marked by gender, class, ethnicity, religion and various other dimensions of difference and inequality. In keeping with the universal assumptions of Western liberal thought, it was assumed that differential patterns of access and inclusion would simply wither away, once the formally instituted social divisions of the colonial era were abolished. While there were various policies strategies directed at indigenization/ Africanization, and at overcoming regional and ethnic divisions, positive action to eradicate gender inequality was deferred.[3] Only in recent years have a minority of African nations introduced specific policies to increase the intake of women, despite the empirical evidence of pervasive under-representation most countries (Bennett 2002; Mama 2003).[4] The persistence of ethnic, religious and regional disparities in access has not been adequately monitored, but the available evidence indicates that the expansion of the public university sector allowed significant numbers of women and other previously disadvantaged groups to acquire tertiary education for the first time in history.

This means that African universities have served as key routes to social mobility, enabling steadily increasing multitudes of Africans to gain the credentials and training to pursue professional careers, first at home and later abroad too.[5] It is therefore worth recalling that until the crisis and reform of African higher education, locally trained doctors, lawyers, teachers, scientists, social scientists, artists and media professionals were being produced in sufficient numbers to staff government and private sector institutions established all over the continent.

The well-documented deterioration of Africa's higher education sector during the 1980s and 1990s need not be detailed here (see Federici et al. 2000; Zeleza 2003). Life simply became untenable for new generations of Africans who might reasonably have been expected to play keys roles in national and regional development. Significant numbers migrated overseas, only a minority were able to pursue academic careers, and those who remained found their brains drained in other ways – into various entrepreneurial and consultancy activities that soon became more essential to their survival than their professional employment as highly trained academics. The long-term consequences of the deterioration of African higher education for the development capacities of the region, especially

intellectual development, are probably immeasurable. One of the consequences of the decline has been the diminution of both academic freedom
and institutional autonomy, not just from the state, but more invidiously
from international financial institutions and other external interests (Diouf
and Mamdani 1994; Federici et al. 2000).

Who are the architects of the decline and ongoing redirection of African
academic institutions? While the growing leverage exercised by international financial institutions and interests during the seemingly endless
economic crisis is commonly invoked, it is also clear that authoritarian governments and officials have had their own reasons for embracing external
directives. Even the more democratically inclined regimes, however, which
initially placed a premium on education, eventually themselves complied
with economic conditionalities that led to the rapid erosion of educational
institutions, even as the demand continued to grow.

Gender politics in African academic organizations

Despite the modernizing and emancipatory imperatives guiding African
universities, and the gradual increase of the proportion of women accessing tertiary education, the empirical profile is one in which inequality has
been sustained across the first three decades of independence. In the
mid-1990s the available figures suggested that only about 3 per cent of
Africa's professorate were women (Ajayi et al. 1996). More recent calcula-
tions indicate a high level of variation, but place the number of women
faculty at 6.1 per cent in Ethiopia, 12 per cent in Ghana and Nigeria, and,
after a decade of affirmative action, 19 per cent in Uganda. Only 25 per
cent of students on the continent were women in the mid-1990s (ibid.).
At the present time the statistics are still incomplete, but the percentage
of women enrolled as students varies widely from a low of 9 per cent in
Central African Republic and 15 per cent in Ethiopia to over 40 per cent
in Morocco, Egypt and Senegal. Libya and Swaziland are the only countries
approximating numerical parity, both showing 51 per cent (Tefera and
Altbach 2003).

These global figures address only access to study and employment, and
tell us very little about the institutional cultures and conditions facing
women in Africa's universities. For the time being, deeper analysis must
rely on qualitative evidence and the accumulated experience and knowledge among Africa's more gender-conscious academics (see *Feminist Africa*
2002). What is clear from these disparate sources is the fact that Africa's
campuses remain difficult and challenging places for women at many
levels, in ways that are complicated further by the dynamics of growing
poverty, and by persistently inequitable ethnic, religious, sexual and other

social relations. The persistence of patriarchal and misogynistic campus cultures, the growing public sensitivity to sexual harassment and abuse, and the complex links between sexual transactions and the spread of HIV/AIDS undoubtedly fuel interest in gender and women's studies, if not in the more assertive manifestations of feminist politics.

As a field in which women are taken seriously as scholars and intellectuals, gender and women's studies offers women students and academic staff alternative routes to academic and professional development. Gender and women's studies departments also offer women possibilities of collegial and mentoring relationships less likely to be subverted by the interpersonal dynamics of gender and sexuality. Feminist methodologies tend to be learner-centred and empowering, and to privilege collegialism and collective intellectual work as well as a plethora of innovative research methodologies sensitive to power relations and gender dynamics. At the analytical level, feminist theory and gender analysis offer tools that problematize and explore the myriad experiences of marginalization that still constitute many aspects of women's lived experience in and beyond the academy.

Other, more positive developments have occurred during the period of crisis and reform. The African intellectual community has responded in many ways, but the most strategic has been the organization of independent intellectual work outside the academic establishment. The 1970s saw the emergence of several regional scholarly associations and networks that sought to facilitate trans national intellectual dialogue. Perhaps the most significant of these are the Council for the Development of Social Science Research in Africa (CODESRIA) in 1973, and the Association of African Women for Research and Development (AAWORD) in 1977. Both were autonomous pan-African networks which reaffirmed, and later came to sustain, earlier intellectual traditions that challenged imperial legacies and committed African scholarship to new and trans-disciplinary methodologies, to multi-lingualism, to egalitarian and radical research and scholarship grounded in African social realities and concerns, and to the defence of academic freedom.

During the ensuing period, as the crisis in the university sector deepened, the relative importance of the NGO sector in African intellectual life has grown, especially in terms of research and publication. In the end it is these independent bodies which have ensured the presence of a vibrant and exciting intellectual culture closely attuned to the changing conditions and challenges facing Africans at all levels of their diverse and complex societies. CODESRIA and AAWORD were joined by the Addis Ababa-based Organization of Social Science Research in East Africa (OSSREA) and the

Southern African Political Economy Trust (SAPES) based in Harare. Later, nationally focused NGOs such as the Centre for Basic Research in Kampala, the Port Harcourt-based Centre for Advanced Social Studies, the Kano-based Centre for Research and Documentation, both in Nigeria, and the Forum for Social Studies in Addis Ababa were also established as key sites for radical research. Women have been actively involved in bringing feminist theory and gender analysis to these forums, but they have also established a plethora of women's organizations engaging in research, documentation and training from an activist orientation. These include the following: the Tanzanian Gender Networking Programme, the Women and Laws in Southern African research network, the Zimbabwe Women's Resource Centre and Network, the Women's Law and Development Network, the Nairobi-based FEMNET, the ISIS-WICCE network based in Uganda, the Southern African Network of Tertiary Institutions Challenging Sexual Harassment and Gender-based Violence, and the Feminist Studies Network, hosted by the African Gender Institute.[6] These more independent organizations have been valuable and exciting sites for the pursuit of feminist studies and activism in various fields, unhindered by the weight of university bureaucracies and institutional politics, and less constrained by the disciplinary requirements that often direct and limit academic research.

It needs to be borne in mind, however, that the non-governmental sector is altogether much smaller than the university sector in the region, and is far more vulnerable to political pressures, donor interests and other pressures than public institutions. The importance of these scholarly and research NGOs is therefore not so much their scale and reach as their intellectual politics, something that has assumed particular importance throughout the period of crisis and reform. In offering space for conceptual and methodological innovation and critical enquiry and analysis, they have made a significant contribution to African research and intellectual culture, at a time when this has been under siege from a formidable array of forces. Organizations such as CODESRIA have played a key role in ensuring that African intellectual life has retained a degree of vibrancy and radicalism, offering intellectual support, research funding and training to scholars concerned about maintaining critical and socially responsive orientations. The value of this has become more salient in a context in which academic freedoms have been compromised within many of the region's conventional academic institutions, first by governmental controls and censorship, and later by the intellectual consequences of globalization and higher education reform.

Often able to draw on well-developed international connections for support, these forums carry out activities which reflect a deep collective commitment to maintaining and strengthening critical intellectual work in Africa. The women's organizations carrying out research and documentation have sought to maintain a close and reciprocal engagement between theory, policy and practice.[7] The immediacy and intensity of lobbying and advocacy work, however, may often have led to it taking priority over more reflective modes of intellectual engagement and reflection. What has become clearer with experience is the fact that maintaining the synergy between theory and practice, between research and activism, presents challenges that require both intellectual skill and strategic competence.

Coming back to the broader societal conditions, I noted that feminist activism has made it incumbent on governments, international agencies and other policy-makers to display some level of engagement with the gender implications of development strategies, policies and projects. This has in turn created a demand for gender experts who can lay claim to enough technical proficiency to be contracted to provide 'gender services' to mainstream institutions. The fact that all the gender servicing of mainstream institutions of the last three decades or so has failed to bring about substantive improvements in the status of women vis-à-vis men, however, only further underlines the need for more critical and conceptually profound approaches than might initially have been apparent. In the meantime, the demand for gender expertise looks set to persist under the various development rubrics – women in development, women and development, gender and development, gender mainstreaming, and so on. Feminist critics of the whole business of development can be forgiven for suggesting, at times furiously, that all these shifting terms signify is a parasitic relationship of appropriation and neutralization, as women continue to be oppressed and exploited in old and new ways.

The following section critically reviews the intellectual and institutional capacities within the field of gender and/or women's studies (GWS) in African academic institutions.[8]

Feminist scholarship

Feminist intellectuals have generated a large and diverse body of theoretical and conceptual tools, research methodologies and pedagogical innovations and adaptations which are deployed by teachers, trainers, researchers and activists all over the world. They have also produced a substantial body of knowledge, both local and international in scope, which displays a rich tapestry of diverse and dynamic political and intellectual trajectories (Mohanty et al. 1991; Alexander and Mohanty 1997; Basu 1997).

GWS departments place a premium on their relevance to political and policy considerations, and many of those in the West have internationalized their offerings in an effort to rise to the challenges of globalization. Mohanty (2002: 518–23) describes three variations of this process: the feminist-as-tourist/international consumer, the feminist-as-explorer who is more open-minded but no less voracious a consumer; and finally the feminist solidarity/comparative feminist studies type. Without going into the same level of detail, let me simply note that all these are US-based, and that while we might recognize the 'types' and even encounter them all quite frequently, I am more concerned to address the epistemological and practical challenges that face feminist scholars living and working in African contexts.

In this respect it is worth recalling that one of the major contributions of contemporary feminist theory, enriched as it has been by the interventions of Southern-based feminists, is an insistence on being constantly alert to the politics of location and diversities of class, race, culture, religion and sexuality. Feminist epistemology also seeks to build an understanding of the connections between the local and global, between the micro-politics of subjectivity and everyday life and the macro-politics of global governance and political economy. This reflects a commitment to a certain holism, offering conceptual tools that traverse the various layers of social realities, so challenging and subverting the disciplinary and locational fragmentations that have characterized Western academic traditions.

Feminist theorists therefore straddle many intellectual and institutional arenas, in which they face the challenge of keeping global and local levels of analysis in their sights. They must therefore cultivate the navigational and strategic skills required to move between the different levels of analysis, while remaining alert to the fact that these heuristically discernible layers are often interlaced in complicated ways.

In the academic arena, whether one refers to women's studies, gender studies or feminist studies, it is clear that feminist thought has generated a great deal of intellectual ferment across all the disciplines. Feminist studies have often been deeply subversive, overturning pre-existing assumptions, pre-existing histories of knowledge, and transforming pre-existing accounts of human history with rich and interesting herstories that function to complete and to subvert the masculine-dominated canons that went before.

Several features distinguish feminist thought in African contexts. First and most obvious are the historical relations that have constructed Africa and notions of Africa from the outside. African philosophers have drawn our attention to the fact that for centuries Africa has occupied a peculiar place in Western mythology, a dark land of fables and fantasies, the antithesis of Western civilization, enlightenment and reason.[9] The advent of modern science did little to interrupt this fantastic status, but rather continued to legitimize exploitative and extractive agendas, constructing the continent as a series of myths that grew more Gothic with every generation. Once the destruction of earlier civilizations was complete, systems of occupation and exploitation ensured that underdevelopment gained ground.[10]

The demythologization of Africa has been a central project of the modern-day African intelligentsia, ever since Africanus Horton dreamed of an African university, back in the nineteenth century. Nationalist intellectuals, political visionaries and philosophers have continuously asserted their own visions of Africa and Africanness (or Africanity). Whether their consciousness was nationalist or pan-Africanist, however, African intellectuals have continued to display a quite remarkable reticence over questions of gender. What the dominance of male interests and concerns has meant for African thought and intellectual development has yet to be properly addressed within the African scholarly community. For the time being, it would seem that African and feminist intellectual trajectories have largely continued to develop in parallel universes, in a manner that restricts the value and relevance of work being produced by mainstream scholars (Pereira 2002). In the meantime there continues to be a fair amount of myth-making about African women, African femininity and, of course, African feminism. African men and masculinity, and gender-blind intellectual and analytical perspectives, continue to hold centre stage, while the impact of persisting male domination on all aspects of social and political life remains unproblematized and normative.

While there is some receptiveness to feminist interventions within the independent scholarly bodies, mainstream academic institutions have proved far more intransigent, the majority insisting that feminism, and therefore GWS, has no local currency. Only a small minority of African male academics are aware of the now substantial body of gender research that documents, historicizes and locates women's activism and women's intellectual contribution to African societies and scholarship.[11]

Whatever the local trajectories and conditions that have given rise to feminist activism in African contexts, it is clear that the development of GWS in Africa has been complicated by the global inequalities in knowledge production that favour Western scholarship, as well as by the impact of international development institutions, and their particular gender discourses in African contexts.

Development policy interest in gender has clearly facilitated the growth of gender studies as a field, but there is also evidence to suggest that this has also led to a high level of instrumentalism, seen in the emphasis on policy studies, technical skills and application. The examples discussed below indicate that the developmental interest may also have led to the premature overburdening of a nascent intellectual community that has yet to acquire the institutional capacity to meet the multiple demands for services coming from various quarters. The question of intellectual capacity also arises. Today's university teachers are required to administer and deliver teaching and research under increasingly challenging institutional and financial conditions. Those who are women often find themselves playing multiple roles in institutional maintenance, and social support roles to students and colleagues too. Those with activist inclinations, as is the case for many working in the field of GWS, also need to be conceptually equipped to do more than passively service disparate policy agendas, and to take on higher levels of critical analysis and engagement in the policy arena.

From the practical arena come extra-institutional demands and expectations from international agencies, governmental officials, politicians, policy-makers and activists across all the sectors seeking to bring gender into their work (or at least to demonstrate that they have attempted to do so). Many of these are women seeking support in advancing gender agendas in the national political and policy arena; others come from international development agencies seeking local informants or gender consultants; yet others come from international, national and community-based NGOs and networks. While the exigencies of funding might privilege the use of Western gender consultants in this market, it is apparent that local gender expertise is also in demand, and increasingly seen as a way of reducing costs. Even so, it is a need that GWS units seek to address, knowing as they do that they might well be more effective, given the specific nuancing and complexity of gender relations in any particular context. The yawning gap between legal and policy prescriptions on the one hand and persisting inequality on the other may well have something to do with the prevalence of generic recipes and tools that may often be insensitive to local conditions, subtleties and sensibilities.

In what follows I review the institutional capacity for gender and/or women's studies in Africa, with particular attention to the university departments at Makerere and Cape Town. The purpose of this exercise is to consider the prospects for gender studies realizing its potential as a critical and independent field of work.

Mapping the terrain[12]

GWS has been a growth area over the last two decades. The African Gender Institute's tracking of this growth indicates that from just a handful of sites in the early 1990s the field has grown substantially.[13]

A total of 30 universities across the continent responded to the survey, identifying their institutions as sites for teaching and researching gender and women's studies. These universities are Addis Ababa University in Ethiopia; Ahfad University in Sudan; Ahmadu Bello University, Lagos State University, Obafemi Awolowo University, University of Benin, University of Ibadan, University of Nigeria and Usmano Danfodiyo University in Nigeria; Makerere University in Uganda; the Universities of Buea and Yaounde in Cameroon; the University of Cape Coast and the University of Ghana in Ghana; the University of Malawi; the University of Namibia in Namibia; the University of Sierra Leone; the University of Zambia; the University of Zimbabwe; the Institute for Gender and Women's Studies at the American University in Cairo, Egypt; and Rhodes University, the University of Cape Town, Fort Hare University, the University of Durban-Westville, the University of Natal, the University of Pretoria, the University of Stellenbosch, the University of South Africa (UNISA) and the University of the Western Cape in South Africa. South Africa has the greatest number of Gender and Women's Studies teaching sites, with 9 out of the country's 27 universities offering some degree of gender and women's studies teaching. With seven universities out of forty teaching gender and women's studies, Nigeria has the second largest number of gender studies sites on the continent. Ghana and Cameroon identified two universities each serving as gender studies teaching and research sites, while most other countries included in this survey had only one.

The oldest of these are those at the Women's Documentation Centres in the Institute of African Studies at the Universities of Ibadan and Dar es Salaam, while the largest is the Department of Women and Gender Studies at Makerere University.[14]

The number of faculty and students has increased substantially too, and there are signs that gender studies is indeed gaining institutional ground, as the number of sites recognized as full academic departments has also risen during the last few years. The AGI's survey responses indicated that:

Sites for teaching and researching gender and women's studies are structured and administered in a number of different ways. Certain institutions have departments, units or programmes dedicated to gender and women's studies teaching and research, while other institutions have gender interwoven or 'mainstreamed' within other, more traditional disciplines or taught courses. Of the 30 institutions 17 have dedicated gender teaching and/or research units, programmes or departments, while the remaining 13 institutions offer gender studies as courses or modules within other institutional departments or courses. Dedicated gender programmes, units or departments, for the purpose of this study, are defined as units which specialise in, and have as their core function, gender teaching and/or research, with dedicated staff and a dedicated coordinator, director or chair. The existence of a dedicated gender studies unit can be taken as a superficial indicator of institutional commitment, but for this to be meaningful requires additional investment in infrastructural and highly-trained human resources in gender and women's studies.

Of the dedicated units, however, only four have full departmental status: the University of Makerere's Department of Women and Gender Studies, the University of Buea's Department of Women's Studies, the University of Cape Town's African Gender Institute, and the University of Zambia's Gender Studies Department.

Only five universities out of 316 on the entire continent offer undergraduate degrees.[15] Twelve of the identified sites teach masters programmes (six of these being in South Africa). Doctoral provision is also scarce, with only two sites offering doctoral degrees – the African Gender Institute in Cape Town and Makerere's Department of Women and Gender Studies. Despite the demand for places, graduate programmes have relied heavily on throughput from strong undergraduate teaching courses, as indicated by the experience of attempts to establish graduate programmes in response to demand for gender studies at the universities of Stellenbosch and Witwatersrand in South Africa, both of which have since retracted. The shortage of doctoral programmes seems to reflect the dearth of senior-level teaching capacity, as there are hardly any full professors with specialized skills in gender studies, and those willing to supervise doctorates find themselves unable to accommodate the demand. This may change as a few more African women working in GWS obtain doctorates with each year that passes.[16]

The intellectual content of the teaching varies, but even a cursory survey indicates that the vast majority teach in the area of development. Very few teach, or publicly admit to teaching, in more controversial fields, such as sexuality, and those who do place it under the respectable rubric of health or population studies, rather than treating it as a key aspect of gender, or even gender and development. This suggests a degree of intellectual pragmatism, and a compliance with administrative rationales, and with development servicing, accommodating gender and women's studies only in so far as they present a funding opportunity.[17] Those pouring energy and labour into GWS are often motivated by feminist politics, and pursuing a radical and transformative intellectual agenda, perhaps with a degree of discretion. The result is that administrators and feminist scholars find themselves coming into conflict over disparate and poorly articulated agendas that play out in invidious and contradictory ways. For scholars, it is increasingly becoming apparent that the boundary between intellectual pragmatism and institutional opportunism is a slippery one, and the more radical among feminist scholars articulate a concern over the fact that teachers are becoming increasingly conventional and less activist in their work on Africa's campuses.[18]

Those engaged in teaching point to a number of constraints. Beyond the salient problems of overload and poor remuneration, a major challenge to the development of locally relevant teaching that can support and/or develop activist agendas with local women's movements is posed by the limited availability of locally generated research and publications, and the constrained access to those that do exist (AGI 2002).

The existing programmes and departments face many challenges. Kasente (2002) provides us with a frank and honest appraisal of the achievements and compromises at Africa's largest gender studies department, the Department of Women and Gender Studies based at the University of Makerere:

> ... the department's experiences in its first decade demonstrate considerable quantitative growth in terms of student numbers, the development of a national and international profile and the expansion of research. This however has occurred alongside a diminishing sense of internal cohesiveness, accountability to the women's movement and engagement with issues of gender transformation in the broader society. (Kasente 2002: 91)

The wider reform effort at Makerere has created a situation in which there are now over a thousand students enrolled at the department, while half of the ten faculty are away pursuing doctoral degrees, now a prerequisite for promotion. The rapidly increased teaching load has been accompanied by competing demands coming from stakeholders within and outside the university. From within the university have come demands related to gender mainstreaming, notably the work of ensuring that various players are kept aware of the cross-cutting importance of gender, coupled with demands that burden the department with the task of providing all the conceptual and practical resources for implementing 'gender mainstreaming'. From without have come the competing requests from government for support for the ministry and various women's organizations, and from international donors seeking the training of local development workers. The department tried to respond to these needs by negotiating partnership arrangements with northern institutions. These enabled the department to establish an outreach programme in gender training, which set out to achieve the commendable goal of creating '... a critical mass of development workers who would work directly with communities to enhance their capacities to meet women's practical needs and to advocate for change where required'. Despite its popularity with the constituencies for whom it was designed, however, the gender training programme could not be sustained once donor funding was discontinued.[19]

The AGI, faced with a similar multiplicity of opportunities and requests from within and beyond the campus, has also been subject to shifting donor interests that have undermined the key national programme focused on policy analysis, training and organizational transformation in South Africa, leading to its suspension in 1999. Following this experience the AGI moved to prioritize the long-term development of critical intellectual capacities and knowledge production, pursued through strong, Africa-focused academic teaching with an emphasis on feminist methodologies and research. Given the minimal core staffing, this necessitated a reduced engagement with policy-makers and practitioners. The ensuing years saw the AGI develop a full undergraduate major degree in Gender and Women's Studies, initiating a postgraduate programme offering honours, masters and doctoral degrees in Gender and Transformation, while continuing to host African women scholars, produce research and publications and run an active website. While struggling to deliver a full academic programme designed to produce teachers and researchers, the AGI continued to lobby and strategize with a view to strengthening its institutional capacity within the university. The strategy of pursuing institutional consolidation through core academic programming, however, has not proved successful, despite the broad expressions of commitment to equity and transformation reflected in university policies.[20]

Ironically, the same recent period of local institutional losses has seen the AGI pursuing its explicitly articulated transformative intellectual agenda on the much broader continental and international fronts, which initially appeared to be a far more ambitious undertaking. The year 2001 saw the initiation of a continent-wide academic networking and intellectual capacity-building programme, Strengthening Gender Studies for Africa's Transformation (GWSAfrica). The broad vision behind this programme is that of an African continent enriched by a robust and dynamic intellectual environment which supports African teaching and research in the field of GWS as a substantive contribution to gender justice. This is pursued through a programme of activities to strengthen African teaching and research in GWS by bringing teachers and researchers based in African universities together in a series of carefully designed intellectual engagements.

The GWSAfrica programme was launched at a regional workshop whose participants set out an action plan. This has led to the following activities:

- A regional network of scholars, researchers and ITC activists has been established.
- A listserve has been established and has maintained ongoing discussion and intellectual engagements among network members.
- A project website of teaching and research resources has been established and maintained, with content areas that so far include review essays and bibliographies, policy papers, resources on politics, identity and culture, religion, health, gender-based violence, education, ICTs, and land/economics. Special sections are dedicated to student writing and current debates.
- A continental gender studies journal, *Feminist Africa*, has been established as an online and hard-copy publication.[21]
- A core curriculum and supporting resources for those teaching GWS in African tertiary institutions are being developed by a curriculum working group convened within the network.

With a small team of project staff, the programme relies on a high level of input and engagement within the primary target community of gender scholars in African institutions, and on the maintenance of close synergy between the different components. So far both have been achieved, as the listserve, websites and journal all support one another, and the intellectual dialogue that has arisen through these systems has informed the curriculum work.

Overall, it is clear that the AGI places great emphasis on working with the community of African feminist scholars to create a supportive intellectual environment and strengthen critical analytical and research capacities. In this sense it differs from conventional academic departments, yet as a strategy it relies on partnership with other centres. To this end the AGI maintains close contact with other sites, and envisages further partnerships with these, particularly with regard to gender research.

The emphasis on continental networking clearly draws on the positive experience of and connections with the more independent NGO-based organizations and scholarly networks listed above. The AGI attaches particular importance to intellectual transformation, and it is to this end that it seeks to rehabilitate and claim space within academic institutions and to insist on regarding universities as legitimate and strategically important sites for feminist work in African contexts. This is particularly challenging given the prevailing academic climate of financial and administrative stringency, in which many African scholars have been habituated to compromise and constraint, and to the ongoing commodification of knowledge. The recent experience of African higher education institutions has posed profound challenges to the emergence of strong, well-rooted, critical perspectives of any kind, including those discussed here, which emanate from feminist concerns though rooted in the unique vantage points offered by diverse African contexts.

Conclusions

I have argued that African GWS has emerged out of both the particular historical and present-day challenges facing the continent and African women in particular. The development nexus has complicated the expansion of the field, but at the same time this has enabled it to grow despite the overall deterioration of higher education.

At an institutional level, most GWS sites are under-resourced and understaffed, having been brought about by high levels of voluntarism from a few dedicated women. Their initial establishment has often been facilitated by instrumental interests rather than by any appreciation of what feminist intellectual work entails or offers. This has meant that GWS has been started, but often without the institutional support that would guarantee consolidation. Most universities are willing to accept donor funding for such initiatives, while failing to make them sustainable in terms of university budgets and staffing plans. In the long run this will ensure that even the most vibrant and productive sites remain precarious, highly exploitative places in which to work, relying on dedication and idealism, not to mention the resilience to withstand over-archingly masculinist institutional cultures that remain intolerant if not hostile to feminist ideas and to those identified with them.

The current climate of marketization and cost recovery seems set to intensify the contradictions between politically correct rhetoric on the one hand and the financial and administrative stringency that under-fund social justice concerns on the other. This is likely to stimulate the development of further critique and analysis, even as it exacerbates the institutional challenges constraining the consolidation of the many sites already in existence. It is in this context that intellectual networking of the type carried out through the regional programme to strengthen gender studies assumes heightened intellectual and political importance.

I have argued that the development nexus has been responsible for as many constraints as opportunities, both of which are worth exploring and analysing. More politicized approaches, such as those offered by feminist theory emerging across the post-colonial capitalist periphery, can and do provide critical conceptual and analytical lenses. These offer valuable tools for demystifying the realities of contemporary Africa and African gender relations by isolating and addressing some of the fallacies currently circulating under the variously named rubrics of women in development, women and development, gender and development, and gender mainstreaming.

To conclude, feminist intellectual capacities grounded in contemporary African social and political realities need to be pursued and developed as a means of attaining new levels of activism demanded by the complexities of the times. Existing disciplinary-based academic paradigms largely fail to do justice to the diverse, complex and changing subjectivities, social arrangements and material realities that characterize the lives and realities of African women and men. Rather than simplifying, fragmenting and reducing the many truths out there, we need to embrace new levels of intellectual sophistication, cosmopolitanism and competence, as we – with the rest of the world – move into a new era replete with new challenges.

Notes

1 Earlier versions of this paper were presented in the Millercom lecture series at the University of Illinois, Champaign Urbana, 12 November 2003, and at the CODESRIA Anniversary Conference in Dakar in December 2003.

2 The body of work emerging from African scholars working with feminist and gender theory has grown substantially in recent years and cannot be reviewed here (but see Mama 1996; Imam et al. 1997; *Feminist Africa* 2002, 2003; Lewis 2003, available at <www.gwsafrica.org>; AGENDA 2001).

3 Nigeria has never countenanced affirmative action to increase women's access, but it has long had a policy of 'federal character' designed to ensure that all federal universities maintained intake quotas from the different regions of the country. Uganda introduced affirmative action for women when the NRM came to power.

4 Uganda's affirmative action policy involved lowering the entry requirements for women, and while it has proved highly controversial, there has been a marked increase in the intake of women, although they still remain in the minority.

5 Albeit not to an extent that compares with Asia, which has not suffered the same degree of under-provision.

6 Survey report and directory available at <www.gwsafrica.org>.

7 See the WLSA 19 and the AGI mission statement at <www.uct.ac.za/org/agi>.

8 This is a convenient appellation used to address the fact that the naming of departments includes the use of both or either term, but most include teaching of feminist theory, methodology and research, as well as the more institutionally acceptable interest in women and development, and gender and development.

9 Particularly the work of Paulin Hountoundji, Valentin Mudimbe and Kwame Appiah.

10 'Underdevelopment' is used here to refer to an unequal relational process, following Rodney (1972).

11 Listed in the annotated bibliographies and review essays available at <www.gwsafrica.org> (Mama 1996; AGI 2002; Lewis 2003).

12 See Boswell (2003); survey report at <www.gwsafrica.org>.

13 There are currently over eight hundred degree-awarding departments and programmes in GWS in the USA.

14 Further details available at <www.gwsafrica.org>.

15 These were Makerere Unversity, the University of Cape Town, the University of Pretoria, the University of the Western Cape and the University of Buea.

16 E.g. the universities of Cape Town, Ghana and Makerere (and probably others) have all seen individual existing faculty return with doctorates in 2003, but restrictions on new hiring continue to pose a constraint and perpetuate brain drain.

17 There are parallels with the government structures and projects for women, which tend to be accommodated where external funding is available, with little allocation in national budgets.

18 The discursive shift towards 'mainstreaming gender' has further muddied the terrain, as it becomes less and less clear exactly what this means in relation to feminist agendas.

19 This experience with donor funding has been repeated at many other sites, including a number of continentally based NGOs specifically dedicated to providing gender training.

20 As can be seen in the fact that by 2004 the AGI was more reliant on donor funding than ever. As a result of the constraints within the university, the AGI has temporarily suspended the undergraduate major offered since 1999, in the hope of restarting it with new faculty in 2006, while maintaining the newer and smaller graduate programme.

21 The full text of issues 1 and 2 is available at <www.feministafrica.org>.

References

AGENDA (2001) Special issues on 'African Feminism', 1 and 2, Durban

AGI (2002) 'Strengthening Gender and Women's Studies in African Contexts', Workshop report available at <www.gwsafrica.org>

AGI/AGENDA (1999) 'Translating Commitment into Practice', Durban

Ajayi, J., L. Goma and G. Ampah Johnson (eds) (1996) *The African Experience with Higher Education*, Oxford: James Currey/Accra: Association of African Universities

Alexander, J. and C. Mohanty (eds) (1997) *Feminist Genealogies, Colonial Legacies, Democratic Futures*, London and New York: Routledge

Appiah, K. A. (1992) *In My Father's House: Africa in the Philosphy of Culture*, London: Methuen

Basu, A. (ed.) (1997) *The Challenge of Local Feminisms*, Boulder, CO: Westview Press

Bennett, J. (2002) 'Exploration of a Gap: Strategising Gender Equity in African Universities', *Feminist Africa*, 1: 34–63

Blackmore, J. (2002) 'Globalisation and the Restructuring of Higher Education for New Knowledge Economies: New Dangers or Old Habits Troubling Gender Equity Work in Universities?', *Higher Education Quarterly*, 56(4): 419–41

Boswell, B. (2003) *Locating Gender and Women's Studies Teaching and Research Programmes at African Universities: Survey Results*, <www.gwsafrica.org/directory/survey/html>

Diouf, M. and M. Mamdani (eds) (1994) *Academic Freedom in Africa*, Dakar: CODESRIA

Federici, S., G. Caffentzis and O. Alidou (eds) (2000) *A Thousand Flowers: Social Struggles against Structural Adjustment in African Universities*, Trenton, NJ: Africa World Press

Gulbenkian Commission (1996) 'The Restructuring of Social Sciences: Open the Social Sciences', Stanford, CA: Stanford University Press

Hountondji, P. (2002) *The Struggle for Meaning: Reflection on Philosophy, Culture and Democracy in Africa*, Ohio University Press

Imam, A., A. Mama and F. Sow (eds) (1997) *Engendering Africa's Social Sciences*, Dakar: CODESRIA

Jackson, C. and R. Pearson (1998) *Feminist Visions of Development*, London: Routledge

Kasente, D. (2002) 'Institutionalising Gender Equality in African Universities: the case of Women's and Gender Studies at Makerere University', *Feminist Africa*, 1: 91–9

Lewis, D. (2003) 'Feminist Studies in Africa', Review essay, <www.gwsafrica.org>

Mama, A. (1996) *Women's Studies and Studies of Women in Africa*, Dakar: CODESRIA

— (2003) 'Restore, Reform, but Do not Transform: Gender Politics and Higher Education', *Journal of Higher Education in Africa*, 1

Mohanty, C. (2002) '"Under Western Eyes" Revisited: Feminist Solidarity through Anticapitalist Struggles', *Signs: Journal of Women in Culture and Society*, 28(1)

Mohanty, C., A. Russo and L. Torres (eds) (1991) *Third World Women and the Politics of Feminism*, Bloomington: Indiana University Press

Mudimbe, V. (1989) *The Invention of Africa: Gnosis, Philosophy and the Order of Language*, Bloomington: Indiana University Press

Pereira, C. (2002) 'Between Knowing and Imagining: What Space for Feminism in Scholarship on Africa?', *Feminist Africa*, 1: 9–33

Rodney, W. (1972) *How Europe Underdeveloped Africa*, Trenton, NJ: Africa World Press

Sall, E. (ed.) (2000) *Women in Academia: Gender and Academic Freedom in Africa*, Dakar: CODESRIA

Sawyerr, A. (2002) 'Challenges Facing African Universities: Selected Issues', Paper presented at the 45th annual meeting of the African Studies Association, Washington, DC, 5–8 December

Teferra, D. and D. Altbach (eds) (2003) *African Higher Education: An International Reference Book*, Bloomington: Indiana University Press

Third World Network (2002) *National Machinery Series*, Accra: Third World Network

WLSA (1997) *Paving a Way Forward: A Review and Research Primer of WLSA Research Methodologies*, Harare

Zeleza, P. T. (2003) *Rethinking Africa's Globalization*, vol. 1: 'The Intellectual Challenges', Trenton, NJ: Africa World Press

Websites

<www.//gwsafrica.org>
<www.//feministafrica.org>
<www.uct.ac.za/org/agi>

6 | The character and formation of intellectuals within the ANC-led South African liberation movement

RAYMOND SUTTNER

Who are intellectuals in the context of the ANC-led South African liberation struggle?

It is common for scholars to see themselves as representing what is covered by the notion of an intellectual and to restrict the scope of the word to those who contribute via accredited journals, within universities or recognized research institutes. Intellectual debate about various issues surrounds what are conventionally called 'scholars' and the 'scholarly community' (CODESRIA 2003). *The Shorter Oxford English Dictionary* (1986, vol. 1: 1,089) speaks of the word 'intellectual', used as an adjective, as 'of, or belonging to, the intellect or understanding. That appeals to or engages the intellect ... Possessing a high degree of understanding; given to pursuits that exercise the intellect ... ' When used as a noun it refers to 'An intellectual being; a person having superior powers of intellect'.

These are very limited definitions of what constitutes an intellectual. Instead, this paper has in mind a category of individuals who, following Gramsci, should be defined by the role they play, by the relationships they have to others. They are people who, broadly speaking, create for a class or people (in the South African case, the majority who were nationally oppressed under apartheid) a coherent and reasoned account of the world, as it appears from the position they occupy. Intellectuals are crucial to the process through which a major new culture, representing the world-view of an emerging class or people, comes into being. It is intellectuals who transform what may previously have been the incoherent and fragmentary 'feelings' of those who live in a particular class or nationally oppressed position, into a coherent account of the world (see Gramsci 1971: 418; Crehan 2002: 129–30).

In a letter of 1931 Gramsci says his definition of an intellectual 'is much broader than the usual concept of "the great intellectuals"' (1979: 204). In his *Prison Notebooks*, he writes:

What are the 'maximum' limits of acceptance of the term 'intellectual'? Can one find a unitary criterion to characterise equally all the diverse and disparate activities of intellectuals and to distinguish these at the same time and in an essential way from the activities of other social groupings? *The most widespread error of method seems to me that of having looked for this criterion of distinction in the intrinsic nature of intellectual activities, rather than in the ensemble of the system of relations in which these activities (and therefore the intellectual groups who personify them) have their place within the general complex of social relations.* (1971: 8. Emphasis added)

In the same way a worker is not characterized by the manual or instrumental work that he or she carries out, but by 'performing this work in specific conditions and in specific social relations'.

If we use such an approach and do not first set formal entry hurdles by way of classifying people in this category, we need to broaden our investigation and examine the many ways of intellectual functioning as well as the processes of intellectual formation that may be found on this continent, now and in the past, which go back to the pre-colonial past, though that is beyond the scope of this paper.[1]

This paper covers a very broad topic. On the level of theory it does not pretend to have exhaustively probed the implications of all the issues that arise, especially in the vast literature examining Gramsci's theories. It is a beginning, working towards providing a theoretical basis that is more adequate in explaining the categories of intellectuals found in the South African liberation movement, led by the ANC. The choice has primarily been to opt for a chronological, albeit very incomplete, account.

ANC intellectuals – from a variety of sources

In the context of the ANC-led national liberation movement, the concept intellectual may be said to apply to individuals created through various processes, some inside the ANC and allied organizations, sometimes deriving from outside, through more conventional institutions, such as universities. In deploying intellectual skills derived from these conventional institutions, it has not been a case of simply applying that knowledge and training. These professionals have needed to undergo various intellectual transformations within the organization(s) in order to perform tasks related to national liberation, to give them the skills that are organizationally specific.

The term intellectual may be said to apply to people deriving from all these processes who perform a specific role – that is, who provide meanings to situations, guidelines for escaping from oppression as well as visions of alternative social conditions, shown to be necessary, possible and potentially realizable. What that entails is not determined for all times, but has a variety of meanings, determined by modified conditions and also by changes in the composition of the organization.

The liberation movement as 'collective intellectual'

The concept 'intellectual', following Gramsci, is also applicable to political parties and by analogy to the national liberation movement itself.[2] Gramsci argues that a political party plays an intellectual role. He ascribes various characteristics to the party as an organization, and in its relationship to intellectuals. Gramsci's focus is on the institutions that produce knowledge rather than on individual intellectuals, and he sees a party as being composed of intellectuals or, as some writers have summarized him, as itself being a 'collective intellectual' or 'collective organic intellectual':[3]

> That all members of a political party should be regarded as intellectuals is an affirmation that can easily lend itself to mockery and caricature. But if one thinks about it nothing could be more exact. There are of course distinctions of level to be made. A party might have a greater or lesser proportion of members in the higher grades or in the lower, but this is not the point. What matters is the function, which is directive and organisational, i.e. educative, i.e. intellectual. (ibid.: 16)

The notion of a 'collective intellectual' is not analogous to 'one individual writ large', but comprises a multiplicity of individuals, unity and cohesion among whom is by no means automatic.

The intellectual role of the party or liberation movement, like intellectual functioning generally, is related to organizational tasks, qualities that are necessary in order to perform specific work. Those who already have these qualities apply them in a particular way; those without these qualities may develop them through various processes within the organization. These qualities are directed towards achieving goals, and many of these Gramsci sees as inherent in a political party aiming to establish its hegemony. They have an intellectual character. By definition, these objectives cannot be achieved without an educational dimension.

The ANC-led liberation movement has played an intellectual role in so far as it welded together a variety of intellectuals in forming a common will, contributing towards the voicing of a new national popular will (see ibid.: 15–16). This is not a simple process but a product of struggle and contestation as well as the creation of and transformation of the character of various categories of intellectuals. Its meaning was different in 1912 from what it was to be in the 1950s, 1960s and today. Who contributes towards that role and with what weight varies in different periods and conditions, including the influence wielded by contributions from outside the organization or, in more recent times, from allied organizations that may have overlapping membership.[4]

But the political party, or in this case national liberation movement, as collective intellectual, is also manifested in some of the products of its activities. In so far as a consensus among its components results in interpretative documentation and media of various sorts, which are presented to its membership and the public at large, that is an intellectual function. It may be empowering in so far as it renders visible what was opaque. It may provide explanations for what is difficult to understand or what is intended by the oppressors/exploiters to be understood in a way that is disadvantageous to the oppressed and exploited people.

It is common knowledge that conquest is often accompanied by various mechanisms instituted in order to divert resistance or instil in the native peoples a sense that resistance is futile or too costly to risk. At various stages of the South African struggle, starting in the pre-conquest period, a variety of forms of resistance were employed. These were based on analyses and estimations of what was at stake, what the threat of colonial rule or the fact of conquest meant, whatever the colonialists may have used to disguise it. These organic intellectuals of the liberation movement in the first place sought to provide explanations of colonial/apartheid conquest and repression, to unmask it where it was disguised, and to explain causality where that too was not evident. Some of these explanations have been very elaborate, relating as they did to fundamentally changed conditions.

Intellectual work has often provided hope of something different where everything was done to suggest that what existed was unalterable (see Seme 1972 [1911]; Jordan 1988). This was especially significant in periods of defeat, as was the case at the time of the Act of Union and more recently when the major leadership figures were sentenced in the Rivonia trial in 1964.

The ANC-led national liberation movement as creator of intellectuals

Furthermore, a key element of the national liberation movement functioning as 'collective intellectual' which this paper wants to highlight is its role in creating its own intellectuals through various processes. This is not to suggest, as Gramsci indicates, that all such intellectuals were of the same level and calibre. Some were simply inducted into the ANC or an allied organization and became communicators of a vision and organizers in a more limited way. Others became major thinkers, after passing through the institutional structures of the ANC and/or allied organizations.

The job of intellectuals has been to try to contribute through theory to finding a way out, a way of escape from the dehumanization of apartheid colonialism. The solution has varied, as will be shown later in this paper. But all the enquiries, which may be described as activities of organic intellectuals, have related to the question of how to resolve the status of the oppressed people in South Africa.

It is true that some answers may have related to the class basis of the intellectuals who provided them, setting limits on what they advanced as 'the possible or feasible or realistic' (without necessarily using such words). It is not therefore only the situation of conquest but also the historical development and composition and social basis of the liberation movement which has conditioned the role intellectuals have played at different times. And of course these are mediating factors that continue at this very moment. Some conditions in the past led to a radical intellectual intervention as part of the collective intellectual input of the alliance as a whole. These may now be under threat, under new conditions, which include the formation of an ANC-led government and the possible creation of a new ruling bloc, where the weight of the working class is counterbalanced by the perceived demand of a globalized world for economic 'fundamentals' to be respected, simultaneously with the increasing strength of an emerging black bourgeoisie.

In focusing on the ANC and its allies I am not suggesting that they are the only movements that have performed a substantial intellectual role or had an important intellectual component in the liberation struggle. In fact, the Trotskyist Unity Movement of South Africa gave primacy to educational tasks, though it may be that this was mainly in relation to people passing through formal educational institutions or in debates among an intelligentsia.[5] I am however aware that many of these Unity Movement scholars made an insufficiently acknowledged intellectual contribution, rewriting history from the point of view of the oppressed people and the working class in particular (e.g. Majeke 1986 [1952]; Mnguni 1988 [1952]).

Intellectual role and processes of intellectual formation

The early ANC In the years prior to the Act of Union, the small stratum of British- and American-trained African intellectuals, together with mission-trained individuals and a limited number of self-trained intellectuals, were very active in the emerging African press, the Church and the small number of associations that were the forerunners of the ANC (Jordan 1973; Odendaal 1984).

In a sense, these professionals were part of the transition and the interpretation of the transition from one form of struggle to another, from the 'spear to the book' (Kunene 1968). In the type of politics inaugurated by the Act of Union it was clear that for the moment the time of the spear or other forms of military resistance was over. But opportunities to participate in parliamentary politics had been open in a marginal sense mainly in the

Cape, from the mid-nineteenth century. This was one of the key areas of intervention for intellectuals and for much of the press, and related to African votes for white politicians, especially in the few constituencies where African voters formed a sizeable number (Jordan 1973; Odendaal 1984).

With the Act of Union, it was a wider form of involvement which arose, requiring a conceptualization of a new form of interaction with the white authorities. The ANC was first formed as the South African Native National Congress (SANNC) in Bloemfontein on 8 January 1912. Its initial structure combined elements of continuity as well as rupture with what had preceded it. It included a House of Chiefs, modelled on the House of Lords, recognizing the continuing authority of traditional leaders who had led the tribal resistance against Boer and British conquest in the nineteenth century. But its founders were faced with a completely new situation. Britain had handed the fate of black South Africans to the local white settlers through the formation of the Union of South Africa.

The earliest attempts at characterizing the meaning of Union and the notion of a 'native union' embraced by the establishment of the ANC were ambiguous, but also had potentially revolutionary implications. In advancing, as Pixley ka Isaka Seme, a British- and American-trained advocate did, the notion of a 'native union', what may have been the germs of a new nation appear. Writing in 1911, on the eve of the establishment of the ANC, Seme stated that he wanted to write on the 'simple subject of Native Union, for after all, this is what the Congress shall be' (1972 [1911]: 72).

Seme spoke of the new Congress as the 'voice in the wilderness' aiming to bring together the 'dark races' in order to review the past and reject all things which 'have retarded our progress, the things which poison the springs of our national life and virtue'. The Congress would enable 'members of one household to talk and think aloud on our home problems and the solution of them'.

He therefore advanced the notion of an alternative union to that of the white Union of South Africa, premised on unity within the Congress. But in order to achieve union, certain demons had to be exorcized, in particular the divisions between African peoples that had not only prevented unity but also facilitated colonial conquest: 'The demon of racialism, the aberrations of the Xosa–Fingo feud, the animosity that exists between the Zulus and the Tongaas, between the Basutos and every other Native must be buried and forgotten; it has shed among us sufficient blood! *We are one people.* These divisions, these jealousies, are the cause of all our woes and of all our backwardness and ignorance today ... ' (ibid.: 72. Spelling as in original; emphasis added). This message was immensely progressive, advancing as it did a fundamental alternative to the Union's attempt to create a nation in South Africa that excluded the African people. This alternative aimed to overcome the animosities between different peoples, which had been exploited in the process of conquest, and also to build a unity between African people that could be the foundation for this new nation. But in the context of the times the concept had its own limitations. It was a union of Africans only. It was a concept of the nation that implicitly excluded women, since they were not yet members of the ANC.

It was also a concept of unity that may not only have excluded the use of difference to create divisions but also denied the validity of distinct identities within this unity. In other words, within the overall progressive and even revolutionary character of this early response to conquest there were also the germs of a long-term danger. This lay in the characteristic projection of a national liberation movement as representing the nation as a whole, declaring that the people are one and by implication seeing alternative conceptions of identity as divisive of that unity. While this was then understandable and indeed part of the alternative concept of the counter-nation, the conceptualization was nevertheless potentially problematic, as it has been with all national liberation movements (Suttner 2004b).

But the immediate problem confronting the fledgling organization was to negotiate a way of operating in new conditions. For decades after the Act of Union, appeals to the authorities via deputations and petitions dominated the organization's methods. In order to conduct this type of strategy, a different type of leadership was required. Thus the first executive was composed entirely of mission-trained professionals – lawyers, priests, teachers and self-taught intellectuals such as the writer Sol Plaatje. 'The teachers, ministers, editors, lawyers and doctors who founded the liberation movements', Jack and Ray Simons wrote, 'were constitutionalists. They defended existing rights and resisted new discrimination in a constant struggle against aggressive white supremacists ... ' (Simons and Simons 1969: 116).

While the modes of struggle opened up after 1910 required new skills and practices compared with the military struggle, they established patterns of behaviour, which marked distinct organizational conceptions, of a relationship to the government as well as to its own members (Magubane 1979: 277–8).

Professor Daniel Kunene articulated the new challenge confronting the Congress as follows:

The African had just emerged from a prolonged battle which he had lost. While this battle raged, he had composed heroic lines for the warriors and kings upon whom he placed his trust ... This came to pass – the country perished. But the struggle was not over, it had only shifted from a physical to an intellectual plane. Education was the new weapon, the intellectual the new warrior. A correspondent of the *Isigidimi* ... commenting on the African's suffering under the white man's rule, suggested that 'the spear' was not the solution. 'No,' he said, 'we have tried and failed. The only solution is learning and knowledge. By knowledge I do not mean just book knowledge. I mean that kind of knowledge that will make us realise that each one lives for all.' (1968: 23–4)

In becoming a new leadership the ANC simultaneously started to weld together an organization that performed the intellectual role that Gramsci attributes to a political party. This was to be a rough road. The final outcome, with the ANC as the leading force in government, was by no means preordained and at times seemed totally unlikely. There were periods when the organization was close to non-existent.

The new leadership tried to give meaning to the conditions that Africans encountered, particularly the imposition of a white union on the people of South Africa, and a stream of discriminatory legislation. Simultaneously, some individuals performed individual intellectual roles, organic to that of the liberation movement. What these intellectuals did was to give meaning reflectively, actively and consequentially. Thus, Sol Plaatje famously documented the impact of the Land Act of 1913, and used his writings and research to campaign in Britain (1982 [1916]).

Essential to the period of petitioning and deputations that opened up after the founding of the ANC was a quest for inclusion in the civil rights constitutionally guaranteed to whites. In order to qualify for inclusion leaders of the time professed loyalty to the British Crown and the Union constitution. This was something commonly found in liberation movements of the time (See, e.g., Kiernan 1993: 89; Younis 2000; Apter 1964).

The early characterization of the South African state, and the social order and the strategic perspective of the ANC, were articulated mainly by the small group of African intellectuals. Many commentators dwell on the photographs of this early leadership, in very formal dress, supposedly as a marked contrast to the rise of a later, more 'angry', generation.[6] There is also a tendency to ridicule their petitioning of local and British authorities. It has wrongly been construed as conservative or written off as 'fawning' (Motlhabi 1984: 38) or as going 'cap in hand' to their masters. Leaders of this period are often criticized for naïveté in their appeals to British morality and Christianity, the values with which most of them had grown up.

It would be a mistake to read too much into this approach (Marks and Trapido 1987: 6). Peter Limb has shown that a careful reading of the texts demonstrates that many of these interventions were heavily laden with irony. The idioms and values of the Empire were used partly with subversive intent. Also, there was an attempt in these appeals to pit the former colonial power against the main enemy, the white settlers (Limb 2003; see also Saunders 2000). In a sense they may have tried to practise 'divide and rule' in reverse.

Official politics and parallel politics of a less formal kind Even where one speaks of ANC politics of a particular time being dominated by specific practices, there has always been contestation, difference over direction, different meanings given to oppression and the nation and ways of contesting apartheid colonial structures.

At the same time as the 'elite' leadership of the ANC pursued one type of politics there were simultaneously various manifestations of more radical ideas and organization within the ANC itself – in the Transvaal (see Bonner 1982), among the women (Wells 1993), in the union movement, especially in the early years of the Industrial and Commercial Union (ICU) (Bradford 1987), and in the activities of the Communist Party (Simons and Simons 1969).

Thus, while men were engaged in moderately building a counter-union, they did not at first include women as members of the ANC and, by implication, the future nation was masculine.[7] It was only in 1943 that women achieved the right to full membership. Excluded from the organization, women were not under the same constraints of 'deputation politics'. From an early period, they were freed for what was often a more radical, mass politics where demands were made rather than petitioning the authorities. In Bloemfontein, protesting against the extension of passes in 1913, women marched under the radical banner, declaring 'We have done with pleading. We now demand!' (Wells 1993).

It is also clear that the degree of exclusion of ANC women, in practice, was less absolute than the constitution appeared to lay down. Prior to the establishment of the ANC itself, women in some areas such as the Orange Free State were involved in congresses. Subsequent to the establishment of the ANC, women regularly attended national gatherings. In fact, Congress made provision for the organization of women without their actually being full members. The formulations on the 'role' of women, however, tended to correspond to traditional gender roles, with women providing hospitality and similar functions. The history shows, nevertheless, that the women inside and outside the formal structures continued to transcend these designated functions and played active political roles.

In the early ANC we have seen, using the theoretical categories earlier outlined, that intellectuals contributed to an embryonic sense of nationhood. Their strategies for achieving this were at first hesitant and constitutional, though there were also counter-strategies articulated by the women and other organizational formations. At this point in time, the ANC as an organization was not yet playing a well-defined role as 'collective intellectual', though the various intellectuals associated with the organization articulated a broadly shared vision on which the organization acted, subject to the contestation that has been mentioned.

Communist night schools and early newspapers as intellectual interventions and creators of intellectuals The Communist Party was to have an uneasy relationship with the ANC for some decades after its establishment. On the side of the ANC there was suspicion of communists as being purveyors of a radical ideology that threatened chiefs and others with interests perceived as antagonistic to the communist vision. On the side of the communists, there was some contempt for the ANC, which was seen as comprising primarily petit-bourgeois intellectuals and having little interest in organizing the masses. Thus Sidney Bunting, in addressing the Comintern[8] in the 1920s, declared that the ANC had 'had its day. It was moribund.' Some of these criticisms had validity, for the activities of the ANC were initially primarily related to an annual conference and little else. Equally, the Communist Party at first failed to give adequate weight to dispossession and the importance of addressing the national question. But gradually the communists came to believe that there could be neither liberation nor socialism in South Africa without leadership by the African majority (Simons and Simons 1969).

The early Communist Party played an important intellectual role through the training of new members as well as the publication of newspapers, especially in the African languages. The Communist Party of South Africa (CPSA) was formed in 1921. Initially it looked to white workers, who were more established in industry and unionized, as the core element in its organization. Africans had only recently become proletarianized and were not seen as constituting an adequate base for building socialism. Gradually, however, the party turned towards the African masses, and in this respect the Comintern played a significant and constructive role in relation to the national question, though this also entailed the imposition of decisions against the will of the then mainly white local party. Its most important intervention was to insist in 1928 on the implementation of the slogan calling for the establishment of an 'independent Native Republic'. This was the precursor of the later analytical framework characterizing apartheid

South Africa as comprising 'colonialism of a special type', a formulation initiated by the Communist Party, but later adopted by the ANC as well (see Jordan 1988: 123ff; Simons and Simons 1969).

In its turn towards the African working class, the party confronted workers who were very often illiterate or with only a smattering of literacy. Eddie Roux, a leading figure in the development of the night schools, claimed that members had a vague idea of what membership entailed, and the gradual influx of Africans created further difficulties in a party already finding it difficult to build ideological cohesion (Roux 1964; and see below). This was one of the reasons leading to the development of night schools. The provision of elementary education to people who were hungry for learning made a considerable impact (Roux 1964, 1993; Roux and Roux 1970; Bird 1980; Johns 1995; Drew 2000).

While night schools established by the Communist Party would equip people better in the world in which they found themselves, it simultaneously sought to impart some knowledge of communism. Many who passed through these schools became acquainted not only with the written word in general, but Marxist texts. In some cases, the products of these schools were to become famous leaders and theoreticians, such as Edwin Mofutsanyana and Moses Kotane, both to become general secretaries of the Communist Party, trade unionist Gana Makabeni, and the first Communist martyr, Johannes Nkosi (Drew 2000: 78; Edgar unpub. 2003). Kotane, who was also a major figure in the ANC, believed that the early night schools had been a formative influence for him and had been responsible for his own political initiation (Bunting 1998: 44).

Adrienne Bird writes that the Communist Party started the first 'effective night school movement – effective primarily in that those that passed through it were not simply given the tools with which to better survive in the existing society ... [T]he CP night schools trained many of the blacks who were later to lead the black resistance movement' (Bird 1980: 64).

Eddie Roux describes the first school 'in 1925 in the Ferreirastown slum, in a Native Church building hired on week nights for the purpose. The building had no electric light. There enthusiastic white communists bent their energies to teaching by candle-light, semi-literate Africans to read involved passages in Bukharin's *ABC of Communism*' (1964: 203).

In 1926 a simplified *Communist Primer for South Africa* was developed and printed serially in the party newspaper, *The South African Worker*, as a substitute for the Bukharin text. At the same time continuous consideration was being given to publishing a newspaper in African languages, but was abandoned because of lack of funds. Nevertheless, *The South African Worker* began to print articles in African languages and in late 1925 its price was lowered 'in a conscious effort to attract African readers' (Johns 1995: 186–7). When the party moved its headquarters from the Old Trades Hall to the site of the party school in Ferreirastown in mid-1927, it was also a 'severing of the links with the white trade unions and a conscious identification with the non-white workers. The new party office rapidly became a centre for social activities among Africans, for trade union organization, and for party education among Africans' (ibid.: 188).

A few years later, the school was further developed, though still under very difficult circumstances:

> The school ... was moved to the party office ... Now on the ground floor of a slum tenement ... There were not enough desks to go round: the pupils sat on the floor. Blackboards there were none: the comrades blackened the walls. Lessons, given by inexperienced but enthusiastic teachers, were interrupted by intermittent incursions of the curious. Night passes were a nuisance. Every adult African, if he wished to avoid arrest after nine in the evening, must carry a special pass signed from day to day by his employer. (Roux 1964: 204–5)

On 17 February 1928, *The South African Worker* reported enrolment in the school as being close to one hundred. Three months later it had risen to 150. In an effort to emulate the success of Johannesburg, the Cape Town comrades established an African labour college at their party office. The newer party branches in Vereeniging and Potchefstroom also established more rudimentary schools (Johns 1995: 195).

The continuing work through the schools was complemented by the revival of the party newspaper, which had collapsed for six months, and reappeared in February 1928. This time it was even more consciously directed at black workers. The party began to expand its presence out of the white areas and in some cases, such as Vereeniging, also established new schools (ibid.: 196). This period saw the party claim an overwhelmingly black membership, some 1,600 out of 1,700 in mid-1928 (ibid.: 197).

The influx of large numbers of Africans in this way created problems in developing ideological cohesion and understanding. 'At first many of the new adherents were rather vague as to the nature of C.P. membership. Asked to prove that they were members of the party, they would produce a trade union card or night school pass. It was all very shocking to some of the Comintern purists, but as time went on things began to sort themselves out' (Roux 1964: 207).

While there were these initial problems, there is no doubt that this introduction was an essential basis that made possible the later emergence of many African theorists within the party and the liberation movement as a whole. The schools also helped create the cohesion that was initially lacking.

Another contributing factor to the development of a core of African intellectuals was the role of the Comintern, which provided education in party schools as well as a special university directed at students from the colonized world. Many leading figures were sent there for courses. About fourteen South African communists were educated in Comintern schools or universities (Filatova 1999: 54–5; Davidson et al. 2003: Introduction). Among those trained were leading ANC/SACP figures such as Moses Kotane and J. B. Marks and the Communist trade unionist Betty du Toit (Davidson et al. 2003: 6). Whatever the dogmatism that may have prevailed, leading non-communist scholars argue that the approach adopted to African studies was advanced for its time (Filatova 1999):

> Although education at the Comintern's schools was highly ideological, it still offered a valid and in some respects advanced training of the kind that students could not get in their own countries. In Moscow they were specifically educated and trained as professional politicians and exposed to a broader international scene. Their fellow students came from many countries and from various backgrounds. There were personalities of significance among them, not all necessarily communists, such as Jomo Kenyatta, the future first president of Kenya, and George Padmore, editor-in-chief of *The Negro Worker* and the future ideologue of the Pan-African movement.
>
> The Comintern's schools gave South African students opportunities to publish, first of all in *The Negro Worker* but later also in other journals. In 1933 Albert Nzula, the first black secretary of the CPSA, published a book about the conditions of labour and about the labour movement in Africa, co-authored with Potekhin and Zusmanovich [scholars who taught at Comintern schools] ... More often than not even the authors themselves saw these publications as propaganda materials or at least as 'applied' studies useful to the cause – rather than as constituting serious academic research. However, they contributed a lot to the emergence of new approaches in African studies far beyond Moscow. Suffice it to say that it was at [these institutions] ... that the debate on the existence of an African bourgeoisie and, more broadly, on the nature of social structures of contemporary African societies, began. (Davidson et al. 2003: 7–8)

Early ANC–CPSA relations and tensions This was a period of contrasting visions and practices in the ANC and CPSA, which were in the main far apart from one another, in no sense seeming likely future partners, as they were to become. It was a period where the ANC's practice of petitioning ran its course without success and where what organization there had been was practically non-existent by the 1930s. For a short period during the presidency of Josiah Gumede the organization appeared headed for a more radical direction, only for him to be ousted and the organization to sink into steady decline (Van Diemel 2002; Simons and Simons 1969).

It was only in the late 1930s and the early 1940s, under the Reverend James Calata and Dr A. B. Xuma as secretary-general and president respectively, that the organization started to revive. This was modest and based on attempts to build the administration on a sound footing and establish a carefully monitored membership base (Walshe 1970). But it was nevertheless an organizational foundation that would make realizable some of the interventions that are generally credited to the rise of the Youth League alone.

The interventions of the Youth League may have remained in the realm of ideas had they not also found organizational expression on the basis provided in the period of Xuma and Calata.

Another important achievement of the Xuma presidency was the preparation and adoption of *African Claims in South Africa*, demands drawn up by a committee of leading intellectuals, based on the Atlantic Charter adapted to South Africa. It described itself as a restatement of the charter 'from the standpoint of Africans within the Union of South Africa' and also contained a 'Bill of Rights'. This was regarded as the most authoritative statement of ANC aims since the 1919 constitution (Karis and Carter 1973: 209ff). In many ways this was a precursor of the Freedom Charter, adopted in 1955, though it did not involve the popular process entailed in the creation of the latter (ibid.: 88ff; on the process leading to the creation of the Freedom Charter, see Suttner and Cronin 1986).

The emphasis on the organizational base from which it benefited is not intended to detract from the significance of the rise of the Youth League in the mid-1940s. The Youth League was a profound expression of the anger of youth with the failure of the previous moderate policies of the ANC and a call for a new direction and vision. The league was led by a brilliant lawyer/philosopher, Anton Lembede, who died very young, together with Mandela, Tambo and Sisulu, later to become giants of the ANC.

The Youth League had an Africanist message, not addressing itself to the people of South Africa in general, but stressing the notions of African nationalism and self-determination (Gerhart 1978). Not only did the Youth League resist cooperation with non-Africans, but it was also initially anti-communist. Gradually, however, a degree of convergence developed with the communists based on a common militancy and a developing appreciation on the side of the Youth League of the need for organization.

The early communist schools performed an important role in the development of cadres and leaders which served not only the party but also the entire liberation movement. In that sense the party was conducting the role of a 'collective intellectual', communicating a vision, inducting people with that vision but also creating its own intellectuals. Among these were some of the most important leaders of the entire liberation movement.

Political education in the 1950s One lesson of ANC history is that the leadership from the 1950s was never able simply to embark on any course of action purely because they considered it wise and desirable. The organization was developing a mass following and the members could not be ignored. Mandela explains how important the earlier Indian passive resistance campaign was in influencing the ANC to adopt its Defiance Campaign of 1952. Until then, Africans had considered imprisonment as imposing a stigma, and it was only gradually that they could be persuaded to move towards breaking the law and incurring imprisonment (Mandela 1994). The meaning of imprisonment had to be redefined as being an honour in certain contexts.

Furthermore, there is an additional careful choice of words. 'Defiance' was consciously used instead of 'passive resistance' – the term adopted in the Indian Congress campaign. Sisulu indicated that this was a specific intervention aimed at driving the struggle towards a higher plane, and indeed the notion of contestation conveyed by the word 'defy' was new to the vocabulary of South African politics. Sisulu says: 'The name "Defiance" was deliberately used to make a difference between passive resistance and defiance. The aim here was to incite the people to action so that they should be militant and no longer fear jail. They must go willingly to jail. That was the aim, to arouse the whole nation' (n.d.: 76). The Defiance Campaign was conceived as a break with the past, even as part of a revolutionary break.

> It had the effect of making the people confident and fearless, prepared to defy the laws, to be prepared to go to jail and meet any situation. That was the importance of it. It was the beginning of a new situation which led even to a person facing the death penalty with confidence. The Campaign brought about a situation in which people were not arrested just by chance, but by plan. This meant organization ... The movement called for volunteers. In the Eastern Cape, it was called 'Amadela Kufa', 'defiers of death'. You can see from this that a revolutionary situation was emerging. (ibid.: 79)

During the 1950s the ANC anticipated the possibility of a ban in the light of action against the Communist Party, which dissolved in 1950, and later reconstituted underground (Suttner 2004a). The ANC developed the M-Plan, to undertake street-level organization, as a preparation for future banning and underground operation. One of the elements of this plan was extensive political education (Anon. 1984; Everatt unpub. 1990; Mandela 1994: 135; Suttner 2003b; interviews Mtshali, Nair).

Many people appear to have gone through some form of internal education during the 1950s, where a common understanding of 'Congress politics' was developed through lectures and discussion. These elements helped develop what Gramsci calls 'the national-popular collective will ... ' (1971: 131–2). Those who participated at one level were expected to give the lectures at another.

Mandela explains:

> As part of the M-plan, the ANC introduced an elementary course of political lectures for its members throughout the country. These lectures were meant not only to educate but to hold the organization together. They were given in secret by branch leaders. *Those members in attendance would in turn give the same lectures to others in their homes and communities.* In the beginning, the lectures were not systematised, but within a number of months there was a set curriculum. There were three courses, 'The World We Live In', 'How We Are Governed', and 'The Need for Change'. In the first course, we discussed the different types of political and economic systems around the world as well as in South Africa. It was an overview of the growth of capitalism as well as socialism. (1994: 135. Emphasis added)

Inside and outside these structures, and within this overall perspective, many cadres saw political education as their key task during this period. One significant aspect of this political education is that much of its content seemed to have been informed by a Marxist orientation (Anon. 1984; interviews Nair, Ndlovu; Suttner 2003b). Generally, the widespread diffusion of Marxist thinking within the ANC today tends to be attributed to the exile experience, whereby some cadres were sent to Communist Party schools and much of the political education had a Marxist orientation (interview Serache; see also Sparg et al. 2001; Suttner 2003a). But clearly these Congress Alliance courses indicate that this mode of analysis was already within that paradigm long before the phase of exile.

During this period and even earlier a great deal of political education was conducted in some ANC and communist-aligned trade unions (Suttner 2003b). If one examines the 1940s and 1950s in the province of Natal, now called KwaZulu-Natal, with the embryonic establishment of non-racial trade unions, an elaborate system of internal education was in place, conducted in the main by communists. Through these courses, sometimes called 'social theory', sometimes called Marxism, a number of people received training in a Marxist analysis of social relations.[9]

In one set of interviews Eric Mtshali, a veteran MK member and now a member of the SACP[10] Central Committee, describes having been through such training (interview Mtshali). In a later interview with Cleopas Ndlovu one hears that he attended a similar course at a later stage. When he was moved from the general class to a more advanced course with smaller numbers, his lecturer was Eric Mtshali (interview Ndlovu 2003). What this means is that through the process of internal education within the unions and the Communist Party, of which he was then a member, Mtshali was transformed from a student into a lecturer and, in Gramscian terms, into a person performing an intellectual role.[11]

The internal education conducted within the Congress Alliance during the 1950s helped consolidate a common perspective. In this regard, the process leading to adoption of the Freedom Charter was an important 'intellectual product' of the alliance as 'collective intellectual', presenting a vision of what that alternative should be, opening up debate as to what type of society would remedy the grievances raised in the Congress of the People campaign (see Suttner and Cronin 1986). The internal education was a clear manifestation of the liberation movement acting as a 'collective intellectual', communicating its understanding of vital issues of the struggle. The charter was a product of mass organizational and collective efforts.

All this was subject to contestation within the organization, as is dramatically illustrated by the break-away of the Africanists, objecting to clauses of the charter referring to South Africa belonging to both black and white and possible nationalization of certain means of production.

Political training in exile and especially in the military camps During the 1950s there was increasing discussion about 'fighting back', the need to respond to the violence of the regime with armed force. After the banning of the ANC in 1960, this took concrete shape with the formation of Umkhonto we Sizwe, initially independent of the ANC. With the defeat of the early sabotage campaign, activities shifted mainly towards more formalized military training outside the country, and gradually also towards the initiation of guerrilla warfare.

Throughout the ANC's exile period, despite the increased emphasis on liberation through warfare, political education was taken very seriously. That is not to say it was uniform and all carefully planned. In fact, much of the exile period was unplanned. The first group of exiles had in the main expected to return to the country as trained soldiers within six months (e.g. interview Mtshali). Many were in fact unable to return for almost thirty years. The level of political education received initially was much extended over the years (Sparg et al. 2001).

Even where soldiers were expected to be returned quickly, the emphasis had always been that the political should dominate the military and that what mattered was not holding a gun but who was behind the gun, what understanding that person had.

This is a repeated theme in political education and seems to have been almost a cliché – that the ANC's army was not merely soldiers in a conventional sense, but bearers of a message, ambassadors for a particular vision of society. This is a constant pattern in initial contacts between youths who left the country after 1976, wanting to pick up the gun, and the ANC leadership and cadres whom they met. The tendency seems generally to have been to restrain moves towards militarism and place emphasis on understanding the struggle and its goals. A body of scholarship argues that in practice militarism was dominant, or at least that there was not adequate political control and direction of military activity and not even an adequate connection between the two (Barrell unpub. 1993).

It was emphasized, however, that cadres needed to understand exactly what they were doing and in selecting targets be able to understand what was especially politically significant and which attacks would have particular symbolic importance, because of the specific ways in which apartheid oppression impacted on the people. It was intended that such action should be seen as piercing the apparent invincibility of the enemy.

Just as it was not planned that the initial group of MK volunteers should have remained outside the country for so long, equally the influx of thousands of new recruits after the 1976 rising was unplanned. While underground operatives within the country reported in general terms on a restive atmosphere, and embryonic signs of resistance, the scale and intensity of the rising were unexpected.

The need for political education of the new recruits was urgent. Many were relatively ignorant of the struggle and its objectives and had a militaristic inclination. Hilda Bernstein may exaggerate the extent to which a historical memory of previous struggle may have been absent from their consciousness (see Suttner unpub. 2004), though many interviewees do confirm this point (Thandi Modise in Curnow 2000). But Bernstein does capture some of the problems that had to be dealt with through political training:

> Each wave brought out its own type of people. Those who left in the late fifties and early sixties were mainly adult, often middle-aged, and highly political, with a history of engaging in public political struggle. Those of

the seventies, and specifically of the huge exile wave after 1976, were over-whelmingly young, largely male; and though fired with political passion, they were often without real ideology or political programmes. They were of a generation who had been cut off from access to information about their own country, their own history, and from political theory and the history of struggle. The 'elders' who might have passed on this knowledge were either themselves in exile, or on Robben Island or Pretoria Central prison. Or perhaps keeping discreetly quiet. 'Mandela' was a remote name, used by some parents as a warning of what happens to those who follow the path of resistance to law and authority.[12]

Consequently, the ANC embarked on careful training at various levels. Every cadre was meant to be equipped with a broad understanding of the character of the struggle, and its history. They were connected to the strands of resistance history that the regime had tried to obliterate from public consciousness.

But the process of training, as it evolved, was also intended to produce (and did so) trainers and also new intellectuals. One of the most famous teachers in the camps was Professor Jack Simons, a former leading scholar who provided general tuition and courses, but who also trained a body of more advanced cadres who were to be able to perform Simons's function (Sparg et al. 2001). Passing through this process were some of the most famous intellectuals in the struggle, among them Cde Mzala, the pseudonym of the late Jabulani Nobleman Nxumalo. He was the author of a classic book on Gatsha Buthelezi and many articles (see Mzala 1988).

Among the important features of this period was consolidation of non-racial thinking among the youth. Many had not had experience of whites other than as oppressors. Not only did they meet them as comrades, sometimes undergoing training with them, but also the ideological training consolidated this non-racial perspective.

In the first place, then, the ANC transmitted a concept of the new nation to the youth who were trained. This was not a process whereby the youth were simple recipients of the message. Often they came with a counter-perspective, either militaristic or that of the black consciousness movement. Many of these youths, especially from the black consciousness movement, made a significant impact on ANC thinking, which needs fuller documentation.

Beyond induction, debate and contestation from this generation, a body of new ANC intellectuals emerged – trainers as well as thinkers – who contributed substantially to the direction the organization took.

Political education on Robben Island The prison experience had a very definite impact on the nature of the ANC. Training on Robben Island served to cement a particular conception of history and understanding of the character of the organization. Although prisoners were held in a variety of different prisons, it is the impact of Robben Island which undoubtedly had a decisive influence on the political development of large numbers of people inside the prison, and, after release, on those with whom former prisoners interacted. Although there was political education in most prisons, the Robben Island experience was by far the most important in terms of its long-term impact. Purely for quantitative reasons we are dealing with quite different phenomena. Numbers are important in prison, even for practical matters such as facilitating the smuggling of political material and other activities relevant to political education. The organization needed to transcribe and hide documents used for political education and the more prisoners there were the easier it was to develop a body of resources for the courses conducted.[13]

In the white section of Pretoria prison, male prisoners were continuously engaged in political discussions and 'seminars', though this was intended to be unknown to the authorities. In contrast to the situation on Robben Island, most of these prisoners were already graduates (Suttner 2001). It is not clear, from the existing literature, to what extent political education was conducted among women prisoners. Militating against this was the smallness of their numbers and, in the case of white prisoners, in the first intake, their relatively short sentences.

A large number of young people received much of their political education about the ANC on Robben Island (Sisulu n.d.: 162; Joseph Faniso Mati in Coetzee et al. 2002). Some people first learned to read and write on the island or acquired advanced education and became seasoned political thinkers or analysts there. Mati reports, when he arrived in the early 1960s, 'Fortunately, when we got to Robben Island we found that the ANC was already organised. There were group leaders and a structure ... ' (Coetzee et al. 2002: 38). 'People must study,' the ANC would repeatedly say. 'If you got a matric, you had to teach others how to read and write, had to teach those who were attempting standard six or the junior certificate. Every person on the Island knew that he had an obligation to teach others. Later on when we managed to get study rights the teaching was more formal, but initially we specifically tried to help those who couldn't read or write' (ibid.: 45; see also interview with Monde Colin Mkunqwana in ibid.: 87).

One of the key teachers on the island was the late Walter Sisulu, who at the time of his imprisonment had not progressed beyond primary education at school. Nelson Mandela at one point referred to him as the greatest living historian of the ANC, and in this regard Mandela can be taken to be referring primarily to oral communication (though Sisulu was also an occasional writer). The notion of an 'oral intellectual' may be a very underrated phenomenon in South Africa. Some of the most important political leaders, such as Elias Motsoaledi, had very little formal education and conducted their teachings mainly orally, and this was the case with Sisulu. While the need to acquire literacy was stressed, the notion of being a thinker and an intellectual could definitely not be equated with literacy.

Walter Sisulu explains his role:

> When we settled down in Robben Island ... we had to create machinery for all prisoners, not necessarily the ANC alone, for discipline and all. And in that situation ... one of my tasks was to educate people about the history of the ANC and that is what I did. We were working at the quarry. Now we worked there as groups. So those of us who were taking particular classes would group together, work together. Then a lecture takes place there while we are working. (Sisulu n.d.: 162–3)

Some of the ideas of the leadership were committed to writing (and some have now been published – see Mbeki 1991; Maharaj 2001). This was all strictly illegal and carried out in secret (Harry Gwala, cited in Buntman 1996: 106). The island was decisive in the political education of the young generation of 1976, consolidating their understanding of the history of resistance and in many or most cases 'converting' them to the ANC (see Buntman 2003). Daniel Montsisi, a leader of the 1976 rising in Soweto, records:

> The Island was a political education for me. Firstly, we developed a deep comradeship through discussion with the older leaders, and a deep respect. Before I went to the Island my understanding of the Freedom Charter was not thorough. There I had the time to look back at history ... It was like putting together pieces of a jigsaw puzzle which had been missing all along. We delved into our history. We discovered that we young people were not the first to take up the fight against apartheid, but a new part of a developing process. (Johnson 1988a: 107)

In order to ensure the maximum benefit from political education, it was necessary to tackle illiteracy. According to Harry Gwala, one of the most famous educators on the island, literacy was needed in order to conduct the political theory classes that he and Stephen Dlamini started. Gwala explained that people who were illiterate could not understand the abstract concepts they were teaching and using: 'So we organised ... literacy education' (Buntman 1996: 112–13). One of the beneficiaries of this literacy training was the current deputy-president of the country, Jacob Zuma.

The programmes of political education on the island were not conceived purely to keep prisoners occupied and avoid idleness, though this may have been a factor, since idleness could lead to demoralization. There was, additionally, a very self-conscious motivation, to prepare prisoners to play a significant political role after release. Fran Buntman writes:

> [T]he inmates on Robben Island had always regarded it as their duty to produce capable activists who would eventually go back into their communities. The youth of '76 represented the future of the movements and the liberation struggle. These were the future activists, leaders, and soldiers, and so their recruitment was a necessity. Recruitment was, of course, a starting point for the critical process of training activists, teaching them organizational histories, ideologies and strategies, and preparing them for their political obligations and mandates upon release ... (2001: 156, 168, 170)

Time spent on the island appears to have been a way of crystallizing thinking and developing common positions on various issues. The island graduates' entry into the United Democratic Front (UDF)[14] organizations in the 1980s usually connoted the arrival of people who were seen as having much political maturity, and able to advance non-sectarian and unifying positions.

As mentioned, there had been a rupture in the tradition of Congress organization and in the consciousness of what it represented. While it did continue to have an underground presence, many people grew up without systematic exposure to the ideas, principles and ways of organization of the ANC and its allies. Those released from prison became bearers of a tradition of struggle in the same way as older comrades in exile helped connect a new generation to the history and policies of the past (see Buntman 2003).

Pravin Gordhan speaks of the impact of released political prisoners on the thinking and culture of young activists in mid-1970s Natal: 'They were bearers of history, bearers of experiences, bearers of anecdotes, bearers of the Congress culture, "this is how you do things, this is how you say things, this is how you analyse things", they were bearers of inspiration, because you could relate to them as heroes, and there were not many heroes at the time, and each of them had a different quality because they each played a different role ... ' (interview).

Certainly there was an element of romanticism attached to being in prison. It carried considerable authority, feeding into the hierarchical character of the ANC and especially underground. There was often an assumption that activists in the 1980s could not rely on their own judgement, but needed to buttress this with appeal to a higher authority (see

Suttner 2005 regarding the UDF's 'B team mentality'). The ANC official leadership in exile was not easily accessible (although many people listened illegally to the ANC's Radio Freedom broadcast from Lusaka and other countries on the continent). The next-best option may have been to consult with a prison veteran. Obviously such hierarchical conceptions were factors running counter to building critical thinking.

Each generation that came together on Robben Island possessed distinct knowledge and experience drawn from the different periods of involvement. The time spent on the island helped bridge inter-generational gaps, in ways that would impact on the struggle outside. This is not to suggest that those from any one generation had uncontested versions of what the ANC represented. There were divergent perceptions among the leadership, with Govan Mbeki and Harry Gwala challenging the ideas and leadership of Nelson Mandela and Walter Sisulu (see Buntman 1996: 125). Among the 1976 generation, political positions were often less crystallized and the years of contact with the older generation saw many 'cross over' to the ANC, but a core remained in the BCM (Black Consciousness Movement).

One of the important features of the intellectual evolution of individuals within prisons was the combination of individual and collective work. Many undertook formal courses, but the main process of development was collective. Political education courses have been emphasized here but the collective influence was wider. In prison one did not read a newspaper alone but in dialogue with others.[15] Sometimes it was a formal session, often called 'news analysis', found also in military situations (interview Moche). It is in interpreting such data that many people have the opportunity to grow. In fact in these interactions one often finds wholly new ways of interpreting events.

Given the categories outlined at the beginning of this paper, Robben Island is unique. It has many of the characteristics found in the production of intellectuals in conventional educational institutions, as indicated by the existence of specific course structures. In so far as these related directly to the history of the ANC there was not the same need to transform acquired knowledge and understanding as would have been the case with those fresh from university.

Clearly the lecturers performed an intellectual role. In terms of an overall task carried out by many people, they acted as 'collective intellectuals'. From this process prisoners were inducted into ANC policies, but many also became leading thinkers of the liberation movement. The process of political education created a new cadre of political leadership within the prison, but also many, as indicated, who had considerable impact after their release.

Party/national liberation movement as 'collective intellectual'

The concepts 'collective intellectual' and 'collective organic intellectual', in referring to a political party, we have noted, are ascribed to Gramsci, though he does not appear to have actually used these specific terms. Gramsci speaks of the party playing a coordinating role in regard to intellectuals: 'The political party for all groups is precisely the mechanism which carries out in civil society the same function as the state carries out, more synthetically and over a larger scale, in political society. In other words it is responsible for welding together the organic intellectuals of a given group – the dominant one – and the traditional intellectuals' (1971: 15–16).

Throughout the history of the liberation movement intellectuals trained through conventional means have been drawn into the ANC and SACP. The processes of interaction between these intellectuals in the structures of the organization are one way in which book knowledge drawn from formal institutions is transformed into political understanding, which in combination and debate with others becomes part of the intellectual input of the organization. What is required varies from time to time. Thus Joe Slovo and Joe Matthews (who later left the ANC and SACP) were trained as lawyers and were theorists in the Communist Party, and became theorists of guerrilla warfare. In the period of negotiations, Slovo had again to convert his theoretical expertise into practical analysis of negotiated settlements and transition.

The process of acquiring a university qualification is in the main an individual process. A student sits in the library and at home, attends classes and sits examinations as an individual. For a political party something more than this is required, and it can only be acquired through collective work. Many of the qualities required for obtaining formal qualifications remain applicable – the need to read and study. But there is a much greater collective involvement and the idea is to make the insights derived, not part of the body of organic intellectuals alone, but of the membership as a whole.

Referring to the 'Modern Prince' or Communist Party, Gramsci sees the organization as:

> the proclaimer and organiser of an intellectual and moral reform, which also means creating the terrain for a subsequent development of the national-popular collective will towards the realisation of a superior, total form of modern civilisation.
>
> These two basic points – the formation of a national-popular collective will, of which the modern Prince is at one and the same time the organiser and the active, operative expression; and intellectual and moral reform– should structure the entire work ... (ibid.: 132–3)

The argument presented here is that a political party can perform the role of a 'collective intellectual' in another sense, and this has special importance in the context of the South African liberation struggle. This is where a political party or national liberation movement periodically intervenes and – as a collective – performs an intellectual role. This may be through collectively generated policy documents or strategic interventions or radio broadcasts and other media. What is essentially intellectual about these interventions is that they give meaning to events, conditions or situations that may appear to be fairly settled or, alternatively, to have suddenly changed. The intervention generally also tends to provide direction as to what can be done or should be done in relation to this set of conditions. This is at once a conjunctural analysis and usually also a tactical and strategic intervention (see ANC 1969).

The intervention may be directed at the organization's membership and followers or the public at large. It is meant to be an interpretation as well as a guide. It is a consensus of the body of intellectuals within the party or of a party that has become a body of intellectuals. But that does not signify an unproblematic intervention starting from within the party itself. Every consensus represents a result of struggle, not a simple translation of what is already there. Most products of consensus are themselves subject to further struggle.

The ANC acting as 'collective intellectual' through its strategy and tactics document of 1969

It has been argued that the ANC and its allies, through interventions via documentation and other media, from time to time initiated or entered into debates, gave meaning to situations and as a consequence acted as a 'collective intellectual'. One important illustration of this phenomenon was at the time of the Morogoro consultative conference in Tanzania, called at a time of crisis and demoralization in 1969. The crisis related not only to events immediately preceding the conference but also to the entire situation following the banning of the ANC and its hasty organization underground, initiation of armed struggle and the subsequent arrest of much of its top leadership.

The re-establishment of the organization in exile was a slow process, partly because the ANC was at first over-optimistic in its expectations of a return to South Africa. It was only in 1967 that the ANC headquarters was acknowledged to be outside the country. The immediate result of the Rivonia arrests and subsequent 'mopping up' trials of less senior operatives was to create an atmosphere of overwhelming power on the part of the apartheid state. Very faltering steps to re-establish a presence inside and outside the country on the part of the liberation movement did not initially have great impact. This perception of state invincibility was partly exaggerated but nevertheless corresponded to what many of the organization's supporters believed to be the case. Outside, with many cadres receiving advanced military training, some impatience was expressed with simply waiting. Military action was initiated through engaging Rhodesian forces, together with ZAPU,[16] with a view to fighting a way through to South Africa. This was in two campaigns in 1967 and 1968, in which, despite some impressive showings, the overall impact was limited or even negative.[17] This was partly because the ZAPU guerrillas with whom MK fought were themselves unfamiliar with the local terrain in the part of Rhodesia where they entered.

In their retreat from the battlefield, many cadres sought refuge in Botswana but were arrested and sentenced to several years in prison. On their return to Dar es Salaam there was considerable anger and dissatisfaction and a memorandum (known as the 'Chris Hani memorandum') was produced criticizing the leadership for over-emphasizing diplomacy at the expense of armed struggle (Shubin 1999).[18]

At the same time, the ANC and other southern African liberation movements experienced a serious diplomatic reverse with the adoption of the Lusaka manifesto – decided by states of the region, over the heads of and without consulting the liberation movements themselves, and calling for negotiations with the apartheid regime as a way of solving the conflict (Karis and Gerhart 1997). This was at a time when the emphasis of the liberation movements themselves was on the necessity to show their strength through military and other struggles.

The conference met in an atmosphere of considerable demoralization and some division among the exiled community, as well as some despondency within the country. The 'Strategy and Tactics' document sought to address this situation. Many of its formulations may have been superseded by events or proven to be wrong. But it was nevertheless an intellectual intervention by an organization, an intervention that served to empower people, to instil in them a sense that the enemy was not invincible and could in fact be defeated – albeit through a protracted struggle on many fronts.

The document sets the scene by answering the question as to whether it had embarked on armed struggle too late. There had been talk of 'fighting back' and taking up arms since the early 1950s, with Nelson Mandela secretly asking Walter Sisulu to sound out the Chinese during an overseas visit about the possible supply of arms (Mandela 1994; Sisulu 2002). Likewise, people in the Northern Transvaal spent much time discussing the Kenyan guerrilla experience (Delius 1996; interview Nkadimeng), and others in the Eastern Cape were talking some time before 1961 of taking up arms (see Mhlaba 2001). In fact, many did 'jump the gun' and started burning down the cane fields in Natal in the late 1950s (Magubane et al. 2004). Why, then, did the ANC delay its decision until 1961?

> Why was the decision for armed struggle taken in 1961? Why not 1951 or 1941 or 1931? Is it that the character of the state had so altered fundamentally that only in 1961 did armed struggle become the only alternative? Not at all. There has never been a moment in the history of South Africa since 1952 in which the White ruling class would have given privileges without a physical battle. Why then did organizations like the African National Congress not call for armed struggle? Was it perhaps that they were not really revolutionary or that it was only in the early '60s that they began to appreciate the correct strategy? Is there substance in the accusations by some of our detractors that until the early '60s the liberation movement was lacking in military fervour and the desire for radical change? In other words was its policy not a revolutionary one? What is our measuring rod for revolutionary policy?
>
> To ignore the real situation and to play about with imaginary forces, concepts and ideals is to invite failure. The art of revolutionary leadership consists in providing leadership to the masses and not just to its most advanced elements: it consists of setting a pace which accords with objective conditions and the real possibilities at hand. The revolutionary-sounding phrase does not always reflect revolutionary policy, and revolutionary-sounding policy is not always the spring-board for revolutionary advance. (ANC 1969)

The document proceeds to outline the then current approach to guerrilla warfare. What is important for our present purposes is how it then addresses the question of the strength and weaknesses of 'the enemy'. This is important because it had been some decades since the oppressed people of South Africa had faced colonial conquerors in warfare. Now it was facing a modern state, well equipped with a relatively advanced industrial base.

> On the face of it the enemy is in stable command of a rich and varied economy which, even at this stage when it is not required to extend itself, can afford an enormous military budget. He has a relatively well-trained and efficient army and police force. He can draw on fairly large manpower resources. In addition the major imperialist powers ... have an enormous stake in the economy of our country and constitute a formidable support for the Apartheid regime ... If there is one lesson that the history of guerrilla

143

struggle has taught it is that the material strength and resources of the enemy is [sic] by no means a decisive factor. Guerrilla warfare almost by definition presents a situation in which there is a vast imbalance of material and military resource between the opposing sides. It is designed to cope with the situation in which the enemy is infinitely superior in relation to every conventional factor of warfare. It is *par excellence* the weapon of the materially weak against the materially strong. (ibid.: 150–1)

The document elaborates further, but it is not necessary for our purposes to pursue this. What is important for the argument presented here is that this is an intellectual intervention – it gives meaning to a series of events, situations and a range of forces in a way that empowers the popular masses or, given what was known and believed at the time, it made sense. It may well be that many of these formulations were modified or had to be abandoned, but it remains an intervention of a liberation movement acting as a collective intellectual.

The intervention served as an antidote to those who saw no hope, who analysed the power relationship between oppressor and oppressed as one that could never be reversed. It was a basis for many people to have their commitment to struggle reinvigorated. Others joined the organization on the basis of this analysis because it was seen as providing a meaningful and convincing appraisal of how the struggle might unfold and demonstrating that joining the ranks might not be futile.

Over the years that followed there were many such interventions, though this may have been one of the more powerful. The later interventions had significance mainly because they addressed changed situations and new possibilities. One of the most famous interventions was when the ANC leadership called on the people of South Africa to make apartheid 'unworkable' and South Africa 'ungovernable'. Much of this reached activists through the ANC's illegally broadcast Radio Freedom, on the air every evening at 7 p.m. For a while there was ungovernability, and one of the reasons why a negotiated settlement became possible was because, while the forces of resistance could not defeat the apartheid regime, governability was not possible or sustainable.

The importance of these interventions, which can all be characterized as intellectual interventions, was that they sensed the mood of the masses and the disarray in the ranks of the regime and offered arguments and slogans that could be realized. In some cases, such as the call for the establishment of embryonic organs of 'People's Power', the action on the ground took shape in a way that could not be envisaged in Lusaka. Nevertheless, the ANC provided the overall strategic direction within which these cadres acted. This was done with special potency in the annual 8 January statement of the ANC, delivered by its president on the day of the organization's anniversary, providing a conjunctural analysis as well as 'tasks' for various sectors.

Throughout this period the Communist Party was also producing literature of various sorts – underground publications, illegal journals and various statements. Some of these made a direct impact on the ANC, as can be seen by the latter's adoption of the 'Colonialism of a Special Type' thesis as a way of explaining the South African social formation.

Consensus and contestation in producing an intellectual product

The intellectual products of the liberation movement were a result of debate and contestation. There was debate at all levels, sometimes starting in Maputo, passing on to Angola, then to Lusaka and so on (interview Jordan). But a debate is obviously not the same as a debate that feeds into a decision. The degree to which the membership has been involved has varied, depending on the conditions of the time. In the exile period, where there was a considerable security threat, the tendency was for decisions to be made at the top and communicated downward. But in crisis situations, dissatisfaction or 'rumblings' among the membership resulted on occasions in general meetings and consultative conferences with de facto powers to make decisions. This was the case in 1969 and again in 1985 after a mutiny had been suppressed.

That decisions may have been made at the top did not mean that the consensus that was formed was unproblematically achieved or that it represented a decision or statement or viewpoint that was open to only one interpretation. The ANC speaks of itself as a broad church embracing various tendencies, and it has for some time had within its ranks people with a variety of political views. In ANC matters it is not, however, uncommon for some who are supposed to come from the same tendency to disagree with one another when 'wearing their ANC hat'. Thus communists did not always speak with one voice, though it appears that this was the case at one stage when they were operating underground in the 1950s (interviews Kathrada, Mtshali, Nair). At some stages there were important differences in emphasis related to the extent to which the party saw itself as an independent organization or whether it lost much of its independent existence in relation to the ANC (Suttner 2004a).

But there were debates and divergences over how to conduct the struggle throughout the ANC's history, and in the exile period over the type of military campaign to wage, how it should be combined with political struggle, and what the organizational implications should be.

145

New conjuncture after 1990 and again after 1994

The character of organizational inputs into debates, the documentation that was produced, was generally a result of a consensus that emerged within the ANC itself and in consultation with its 'revolutionary alliance' partners, SACP and the South African Congress of Trade Unions, SACTU (later replaced by the Congress of South African Trade Unions, COSATU). In the period prior to 1990 there was no significant divergence in the perspectives of the three partners.

The unbanning of the ANC and SACP created conditions that placed strain on the relationships within and between the organizations. In the first place the ANC had to re-establish itself inside the country, combining elements from a variety of different traditions (Suttner 2003a). And the conditions under which negotiations were conducted caused tensions, especially among the military, who were not all convinced of the need to suspend armed action, and also among the mass democratic movement, which resisted attempts at demobilization or curbing mass-based activity.

The election of the ANC as the leading force in government again created new relationships. The distinction between government and organization became blurred. GEAR (the acronym referring to the government's conservative macro-economic policy, adopted in 1996), for example, was announced by government, but declared to be ANC policy before going through any process within the organization or within the alliance. The ANC as an organization appeared to be less of a factor than the ANC in government, and the membership appeared to enjoy a very limited role between elections.

In the case of the alliance, increasingly the post-1994 period has seen the development of tensions over the relationship between its components. One of the reasons may be a blurring between the notion of ANC as government and ANC as organization. It is not clear whether the SACP and COSATU are relating, in the alliance, to government or to an equal partner, as fellow organizations. If it is a relationship to government, as it increasingly appears to be, the SACP and COSATU may be cast more in the role of petitioners than equal partners.

The period has also seen volatility deriving from electoral politics. The identity of enemies and allies has reflected a degree of fluidity that was unimaginable some years back. The ANC formed an alliance with the Inkatha Freedom Party, responsible for many deaths of ANC/UDF supporters – but motivated by a much-needed desire for peace in the province of KwaZulu-Natal. The organization later also formed an alliance with the NNP, the former ruling party of the apartheid regime. This was depicted as part of a nation-building process, though the NNP's limited strength means it now brings little to such a relationship.

At the same time tensions between its alliance partners – the SACP and COSATU – escalated into public attacks. Documents were issued calling the SACP and COSATU ultra-left and attacking their left credentials (see, e.g., Moleketi and Jele 2002). A minister commended Lenin's *Left Wing Communism – an Infantile Disorder* to COSATU. Ironically, and showing some of the complexity of the South African political scene, the particular minister was at that time a leader of the Communist Party.

But the trend is for yesterday's allies sometimes to become opponents or to be cast that way and for yesterday's enemies to become allies. Significantly the discourse used by the ANC remains primarily Marxist or Brezhnevite Marxist[19] in its attacks on its allies. Paradoxically it is the classic texts of Marx and Lenin which are deployed to defend the government's macroeconomic policies. The differences within the tripartite alliance are not irreparable, but they do indicate that there is no longer a sense of equality and that the conditions of the relationship have been fundamentally altered.

What this also means is that the notion of a collective intellectual function may be restricted to the utterances of the ANC/government, and in so far as SACP and COSATU perform such functions this may tend to be more independently of the ANC than in the past.

The theoretical basis for this collapse of the alliance as collective intellectual is interesting. As noted, the ANC depicts itself as a broad church, meaning that it is open to people from a variety of political tendencies – Christians, communists, African nationalists, capitalists and so on. But the notion of a broad church or any church may also imply priesthood, often with superior powers of scriptural interpretation.[20] This notion may be symbolically represented by the president or whoever is a leading theoretician, though this function may be dormant in certain phases and more prominent in others.

What has tended to happen in the post-1994 period, however, is that statements of the leadership have often been presented as fait accompli or interpretations of leadership have not met with much challenge. This is partly because, rightly or wrongly, powers of leadership are now associated with powers to make appointments that may carry prestige or high remuneration. Consequently the authoritative statements of certain leadership figures may limit debate within the 'broad church'. The president himself, Thabo Mbeki, is a leading intellectual, whose speeches have now been published in two books and appear regularly on the ANC website, along with a weekly letter that he writes (Mbeki 1998, 2002). At the same time,

147

these interventions do not appear to be part of a broad debate. They are more in the nature of 'authoritative pronouncements', carrying the weight of leadership. In this sense it may sometimes be that such statements are interpreted by many as signifying closure rather than an engagement in intellectual debate.

Conclusion

There are many issues that preoccupy intellectuals on this continent which are important but are not part of this enquiry. The paper does not address such questions as 'speaking truth to power', the relationship that individual intellectuals should have to a liberation movement or political party, how they should exercise an independent role, and so on. These are different types of problems from those that have been examined.

The object of this paper has been to describe a relatively neglected process of intellectual formation and output, within the framework of a Gramscian paradigm. The value of Gramsci is that he redefines notions of education and intellectuals in a way that enables us to recognize such processes in experiences that normally do not 'qualify'.

Many of the data presented demonstrate these intellectual and educational processes occurring, though they took place in an uneven way. The Robben Island prison experience was obviously much more structured as a process of intellectual creation and intellectual production than the period that preceded it and many others that followed, though all are examples of such processes. The prison experience is unique, for it is inherently more structured and concentrated than any processes can be in 'normal life'. This meant that some educational objectives could be achieved there, possibly much more easily than outside.

There is much more to be added and developed, and it is hoped that future discussion will help take this contribution farther.

Acknowledgements

I am indebted to SIDA, through the Nordic Africa Institute, for funding this research, to the Centre for Policy Studies for hosting me for over two years, and to South African Breweries for additional funding. The University of South Africa has provided an additional and stimulating 'home' in recent months and encouraged much of my work. Claire Kruger, Martin Ngobeni, Soneni Ncube and Portia Santho obtained and photocopied much material and Mary-Lynn Suttie provided additional bibliographical assistance. I am grateful to Peter Hudson and Gerry Maré who read through the paper and made valuable suggestions for improvement. The responsibility for the final product naturally remains mine.

Notes

1 It is well known that in every society there have been strata of people who performed an intellectual role. Certain individuals were charged with various spiritual and ritual duties and other cultural functions that explained the meaning of life, gave explanations for disasters or prognosticated for the future. The accuracy or otherwise of what they did, measured in terms of 'contemporary science', is unimportant. What is significant here is that this constituted an intellectual role, a way of making sense of the world for others.

2 In the context of this paper, I apply this even more widely to the alliance of the ANC and the South African Communist Party (SACP), when that becomes established, and to some extent also the trade union ally, at first the South African Congress of Trade Unions (SACTU), later replaced by the Congress of South African Trade Unions (COSATU).

3 The term 'collective intellectual' or 'collective organic intellectual' may not have been used by Gramsci himself. The term 'collective intellectual' may have first been deployed by Togliatti (1979, e.g. at 155).

4 Members of the SACP and COSATU are allowed to hold overlapping ANC membership.

5 The Trotskyist left did also for a period of time implement training pro-grammes in a night school (Bird 1980: 68–9).

6 The dress and class composition of the 'angry' generation of the Youth League was in the main very similar to that of the founders of the ANC.

7 Natasha Erlank argues that this was a continuous trend (2003).

8 The Communist International (Comintern) was a worldwide organization of communist parties, located in Moscow from 1919 until its dissolution in 1943. During its existence every communist party was described as a 'section' of the Communist International.

9 This raises an interesting contemporary question. Given this Marxist orientation during the 1950s and the apparent popularity of socialism during the exile period and within the country in the 1980s, what has happened to that tradition within the ANC in the present period? Has it simply been obliterated from people's minds and, if so, how was that achieved, or does it mean that the conviction and training were in fact very superficial?

10 When the Communist Party was reconstituted underground in 1953, it was renamed the South African Communist Party (SACP) (see Suttner 2004a). MK refers to Umkhonto we Sizwe (the Spear of the Nation), the ANC's armed wing.

11 At a later stage, with the re-emergence of the independent worker move-ment in the early 1970s, large-scale attention was paid to worker education through a variety of courses and media in the years that followed.

12 Ralph Mgijima indicates, however, that this negative exhortation was one of the ways in which he was made aware of the ANC in the face of a public silence about its existence (interview).

13 Transcription was important because books obtained from libraries were sometimes very important to the prisoners but had to be returned.

14 The United Democratic Front (UDF) was formed in 1983, drawing under one banner some six hundred affiliated organizations, representing over 2 million members. Although legally prevented from open identification with the ANC, UDF affiliates tended to view themselves as carrying out the strategies and tactics of the ANC (see Suttner 2005).

15 Initially political prisoners were denied legal access to newspapers. Prisoners on Robben Island were fairly successful in smuggling these in. In the late 1970s the white political prisoners in Pretoria brought an unsuccessful court action to secure access to newspapers, but after losing the case repeatedly right up to the Appellate Division, all the political prisoners gradually 'won the war'.

16 The Zimbabwe African People's Union, under the leadership of the then imprisoned Joshua Nkomo, later to merge with ZANU (PF), under Robert Mugabe.

17 Regarding successes, see Karis and Gerhart (1997: 27).

18 Hani refers to the assassinated MK commander and leader of the SACP, who faced the possibility of being sentenced to death after submitting this memorandum (see Shubin 1999).

19 Many current ANC leaders who have left the SACP passed through the Lenin School during the Brezhnev period.

20 I am indebted here to David Masondo.

References

ANC (1969) 'Strategy and Tactics of the ANC', < www.anc.org.za/history/stratact. html>

Anon. (1984) 'Internal Education in the Congress Alliance', *Africa Perspective*, 24: 99–111

Apter, D. E. (1964) 'Ghana', in J. S. Coleman and C. G Rosberg, Jr (eds), *Political Parties and National Integration in Tropical Africa*, Berkeley and Los Angeles: University of California Press, pp. 259–317

Bernstein, H. (1994) *The Rift. The Exile Experience of South Africans*, London: Jonathan Cape

Bird, A. (1980) 'Black Adult Night School Movements on the Witwatersrand, 1920–1980', *Africa Perspective*, 17: 63–88

Bonner, P. (1982) 'The Transvaal Native Congress, 1917–1920: The Radicalization of the Black Petty Bourgeoisie on the Rand', in S. Marks and R. Rathbone (eds), *Industrialisation and Social Change in South Africa. African Class Formation, Culture and Consciousness, 1870–1930*, London and New York: Longman

Bonner, P. and L. Segal (1998) *Soweto. A History*, Cape Town: Maskew Miller Longman

Bradford, H. (1987) *A Taste of Freedom*, Johannesburg: Ravan Press

Bunting, B. (1998) *Moses Kotane, South African Revolutionary. A Political Biography*, Bellville: Mayibuye Books, 3rd edn

Buntman, F. (1996) 'Resistance on Robben Island 1963–1976', in H. Deacon (ed.), *The Island. A History of Robben Island 1488–1990*, Mayibuye History and Literature Series no. 60, Cape Town and Johannesburg: David Philip

— (2001) 'Categorical and Strategic Resistance and the Making of Political Prisoner Identity in Apartheid's Robben Island Prison', in A. Zegeye (ed.), *Social Identities in the New South Africa after Apartheid*, vol. 1, Cape Town and Maroelana: Kwela Books and SA History Online, pp. 153–79

— (2003) *Robben Island and Prisoner Resistance to Apartheid*, Cambridge University Press

CODESRIA (2003) 'CODESRIA 30th Anniversary Conference', Dakar, 8–11 December, <www.codesria.org>

Coetzee, J. K., L. Gilfillan and O. Hulec (2002) *Fallen Walls. Voices from the Cells that Held Mandela and Havel*, Nakkadatelstvi Lidove Noviny, Robben Island Museum

Crehan, K. (2002) *Gramsci, Culture and Anthropology*, London: Pluto Press

Curnow, Robyn (2000) 'Interview. Thandi Modise, a Woman at War', *Agenda*, 43: 36–40

Davidson, A., I. Filatova, V. Gorodnov and S. Johns (2003) *South Africa and the Communist International. A Documentary History*, vol. 1, *Socialist Pilgrims to Bolshevik Footsoldiers 1919–1930*, London and Portland, OR: Frank Cass

Delius, P. (1996) *A Lion amongst the Cattle. Reconstruction and Resistance in the Northern Transvaal*, Portsmouth, NH: Heinemann; Johannesburg: Ravan Press; Oxford: James Currey

Drew, A. (2000) *Discordant Comrades. Identities and Loyalties on the South African Left*, Aldershot: Ashgate

Dubow, S. (2000) *The African National Congress*, Johannesburg: Jonathan Ball

Erlank, N. (2003) 'Gender and Masculinity in South African Nationalist Discourse, 1912–1950', *Feminist Studies*, 29(3): 653–72

Filatova, I. (1999) 'Indoctrination or Scholarship? Education of Africans at the Communist University of the Toilers of the East in the Soviet Union, 1923–1937', *Paedagogica Historica. International Journal of the History of Education* 35(1)

Frederikse, J. (1990) *The Unbreakable Thread. Non-Racialism in South Africa*, Johannesburg: Ravan Press

Gerhart, G. M. (1978) *Black Power in South Africa. The Evolution of an Ideology*, Berkeley, Los Angeles, London: University of California Press

Gramsci, A. (1971) *Selections from the Prison Notebooks*, ed. Q. Hoare and G. Nowell Smith, London: Lawrence and Wishart

— (1979) *Letters from Prison*, introduced by L. Lawner, London, Melbourne, New York: Quartet

Johns, S. (1995) *Raising the Red Flag. The International Socialist League and the Communist Party of South Africa, 1914–1932*, Bellville: Mayibuye Books

Johnson, S. (ed.) (1988a) *South Africa: No Turning Back*, Houndsmills, Basingstoke, Hampshire and London: Macmillan in association with the David Davies Memorial Institute of International Studies

— (1988b) '"The Soldiers of Luthuli": Youth in the Politics of Resistance in South Africa', in Johnson (1988a), pp. 94–152

Jordan, A. C. (1973) *Towards an African Literature. The Emergence of Literary*

Form in Xhosa, Berkeley, Los Angeles, London, University of California Press

Jordan, P. (1988) 'The South African Liberation Movement and the Making of a New Nation', in M. van Diepen (ed.), *The National Question in South Africa*, London and New Jersey: Zed Books

Karis, T. and G. M. Carter (eds) (1973) *From Protest to Challenge. A Documentary History of African Politics in South Africa 1882–1964*, vol. 2, *Hope and Challenge*, Stanford, CA: Hoover Institutions Press

Karis, T. and G. M. Gerhart (1997) *From Protest to Challenge. A Documentary History of African Politics in South Africa, 1882–1990*, vol. 5, *Nadir and Resurgence, 1964–1979*, Pretoria: UNISA Press

Kiernan, V. G. (1993) 'Colonial Liberation Movement', in W. Outhwaite, T. Bottomore, E. Gellner, R. Nisbet, A. Touraine (eds), *The Blackwell Dictionary of Twentieth-century Thought*, Oxford: Blackwell

Kunene, D. P. (1968) 'Deculturation – the African Writer's Response', *Africa Today*, 15(4): 19–24

Limb, P. (2003) 'Sol Plaatje Reconsidered', *African Studies*, 62(1): 33–52

Magubane, B. M. (1979) *The Political Economy of Race and Class in South Africa*, New York and London: Monthly Review Press

Magubane, B., P. Bonner, J. Sithole, P. Delius, J. Cherry, P. Gibbs and T. April (2004) 'The Turn to Armed Struggle', in *The Road to Democracy in South Africa*, vol. 1 (1960–1970), Cape Town: South African Democracy Education Trust/Zebra Press

Maharaj, M. (ed.) (2001) *Reflections in Prison*, Cape Town: Zebra Press and Robben Island Museum

'Majeke, Nosipho' [D. Taylor] (1986) [1952] *The Role of the Missionaries in Conquest*, Cumberwood

Mandel, E. (1978) 'The Leninist Theory of Organization', in R. Blackburn (ed.), *Revolution and Class Struggle. A Reader in Marxist Politics*, Sussex: Harvester Press; New Jersey: Humanities Press

Mandela, N. (1994) *Long Walk to Freedom. The Autobiography of Nelson Mandela*, Randburg: Macdonald Purnell

Marks, S. and S. Trapido (1987) 'The Politics of Race, Class and Nationalism', in S. Marks and S. Trapido (eds), *The Politics of Race, Class and Nationalism In Twentieth-century South Africa*, London and New York: Longman

Marx, A. W. (1992) *Lessons of Struggle. South African Internal Opposition, 1960–1990*, Cape Town: Oxford University Press

Mbeki, G. (1991) *Learning from Robben Island. The Prison Writings of Govan Mbeki*, London: James Currey; Athens: Ohio University Press; Cape Town, David Philip

— (1992) *The Struggle for Liberation in South Africa. A Short History*, Mayibuye History Series no. 13, Cape Town: David Philip.

— (1996) *Sunset at Midday. Latshon ilang emini!*, Braamfontein: Nolwazi Educational

Mbeki, T. (1998) *Africa. The Time Has Come. Selected Speeches*, Cape Town and Johannesburg: Tafelberg, Mafube

— (2002) *Africa. Define Yourself*, Randburg: Tafelberg, Mafube

Mhlaba, R. (2001) *Raymond Mhlaba's Personal Memoirs. Reminiscing from Rwanda and Uganda*, narrated to Thembeka Mufamadi, Pretoria and Robben Island Museum: Human Sciences Research Council

Mnguni [pseudonym] (1988 [1952]) *Three Hundred Years*, Cumberwood

Moleketi, J. and J. Jele (2002) *Two Strategies of the National Liberation Movement in the Struggle for the Victory of the National Democratic Revolution*, Johannesburg: [no publisher given]

Motlhabi, M. (1984) *The Theory and Practice of Black Resistance to Apartheid. A Social-ethical Analysis*, Johannesburg: Skotaville

Mzala (1988) *Gatsha Buthelezi. Chief with a Double Agenda*, London and New Jersey: Zed Books

Odendaal, A. (1984) *Vukani Bantu! The Beginnings of Black Protest Politics in South Africa to 1912*, Cape Town, Johannesburg: David Philip

Plaatje, S. T. (1982 [1916]) *Native Life in South Africa*, Johannesburg: Ravan Press

Roux, E. (1964) *Time Longer than Rope. A History of the Black Man's Struggle for Freedom in South Africa*, 2nd edn, Madison: University of Wisconsin Press

— (1993) *S. P. Bunting. A Political Biography*, ed. Brian Bunting with a foreword by Chris Hani, Bellville: Mayibuye Books

Roux, E. and W. Roux (1970) *Rebel Pity. The Life of Eddie Roux*, London: Rex Collings

Saunders, C. (2000) 'African Attitudes to Britain and the Empire before and after the South African War', in D. Lowry (ed.), *The South African War Reappraised*, Manchester and New York: Manchester University Press.

Seme, P. ka I. (1972 [1911]) 'Document 21. "Native Union"', in Karis and Carter (1973)

Shubin, V. (1999) *ANC. A View from Moscow*, Bellville: Mayibuye Books/UWC

Simons, J. and R. Simons (1969, reprinted 1983), *Class and Colour in South Africa 1850–1950*, London: International Defence and Aid Fund for Southern Africa

Sisulu, E. (2002) *Walter & Albertina Sisulu. In Our Lifetime*, Claremont: David Philip

Sisulu, W. (n.d., c.2001) *I Will Go Singing. Walter Sisulu Speaks of His Life and the Struggle for Freedom in South Africa*, in conversation with George M. Houser and Herbert Shore, Robben Island Museum in association with the Africa Fund, New York

Sparg, M., J. Schreiner and G. Ansell (eds) (2001) *Comrade Jack. The Political Lectures and Diary of Jack Simons, Novo Catengue*, Johannesburg: STE/ANC

Suttner, R. (2001) *Inside Apartheid's Prison*, Melbourne, New York, Pietermaritzburg: Ocean and University of Natal Press

— (2003a) 'Culture(s) of the African National Congress of South Africa: Imprint of Exile Experiences', *Journal of Contemporary African Studies*, 21(2): 303–20

— (2003b) 'Early ANC Underground: From the M Plan to Rivonia', *South African Historical Journal*, 49: 123–46

— (2004a) 'The Reconstitution of the South African Communist Party as an Underground Organization', *Journal of Contemporary African Studies*, 22(1): 43–68

— (2004b) 'Democratic Transition and Consolidation in South Africa: Advice of "the Experts"', *Current Sociology*, 52(5) (forthcoming)

— (2005) 'Legacies and Meanings of the United Democratic Front Period for Contemporary South Africa', CODESRIA (forthcoming)

Suttner, R. and J. Cronin (1986) *30 Years of the Freedom Charter*, Johannesburg: Ravan Press

Togliatti, P. (1979) *On Gramsci and Other Writings*, ed. and introduced by D. Sassoon, London: Lawrence and Wishart

Van Diemel, R. (2002) *In Search of 'Freedom, Fair Play and Justice'. Josiah Tshangana Gumede 1867–1947*, Belhar, Cape Town: privately published

Walshe, P. (1970) *The Rise of African Nationalism in South Africa. The African National Congress 1912–1952*, London: C. Hurst & Co.

Wells, J. C. (1993) *We Now Demand! The History of Women's Resistance to Pass Laws in South Africa*, Johannesburg: Witwatersrand University Press

Younis, M. N. (2000) *Liberation and Democratisation. The South African and Palestinian National Movements*, Minneapolis, London: University of Minnesota Press

Unpublished references

Barrell, H. (1993) *Conscripts to Their Age: African National Congress Operational Strategy, 1976–1986*, DPhil thesis, Oxford University

Edgar, R. (2003) *The Making of an African Communist: Edwin Thabo Mofutsanyana and the Communist Party of South Africa, 1927–1939*

Everatt, D. (1990) *The Politics of Nonracialism: White Opposition to Apartheid, 1945–1960*, DPhil thesis, Oxford University

Suttner, R. (2004) *ANC after Rivonia – Dead or Alive?*

Interviews

Gordhan, Pravin, 13 April 2003, Pretoria

Jordan, Pallo, 20 February 2003, Cape Town

Kathrada, Ahmed, 18 February 2003, Cape Town

Mashigo, Petros 'Shoes', 12 April 2003, Pretoria

Mgijima, Ralph, 15 July 2003, Johannesburg

Moche, Victor, 23 July 2002, Johannesburg

Mtshali, Eric, 8 February 2003, Johannesburg

Nair, Billy, 1 February 2003, Cape Town

Ndlovu, Cleopas, 30 June 2003, Durban

Nkadimeng, John, 2 February 2003, Johannesburg

Serache, Nat, 31 August 2002, Johannesburg

Shoke, Solly, 20 September 2003, Johannesburg

Tshabalala, Phumla, 13 July 2003, Johannesburg

7 | Europhone or African memory: the challenge of the pan-Africanist intellectual in the era of globalization[1]

NGUGI WA THIONG'O

The current global situation – a world being shaped by the imperative of capitalist fundamentalism with its quasi-religious ideology of privatization and imperial requirements for the unfettered movement of capital across national borders – poses a special challenge to social science and the organization of knowledge in Africa today. Fundamentalism, secular or religious, is a belief, a claim and assertion that there is only one way of organizing reality – it demands that all conform to that idea or else be excommunicated from the global temple of true believer, and in some cases be hauled to hell. The economic panacea dished out to all who seek loans from the World Bank and the International Monetary Fund has the same identical demand – privatize or perish – and homily – leave everything, even your social fate, to the tender mercies of the market. This fundamentalism of finance capital and the elevation of the market to the status of a universal deity generate other fundamentalisms, religious and secular, either in alliance with them or in opposition. These forces are at the heart of globalization, itself not necessarily a new historical phenomenon, but one that is nevertheless moving at breakneck speed, towards a possible mutation into a form qualitatively different from its earlier manifestations in the evolution of capitalist modernity. The speed and sophistication of technologies of information hasten this economic integration of the globe. They facilitate, for instance, the management of global enterprises from a single centre and the instant movement of capital across national borders. But they also speed up the social integration of the globe, with the world being shaped in the image of a consuming West. A global middle class with similar tastes and style of life is emerging. The knowledge and information shared in a global neighbourhood result in a global intellectual community. And yet what emerges from this global neighbourhood is not equality, fraternity, sisterhood, liberty – the mutual dependency and care of the traditional peasant neighbourhood where neighbourliness is truly a moral value, with its emphasis on hospitality over hostility. No, this global neighbourhood hosts hostile camps.

Thus the major character of the emerging globe is the division of the world into a minority of very wealthy creditor nations, mostly Western (and which, incidentally, also harbour weapons of mass destruction), and the majority debtor nations, mostly African, Asian and South American (which, incidentally, are always buying arms from the same dominant group); and within each nation a yawning gap between a wealthy tiny social stratum and a poor social majority. The world is now occupied by opposing extremes of poverty and wealth, the poor ironically adding to the wealth of the wealthy through debt slavery. It has happened before in history, when slavery fuelled the beginnings of capitalist modernity in the seventeenth century. The tragedy of the dawn of capital is being replayed, almost four hundred years later, as a grim comedy of the wealthy nations and social classes within nations consuming 90 per cent of the results of global social production. This consumption includes that of information and knowledge – and as the saying has it, information is power.

Despite its vast natural and human resources – indeed, despite the fact that Africa has always provided, albeit unwillingly, resources that have fuelled capitalist modernity to its current stage of globalization – this continent gets the rawest deal. This is obvious in the areas of economic and political power. But it is also reflected in the production and consumption of information and knowledge. As in the political and economic fields, Africa has been a player in the production of knowledge. The increase in universities and research centres, though with often shrinking resources, has resulted in great African producers of knowledge in all fields, such that brilliant sons and daughters of Africa are to be found in all the universities in the world. The constellation of thinkers and researchers around CODESRIA is testament to this. So why the raw deal for Africa, despite the consumption of knowledge produced by its sons and daughters?

It is only fitting and proper that we raise this question at this gathering to mark and celebrate thirty years of the existence of CODESRIA, founded in 1973 by African social scientists with the noble and most appropriate aim of developing scientific capacities and tools that further the cohesion, well-being and development of African societies. The founding visionaries were very conscious that the council would be meaningful only if a deliberate effort was made to foster a pan-African community of intellectual workers active in and connected to the continent, the accent being placed on the commitment to that connection. Thus pan-Africanism has always been embedded in the ideals and ambitions of CODESRIA. The fact that thirty years later we are all gathered here, on African soil, from the different parts of the continent and four corners of the globe, bespeaks the success of those laudable aims; thus it is only fitting that the grand finale should be organized around the theme of pan-Africanism. It is indeed a remarkable continuity, an intellectual effort and output of which Africa should be proud, for it is a continuity that has resulted in the production of a dazzling array of books, journals and monographs. CODESRIA is reflective of the vitality of intellectual production in Africa and by Africans all over the world.

Has this vitality resulted in the enhancement of a scientific and democratic intellectual culture? Are African intellectuals and their production really connected to the continent? Even a cursory glance shows that there is clearly a discrepancy between the quality and quantity of this knowledge production and the quality and quantity of its consumption by the general populace. Ours has been a case of trickle-down knowledge, a variation on that form of economics characteristic of capitalist modernity, reflected more particularly in its colonial manifestation, which of course is the root base of modern education in Africa. And here I am talking of social production and the consumption of knowledge and information in the whole realm of thought, from the literary to the scientific. Since our very mandate as African producers of knowledge is to connect with the continent, it behoves us continually to re-examine our entire colonial heritage, which includes the theory and practice of trickle-down knowledge. This means having to continually examine our relationship to European memory in the organization of knowledge. Wherever Europe went in the globe, it planted its memory. First on the landscape: Europe mapped, surveyed the lie of the land, and then named it.[2] The classic text of the colonial process, Shakespeare's *The Tempest*, illustrates this. Remember that when Prospero first arrives at the Caribbean island inherited by Caliban from his mother Sycorax, he learns everything about the island from its own native, and then renames whatever Caliban shows him. The colonial explorer's journal is a record of efforts to plant memory on the landscape. Consider other examples. The east coast of America, for instance, becomes New England. The Great Lake that links Uganda, Kenya and Tanzania – and the most important source of the Nile – becomes Lake Victoria. In fact, after 1884 the African landscape becomes covered with French, British, German, Italian or Portuguese memory. It is in the naming of the landscape that we can so clearly see the layering of one memory over another, a previous native memory of place buried under another, a foreign alluvium becoming the new visible identity of a place.

The same Europe planted its memory on the bodies of the colonized. One could easily regard Western Christianity, for instance, as a vast renaming ritual. To name is to express a relationship, mostly of ownership, as was seen in plantation slavery, when slaves were branded with the name of their owners; when they changed plantations or when the same plantation was taken up by another owner, they were made to take up the new names – a marker of their new identities as the property of the new owner – and were branded accordingly. There is that horror scene in Sembene Ousmane's film *Ceddo* where this ownership and identity are branded on the body of the owned with hot iron. Forcible religious renaming is very much a continuation of this violent tradition. In colonized Africa, Christian converts had to abandon their names and assume holy ones such as James, Margaret, or Bush. One could never be received in Christian heaven without a European name. As a result, European names, like the iron brands of Sembene's film, cling to the bodies of many African peoples, and whatever they achieve that 'name' is always around to claim its ownership of that achievement. A name given and accepted is a memory planted on the body of its grateful or unquestioning recipient. The body becomes a book, a parchment, where ownership and identity are forever inscribed.

Europe went farther and planted its memory on the intellect. This was achieved by imposing European languages on the conquered. In Africa this meant raising European languages to the level of an ideal whose achievement was the pinnacle of pure enlightenment. But language of course comes with culture; for instance, in recruiting new servants of the empire from among the colonized, Lord Macaulay believed that teaching English in India would produce a class of natives, Indian in blood and colour, but English in taste, opinions, morals and intellect, who would stand as interpreters between them and the people they governed – a buffer between the real owners of the empire and the vast masses of the owned. Language is a means of organizing and conceptualizing reality, but it is also a bank for the memory generated by human interaction with the natural social environment. Each language, no matter how small, carries its memory of the world. Suppressing and diminishing the languages of the colonized also meant marginalizing the memory they carried and elevating to a desirable universality the memory carried by the language of the conqueror. This obviously includes elevation of that language's conceptualization of the world, including that of self and otherness. There is the famous encounter between Friday and Robinson Crusoe in Defoe's novel of the same title. Here Friday is assumed to be a kind of *tabula rasa* with no previous knowledge of the world, and Crusoe takes on the duty and responsibility of educating his new human possession. He starts with language – Crusoe's language, of course. 'Your name is Friday because I found you on a Friday. And my name is Master.' Their relationship of inequality is defined and normalized by language.

Europe also planted its memory on method. Reverting to the *The Tempest*, we find in the relationship between Prospero and Caliban illuminations of colonial knowledge and scholarship and, in fact, its very method. Initially it is the native informant who knows everything about the immediate environment, including the location of water and means of survival. It is the native informant who imparts this local knowledge to the colonial intellectual, in the form of an explorer or administrator who codes it into his language. Historically, we get the same process in the encounter between Christopher Columbus and the Amerindian world he thinks is Asia. Columbus's journal shows him to be one of the first in a long line of intellectual servants of capitalist modernity committed to renaming landscapes. After waxing rhapsodic about the beauty of the Caribbean islands and his generous reception by the natives, Columbus seizes some of them 'in order that they might learn and give me information of that which there is in these parts ... I shall take them with me.'[3] Learning – or shall we say education – is tied in with capture and enslavement. Presumably what he learns from the learned captives is coded in Columbus's European language, in this case Portuguese. Somewhere in this process, the original text and memory of place is lost or becomes forever buried under that of Europe, for at the end of the process a European language becomes the only store of knowledge about the place. Note also that the entire method is that of an outsider, helped by native informants – call them research assistants – looking in. Helped by the assistant, he records primary state-ments, codes them into, say, English, and these notes become the primary data. Somewhere along the line, the original text, in the original language, is lost for ever. In this curious reversal, what the outsider now says of place, his memory of place, becomes the primary source of subsequent additions to knowledge of place, even by the nationals.

The result is really 'the subjection of the colonized to Europe's memory', to paraphrase Sylver Winter, its conceptualization of the world, including, for instance, its notions of democracy, its commitment to a state in the form of the nation-state, or its rationality and epistemology: let's call the latter its 'organization of knowledge', including methods for interpreting and coding that knowledge. Whether such notions are right or wrong, just or unjust, enlightening or not, they result from the colonizer's gaze, shaped by his field of experience and expectations. It is knowledge shaped by the colonial context of its acquisition. Note how even the thinking about the world by the philosophers of enlightenment, David Hume, Immanuel Kant – the whole lot, including later the great dissector of rationality, Hegel himself – is shaped by their years of reading explorer and missionary narratives of other places. The work of the Nigerian philosopher-scholar Eze, particularly his piece on the colour of reason, should be a must for studies of genealogies of Western rationality and epistemology.

I want to suggest that our various fields of knowledge of Africa are in many ways rooted in that entire colonial tradition of the outsider looking in, gathering and coding knowledge with the help of native informants, and then storing the final product in a European language for consumption by those who have access to that language. Anthropology, the study of the insider by the outsider, for the consumption of those who share the culture of the anthropologist, permeates the genealogy of European studies of Africa. We, the inheritors and continuants of that tradition, in many ways anthropologize Africa, especially in method. We collect intellectual items and put them in European language museums and archives. Africa's global visibility through European languages has meant Africa's invisibility in African languages.

How many social scientists have ever written even a single document in an African language? How many researchers have even retained the original field notes in words spoken by the primary informant? Our knowledge of Africa is largely filtered through European languages and their vocabulary. There are those, of course, who will argue that African languages are incapable of handling complexities of social thought, claiming that they do not possess an adequate vocabulary, for instance.

This objection was long ago answered by one of the brightest intellects from Africa, Cheikh Anta Diop, when he argued that no language has a monopoly on cognitive vocabulary, that every language could develop its terms for science and technology, a position being maintained by contemporary thinkers such as Kwesi Kwaa Prah, whose CASAS (Centre for Advanced Studies of African Society), based in Cape Town, South Africa, is doing so much to advocate the use of African languages in all fields of learning, even in scientific thought. Similar advocacy is to be found in philosopher Paulin Hountondji's African Centre for Advanced Studies (Centre Africain des Hautes Études), based in Porto-Novo, Benin, which now intends to promote African languages as media for African scientific thought. There are other individuals, such as Neville Alexander of Cape Town, South Africa, who chaired the committee that came up with the new, very enlightened South African policy on languages, or Kwesi Wiredu, who long ago called on African philosophers to engage issues in African languages. This advocacy has a long history going back to the Xhosa intellectuals of the late nineteenth century and continued among Zulu intellectuals of the 1940s. The advocacy of Cheikh Anta Diop is well known. All these intellectuals have tried to debunk the claims of inadequacy of words and terms. In practice, the continued Ethiopian scholarship in African languages belies the negative claims, and it should not be forgotten that even English and French had to overcome similar claims of inadequacy as vehicles for philosophy and scientific thought as against the once dominant Latin. Those languages needed the courage of their intellectuals to break loose from the grip of Latin memory. In the introduction to his *Discourse on Method*, Descartes defends his use of vernacular for philosophic thought against similar claims of inadequacy of concepts in French. What African languages need is similar commitment from African intellectuals. In this we may need to read and reread the words of the Asmara Declaration, which, while calling on African languages to take seriously the duty, the challenge and the responsibility of speaking for Africa, also called on African intellectuals to develop the capacities of African languages for science and technology. It can be done. It *has* been done in Tanzania, where Kiswahili has now developed a massive vocabulary in all the branches of learning. It only takes courage and hard work.

It is in this context that I want to cite the case of Gatua wa Mbugua. Gatua wa Mbugua is a graduate student at Cornell University, and in May 2003 he presented and successfully defended his masters thesis on bio-intensive agriculture to the Department of Crop Science at Cornell University. There is nothing unusual in this. What was new was the fact that the entire masters thesis was in the Gikuyu language. *Nditi ya UrÐmi wa MbayotehibØ Kenya kØrð magetha ma thØkØma na Maguni Thðinði wa Cio. Ugo mØneane kØrÐ arutani a Thukuru ya NgiranjuÐti ya Yunibacðtð ya Cornell kØhingia gÐcunÐi kÐmwe kÐa mØtaratara wa Ndigirii ya MØramati wa Thayathi, gÐthathanwa 2003.* Gatua wa Mbugua's manuscript was the result of sheer dedication and lots of hard work, for he had to provide an English translation: *The Impact of Bio-intensive Cropping on Yields and Nutrient Contents of Collared Greens in Kenya, a Thesis Presented to the Faculty of the Graduate School of Cornell University in Partial Fulfilment of the Requirements for the Degree of Master of Science, May 2003.*

Writing scientific works in African languages is not novel in places such as Ethiopia, but for most of Africa it is. As far as I know, Mbugua's work is the first ever scientific work in Gikuyu at any university in or outside Africa. He had no tradition to fall back on, not even that of a stable scientific vocabulary, but this did not daunt him. All his fieldwork and fieldwork notes in Kenya were in Gikuyu. He wrote the entire thesis in Gikuyu before translating it for his teachers, who, of course, had to evaluate the scientific content.

There are cynics who will respond to this with: so what? The Gikuyu language cannot sustain a written intellectual production. The Gikuyu people number about 6 million; the Danish people about 4 million. All books written and published in Gikuyu would not fill up a shelf. Books written and published in Danish number thousands and fill up the shelves of many libraries. The Yoruba people number more than 10 million; the Swedes about 8 million. But intellectual production in the two languages is very different. Why do some people believe these 10 million Africans cannot sustain such a production if 8 million Swedes can? Icelanders number about 250,000. They have one of the most flourishing intellectual cultures in Europe. What a quarter of a million can do, surely 10 million people can.

But does the existence of many languages not contradict the ideology of pan-Africanism and dreams of continental unity? This is a genuine concern, but the perception of irresolvable contradiction is largely based on the assumption that mono-lingualism was a sine qua non of modernity and the historical fiction that some societies, and not others, are marked by mono-culturalism. The existence of many languages is not a peculiarly African problem. It was this which made Cheikh Anita Diop, in 1948, respond to 'the objection, usually raised, that Africans can never have linguistic unity' with the dismissive rejoinder: 'Africa does not need such linguistic unity any more than Europe does.' It is a fact that each African country, never mind the entire continent, has many nationalities and languages. Furthermore, colonialism divided peoples of the same language and culture across different borders, factions of the same historically constituted peoples owing allegiance to different territorial states of a more recent ilk. Should we not accept that reality as the starting point and then pose the questions? How can we turn the division of peoples of the same language and culture across different borders into a strength? How can the many languages be used to bring about the unity of African peoples within a given country and the continent more broadly? In short, how can these languages and cultures serve the pan-African ideal of our dreams?

We have to look at pan-Africanism as a people-to-people relationship and not one between the heads of states or that of the intellectual and Western-educated elite held together by their common inheritance of European languages and their roots in a European memory of place, organization of knowledge and conceptualization of reality. There is no rational basis other than convenience for regarding colonial boundaries as sacrosanct and by implication the residents of either side of the colonial border as foreigners. These borders were historically constituted, markers of European memory on Africa, to meet colonial needs, and there is no reason why they cannot be historically reconstituted to meet African needs and reconnect with African memory. The people with the same language, culture and history on either side of colonially drawn borders, what is called border communities, constitute a shared community that culturally links the two territories. A good number of these border communities have a common spiritual leader and, in reality, they refuse to be bound by the colonial borders that divide them. In their cultural practices, they have always challenged the colonially derived nation-state. Again, should we not be using these peoples with a common spiritual authority and history as the basis for projects of unification instead of criminalizing their crossings or impeding them through visa barriers and border police control? For instance, if Kenya, Ethiopia, Djibouti and Somalia itself were to see the Somali people as a shared community, then uniting Ethiopia, Kenya, Somalia and Djibouti does not mean yoking together cultural strangers. There is not a single African country which does not have a shared community on either side of its borders. These shared communities would form the links of chain of African unity from the Cape to Cairo, from Kenya to Cape Verde.

Acceptance of shared communities would not, in itself, solve the contradiction of many languages. But accepting our languages as a fact of our being, enriching them and then encouraging dialogue among them through the tool of translation, is the best way of creating a firmer cultural and democratic basis for African unity. If all the books written in different African languages, including those produced by diasporan Africans, were available in each and every African language – what we at the International Center for Writing and Translation at the University of California at Irvine call the Restoration Project – it would surely create a common intellectual inheritance and become the common cultural basis for more intellectual productions with roots in a common African memory. As long as it does not grow from the graveyard of other languages, an inter-ethnic, inter-regional continental language would be a gain for Africa, adding another dimension to conversation.

What would be the place of European languages? No matter how we think of the historical process by which they came to occupy the place they now occupy in our lives, it is a fact that English and French have enabled international visibility of the African presence. But they have achieved this by uprooting intellectuals from their languages and cultural bases. They have merely invited African intellectuals to operate within European memory. In European languages – English, French and Portuguese principally – there are also immense deposits of some the best in African thought. They are granaries of African intellectual productions, and these productions are the closest thing we have to a common pan-African social property. The names of Samir Amin, Ali Mazrui, Wole Soyinka, Sembene Ousmane, Mariame Ba, Ama Ata Aidoo, Tsitsi Dangarembga, Sédar Senghor, Agostinho Neto and Alex la Guma, to name just a few, are part of a common, visible African presence. They also make possible conferences such as the one we are having here today. The latter example, in fact, defines best the mission we should assign to French and English: use them to facilitate dialogue among African languages and increase the visibility of African languages in the community of world languages, instead of allowing them to disable our efforts by uprooting intellectuals and their production from their original language bases. Use English and French to facilitate, not disable.

This, then, is the challenge of social science in Africa today: how best can we fulfil one of the most basic aims of CODESRIA, to really connect with the continent, in the era of globalization? How do we create and strengthen a common African base from which to engage with the world? African economic, political and cultural unity is surely the answer, but while political unity and economic integration lie in the realm of decisions taken by political leadership, African intellectuals are bound by their very calling as knowledge producers to create a common intellectual basis for that unity. There is the need for a strong body of public intellectuals rooted in the common languages of the people to argue out, rationalize, popularize and make common the case for a genuine people-based African union.

I believe that only through the use of African languages shall we be able to break with European memory and look at Africa and its contact with the world, including its engagement with European memory, from the inside. We cannot afford to be intellectual outsiders in our own land. We must reconnect with the buried alluvium of African memory and use it as a base for the further planting of African memory on the continent and in the world. This can only result in the empowerment of African languages and cultures and make them pillars of a more self-confident Africa ready to engage the world, through give and take, but from its base in African memory. I end my talk with the call I have been making over the last thirty years: that African intellectuals must do for their languages and cultures what all other intellectuals in history have done for theirs. This is still the challenge of our history. Let's take up the challenge.

Notes

1 Keynote address given at CODESRIA's 30th Anniversary grand finale conference and celebration, Wednesday, 9 December 2003, Dakar, Senegal.

2 See B. Anderson, *Imagined Communities*, rev. edn (London: Verso, 1991), ch. 10, 'Census, Map, Museum'.

3 Cited in B. Mills, *Caribbean Cartographics*, unpublished PhD dissertation, Department of Comparative Literature, New York University.

8 | The language question and national development in Africa

BEBAN SAMMY CHUMBOW

Beyond the emotionally charged rhetoric in which the political ideology of pan-Africanism was couched at its inception and after, it is safe to say that its ultimate goal was the development of Africa via the struggle for Africa's liberation and the consolidation of African unity.

After over four decades of action, and despite significant strides on the ladder that leads to the lofty ideal of national development, the ideal itself cannot be said to have been attained. While many plausible explanations can be adduced, it can also be argued that a contributory factor has been the neglect or failure to address the *language factor* in education, science and technology and its crucial role in national development. This is the main thrust of this paper, which leads to the conclusion that whatever economic paradigms are postulated for African development they need to integrate the language issue, with all its ramifications, in order for them to succeed. Thus, for instance, the New Partnership for Africa's Development (NEPAD), the latest in the series of proposals for African development, needs a recon-ceptualization to incorporate a concomitant Language Plan (of Action) for Africa's Development (LAPAD), the contours of which we discuss.

The politics of development and underdevelopment

Development is the ultimate goal of pan-Africanism and the liberation struggle was only the means to this end. Initially, the term 'development' was contrasted with 'underdevelopment' to capture the gap between the rich industrialized nations of Europe and North America and the poor, less industrialized countries of Africa, South America and so on. The former were known as 'developed countries' and the latter as 'underdeveloped' nations. Some African nationalists believed that the 'development gap' could be bridged or at least reduced considerably by the accelerated devel-opment of the economies of underdeveloped countries. They successfully argued for the adoption of the term 'developing nations' to replace the less palatable epithet of 'underdeveloped nations'. Thus underdeveloped nations of Africa came to be called 'developing nations'.

In the economic and political taxonomies of nations, however, most of the developing nations were also known to belong to the 'Third World' and were referred to as 'Third World countries'. Implicit in this appellation is the assumption that from the perspective of the development gap and its impact, there were other countries with higher levels of development that belonged to the 'first' and 'second' worlds, ahead of African countries and others of the Third World.

In 1976, some African leaders, through the voice of President Mobutu Sese Seko (Joseph Desiré) of Zaire (present-day Democratic Republic of Congo), in an address to the United Nations, argued forcefully that all countries are in a state of perpetual development and as such no country, not even the most developed of the so-called developed countries of Europe and America, has stopped developing; therefore they also logically qualify as 'developing' countries. Thus, the term 'developing nations' applied to African countries and their like is at best a misnomer.

This led, in part at least, to the popularization of the current dichotomization and bipolarization of the countries of the world into 'North' (developed countries) and 'South' (underdeveloped or developing countries).

It must, however, be understood that a consensus position has not now been reached in the search for names to distinguish Europe and America from the rest of the world, particularly as there are countries of the South (Japan, Korea, Australia, etc.) which, in terms of current indices of development, belong with the North and vice versa. Experts continue to differ as to the choice of terms to reflect the gap in development between the various nations of the world.

To settle this matter once and for all and avoid a further futile search for names, we invoke the old adage and ask 'what is in a name?'. Call an eagle by whatever name and the reality of the majestic king of the birds soaring over tropical Africa remains; call a snake by whatever name and it remains a snake, a slimy, creeping creature trapped on the ground and incapable of violating anyone's airspace. Put an African country in whatever taxonomic box and the reality of poverty-stricken rural communities, with a few developing townships and pockets of skyscrapers, emerges to stare one in the face. For too long we have been playing ostrich. We have to stop and squarely face the reality of our condition as far as development is concerned and take steps to strategize so as to adequately achieve higher levels of 'development' for the people.

A goal of African development focused on bridging the gap in economic development between the rich and poor countries is predicated on the unreasonable assumption that countries of the North are going to halt industrialization and economic development and wait for countries of the South to catch up with them before proceeding farther up the road to development.

Predictably this has not happened. On the contrary, because of the solid economic base of industrialization consolidated over the years since the Industrial Revolution in Europe, countries of the North have continued to race forward with an unprecedented accelerated velocity in the last four decades, characterized by the advent of the computer age and consequent new technologies of information communication that have propelled the North into the new era of globalization and micro-business.

In Africa (with the exception of South Africa), there are few countries that are making an appreciable effort on the ladder of development. Many countries, despite noticeable mobility, are yet to feel the impact of development. Countries appropriately christened 'the heavily indebted poor countries' (HIPCs) are in this category.

An objective analysis of the situation would therefore show that despite noticeable advances on the ladder of development, because of the differences in the pace of mobility between the North and the South the development gap has instead widened considerably. The most reasonable goal of development for the South should therefore not be the unattainable objective of 'bridging the gap' but the attainable goal of development targets aimed at mobilizing the population out of the underdevelopment zone.

Development

Conceptualization of development Despite the fact that all countries of the world seek development, as exemplified by the existence of well-articulated national development plans, there is no universally accepted definition for 'development'. The first point to note is that development is not synonymous with 'growth', for there can be growth without development – as, for instance, in a situation of population explosion without concomitant economic growth or a rapid increase in the indicators of human development without a commensurate reduction of poverty.

The concept of development proposed by the United Nations (UNDP, UNESCO, WHO, etc.) is one that is 'redemptive' in character in that it underscores the social well-being of the citizenry of the entire nation in terms of the minimum standard of living, which includes health, shelter (housing), food security, life expectancy (reduction of infant mortality), education, work, etc.

In Chumbow (1990) we defined national development as 'the nation's human resources acting on its natural resources to produce goods (tangible and intangible) in order to improve the condition of the average citizen of the nation-state' (in terms of indicators of redemptive development mentioned above).

This definition underscores the inadequacies of development measurable uniquely in economic terms such as per capita income or gross national product (GNP), etc. While the usefulness of these concepts as economic indicators allowing for comparison of the economies of two or more countries is undeniable, they do not capture the *redemptive* character of national development. For instance, despite evidence of growth in most African countries in the last forty years with visible signs of some economic progress (along with considerable population explosion), the situation in most African countries can be characterized as one of growth without development, because of the presence of abject poverty in the rural communities (villages) which surround a few skyscrapers in the urban centres, where conspicuous consumption and a catalogue of economic realizations (in buildings, road infrastructure, etc.) contrasts with the gaping reality of abject poverty, misery, ignorance and disease among the masses throughout the national territory.

Setbacks to development in Africa An evaluation of the efforts of African nations in the enterprise of national development shows that, in most cases, there has been a lot of growth without development (in the sense of redemptive development) as mentioned above. Indeed, a catalogue of the factors adversely affecting the efforts regarding national development in the African context would include the following: (a) demographic explosion, (b) famine and diverse natural disasters and calamities, (c) instability of political regimes, (d) lack of democratic regimes, (e) corruption and inequalities, (f) poor or inadequate exploitation of natural and human resources, (g) non-existence or inadequacy of savings, (h) indebtedness, (i) deteriorating volume of balance of trade between the North and the South, (j) insufficiency of industry and infrastructural duality of juxtaposition of traditional culture with modern culture, and (k) illiteracy and ignorance (Chumbow 1997).

The last of these factors is, perhaps, one of the most important, because most of the other factors can be shown to result from ignorance and illiteracy. Indeed, illiteracy is a major obstacle to national development because it reinforces ignorance by limiting access to scientific, technological and cultural knowledge that is indispensable to self-actualization and full participation in the general effort at national development.

Education, language and national development

Central to any genuine national development endeavour as defined above is the sum total of all activities initiated by *human resources* (through the use of *natural resources*) to improve the material condition (or the quality of life) of the citizenry. The key variables in the national development equation as formulated above are therefore *human resources, natural resources, scientific knowledge* and *technological know-how* set in motion by national consciousness or nationalism. As we have pointed out before (Chumbow 1990), however, it is not sufficient to have an abundance of human and natural resources for development to take place. Available human resources must be transformed into knowledgeable, specialized or skilled manpower by an *education or training process* in order for them to be useful in the national development equation.

In other words, of all the elements in the national development equation *human resources* are the most important. This is evident from the fact that most African countries are very rich in natural resources and yet are underdeveloped. Many Arab countries, with their enormous oil wealth, are nevertheless quite underdeveloped.

Also, as mentioned above, an abundance of population without adequate scientific knowledge and technological know-how or basic skills does not amount to human resources for national development. Only a human population possessing knowledge and skills acquired through education and training can serve as *agents of change* to convert raw materials (natural resources) into finished products for consumption in the national economy. This underscores the crucial importance of *education* in all its forms (formal, informal and lifelong education) in the enterprise of nation-building or national development. All education takes place as a result of effective *communication* of knowledge, skills and techniques by a knowledgeable and competent source to one who lacks such knowledge or skills. *Language* is the normal medium of communication of knowledge and skills in all educational (instructional) systems. Effective acquisition of knowledge and skills can take place only if effective communication via a language medium has taken place.

In industrialized nations it has long been recognized that education is not merely a social service but a necessary national investment. In the words of Mincer (1975), 'education is an investment in the stock of human skills'. According to Striner (1979), 'education is an investment in the formation of human capital'.

Education and training in whatever form require imparting knowledge and skills as well as awakening and developing the intellectual potential of the learner. The role of the language used as the *medium of instruction* in the educational process is therefore very important. Thus, education by means of an appropriate *language medium* provides the knowledge, skills and values necessary for humans to become effective, efficient and qualitatively valuable agents of change in the interest of national development. In a nutshell, the point articulated in this section is essentially that language is important for national development. Since education and manpower training are crucial to national development and the language medium is crucial to education and training, it follows that the language (medium of education) is vital to national development as well. The choice of the language to be used as medium is therefore an important factor in national development and deserves consideration in national development plans, and more importantly it deserves funding in view of its importance for national development.

The use of African languages in education

Education in Africa throughout the colonial era was essentially through the medium of a foreign or exoglossic language: the language of the colonial master (with only a few exceptions). Yet, after over forty years of independence, less than 30 per cent of the adult population of most African countries are literate and educated in English, French, Spanish, Portuguese, Arabic or any other language of the colonial legacy.

Linguists, psycholinguists and anthropological linguists agree, however, that the use of the child's 'mother tongue' as medium of instruction in the school system has significant advantages over the use of an exoglossic or foreign language, where 'mother tongue' is defined as 'the language in which the child first learns to express his ideas about himself and about the world in which he lives' (UNESCO 1953). Since 1951, UNESCO and other world agencies and national bodies have periodically assembled linguists and experts in language-related disciplines to examine the issue of the use of 'vernaculars' in education in all its ramifications. The verdict at the end of all these deliberations has consistently and overwhelmingly been in favour of the use of the indigenous languages of each nation-state or geo-political entity as medium of instruction in the educational system, 'as far up the ladder of education as possible' (ibid.).

The case for the use of African languages in education It is now axiomatic that a child learns better and develops faster cognitively and intellectually if in infancy he or she is taught in the mother tongue continuously over a period of time than when taught in a foreign medium. This, in effect, means that an educational system that favours the use of the child's home language in the teaching process is more likely to approach a maximization of the child's intellectual potential than one that uses an alien medium of instruction. Thus, in Africa, for example, African languages are potentially better options as media of instruction (at least in the early years of schooling) than the foreign languages currently used. To be sure, the use of African languages in education in place of foreign languages such as English, French, Portuguese and Spanish, all of which are legacies of the colonial era, is not without its problems. Expert opinion, however, has generally been that the advantages of the use of African languages in education outweigh the disadvantages by far, and therefore efforts should be made to identify real problems and find solutions to them so as to capitalize on the many long-term advantages of the use of African languages in education.

A fair amount of the research output of language experts in Africa since 1960 has been directed to the issue of the use of African languages in education either as subject or medium of instruction. Research at the policy formulation level has been aimed at selling the idea to individual African nations, presenting the advantages of the enterprise and urging them to adopt it as a policy in part or in whole. Where the idea has been adopted, *applied linguistic* work has been geared towards *standardization* of African languages to make them efficient and suitable for use in the educational system by providing the chosen languages with scientifically based orthographies, pedagogical grammars, dictionaries, primers, readers and literacy materials of various types.

Education in Africa leaves a lot to be desired and efforts at mass literacy in various African countries have failed because education in general and adult literacy in particular have been carried out through a foreign language medium (Chumbow 1982). Literacy efforts in an exoglossic language such as English or French are an even greater obstacle to national development in Africa in that they tend to marginalize the masses of the rural population who are not proficient in these languages. Yet, as we have mentioned already, the effective training of the masses as skilled manpower capable of functioning as viable agents of change in national development requires that they acquire scientific knowledge and/or technological know-how. In other words, the effective mobilization of the masses of the rural population for national development requires the *democratization of access* not in an exoglossic (foreign) language but in a language (or languages) the people know best: an African national language. Consequently, this means that the sum total of knowledge, skills and techniques needed for national development currently confined to and transmitted in an exoglossic language spoken by a relatively small fraction of the population must be made available in an African language (of wider communication) spoken by the masses. This point has been demonstrated beyond doubt in the literature: see, for instance, Bamgbose (1976 and 1991), UNESCO (1953), Ansre (1979) and Chumbow (1982), among others. Monolingual training in a foreign language, no matter how international, does not make the products of the educational programme *effective actors* in a process of lasting development. The proof is that after over four decades of such educational systems, most African nations are yet to take off en route to the much sought-after ideal of national development.

The most important argument in favour of the use of African languages in education is empirical in nature. Two experiments in Nigeria and Cameroon show conclusively that students taught in an African language as medium of instruction, with English and French as second languages, perform significantly better than students taught uniquely in English or French, even when the state examination (the First School Leaving Certificate) is in the foreign-language English or French only (Afolayan 1976; Tadadjeu 1990). This implies that in a well-organized educational programme both languages can be used since knowledge acquired in the mother tongue is transferable to the foreign official language if need be.

Advantages of the use of African languages in education The case for the use of African languages in education has been made in the literature (as indicated above). Arguments in favour of the use of African languages in education are based mainly on well-known advantages of using the mother tongue as a medium of instruction in the school system. It is argued that if there are compelling psychological and educational advantages in using the child's mother tongue (as opposed to a foreign-language medium) in the school system, then African languages (which, in the majority of cases, constitute the mother tongue of African pupils) should be preferred as media in the African school system. The psychological and educational merits of mother-tongue-medium education are complemented by ideological and culturally based arguments in favour of the use of African languages in education.

Some advantages of the use of African languages in education are summarized below:

- The use of African languages in education will lead to a development of African languages in terms of their ability to cope as vehicles of modern thought, science and technology.
- Such a development will lead to a greater participation of African languages in the life of the nation, since with literacy in these languages they can be allocated functions in the area of information as well as in other areas of national development.
- The use of African languages in education will gradually lead to a better development of adult education since more people will be able to read and write in their own language. This has the attendant benefit of eradicating illiteracy and accelerating the rate of national development.

- The languages so developed in this enterprise will better serve as the means of transmitting and preserving cultural values, with the written language complementing oral tradition in this respect. This will enhance cultural independence and linguistic identity.
- The use of the mother tongue will be a greater stimulus to learning and this will lead to a greater and higher level of education.
- The increase in education because of the home language factor will lead to greater interaction between ethnic groups and a higher degree of national awareness and therefore a greater level of integration which is bound to foster national unity.
- From the psychological perspective, as shown by the empirical findings of the experiments of the Six-year Primary Project of Ife (Nigeria) and PROPELCA (Cameroon), students using their mother tongue build up more self-confidence and a sense of initiative which develops their intellectual potential and reduces the rate of drop-out from the school system.
- The use of the mother tongue during the child's formative years (ages one to thirteen years) will minimize learning hardships while maximizing the development of his or her (natural or endowed) intellectual potential.
- It follows that this state of affairs produces, in the long run, a better quality of human resources for national development.
- In the search for a national language, the use and interaction of the indigenous languages of the nation may lead to the emergence of a truly national language.
- The intellectualization of African languages and their use will lead to a democratization of access to scientific knowledge and technology to the benefit of the masses of the rural population who now wallow in ignorance, misery, disease and hunger because such life-saving knowledge and skills are currently confined to a foreign language accessible only to a privileged few.

Arguments against the use of African languages Standard arguments by the general public, some politicians and even some scholars against the use of African languages are of two types.

OBJECTIONABLE OBJECTIONS These are objections that can be considered unsound because they are simply not true or because they are based on false premises and wrong assumptions, or else the argument underlying such objections can be shown to be a logical fallacy.

Most African languages have no grammar. All languages have a grammar.

173

The grammar of many African languages has not been extracted and recorded but that can be done once there is a will to do so (and is currently being done by linguists).

The use of the mother tongue will impede the acquisition of the official language of the nation (English, French, etc.). This is not true. Research evidence indicates that prior acquisition of language and literacy in the mother tongue facilitates the acquisition of the second language. A better command of the second language can be achieved if the child begins learning and writing in the mother tongue and is subsequently introduced to the second language (Afolayan 1976; Tadadjeu 1990; Lambert and Tucker 1972; Engles 1975; Krashen 2001). Besides, Saville and Troike (1971) and Krashen (2001) have shown that the basic skills of language learning (particularly reading skills) are readily transferable from one language to another.

The use of African languages will impede national unity. It is feared that the development and use of African languages in multilingual states will polarize linguistic communities against each other, thus creating disunity. To alleviate this 'potential danger', it is argued that national unity would best be achieved by using a foreign language because 'it is neutral'. As observed by UNESCO (1953), it is not true that tribal traits will disappear and national unity be achieved just by the common use of a foreign tongue as an official language. The provisions of a law requiring the use of English (for instance) as the official language by all can not transform a multilingual state into a monolingual state instantly. In fact, insistence on the use of a foreign (national) language to the neglect of indigenous languages may have a negative effect, leading some linguistic communities to withdraw considerably from national life.

On the other hand, multilingualism can be used as a powerful force for *nation-building*, contrary to some beliefs. Multilingualism and pluralism are, in fact, national resources for developing mutual understanding and a sense of respect for individuality (Ansre 1979). Many African leaders seem to realize this (although it is not clear whether they practise it) when they use the slogan 'unity in diversity'. Expert reaction to the national unity issue is that 'national interests are best served by optimum advancement in education, and this in turn can be promoted by the *use of local languages as medium of instruction*, at least at the beginning of the school programme' (UNESCO 1953).

Most countries of the world are pluralistic in nature. Multi-ethnicity and multilingualism are norms in pluralistic states and yet nationalism is fostered and developed despite the ethnic identities in these states. France and Britain, the two main former colonial masters of the African continent, are pluralistic nations with multi-ethnicity as a hallmark. The

melting-pot example of the USA, known for the high sense of nationalism of its citizens, despite considerable multi-ethnicity, is instructive and
illuminating. With *language planning*, linguistic and ethnic identity can be
harnessed and properly channelled as a concomitant to nation-building
and national development.

*Children who attend schools in which African languages are used as
medium at the beginning of the school programme will be at a disadvantage
vis-à-vis their counterparts who learn in English and French from the onset;
particularly where the latter is the language of higher education and the
language that guarantees access to job opportunities.* This assertion is not
true if the programme of mother tongue medium is organized as provided
by UNESCO (1953) (and successfully tried in many countries), i.e. by using
the mother tongue as medium early while subsequently introducing the
foreign (official) language as a subject, gradually intensifying the latter
with a gradual reduction of the use of mother tongue as medium. This
has been successfully tried in the six-year Primary Project at Ife (Nigeria)
mentioned earlier, where the products of the experimental group were
taught all school subjects in their Yoruba mother tongue as medium with
English as a subject from the second year. It was found that at the end
of the six-year programme, such students performed significantly better
in public examinations (including examinations written in English) than
their counterparts who studied in English as medium all along. Thus, in
a well-organized programme, the use of the mother tongue as medium
does not lead to any such disadvantages. Second, the situation called for
by the experts is not one in which pockets of 'mother tongue first' schools
exist side by side with other schools but one where the government adopts
'mother tongue education' as a *policy* for the entire nation-state, so that
the question of the advantaged versus the disadvantaged student does not
arise. Nevertheless, where the particular situation of the state requires that
the policy be applied to selected areas and languages first, the evidence
from other mother-tongue education projects, as in the Philippines (Ramos
et al. 1967), Mexico (Modiano 1968), Canada (Lambert and Tucker 1972),
Ife, Nigeria (Afolayan 1976) and PROPELCA, Cameroon (Tadadjeu 1990),
shows that such students will not be at a disadvantage with respect to
their counterparts in other schools. In fact, students from such mother-
tongue-medium bilingual schools tend to excel over their counterparts in
the regular school system, as already mentioned in the cases of the Ife
and PROPELCA projects.

PRACTICAL PROBLEMS Under this heading we shall discuss those objections and problems (raised by critics of the use of the mother tongue as

medium of instruction) that are more serious and reasonable, requiring attention. The view of many linguists, language planning specialists and other language experts is generally that such problems are mere obstacles that have to be surmounted in view of the overriding short- and long-term advantages of using African languages in education. Some, in fact, feel that such objections are mere *rationalizations* by those who wish to see the present state of affairs maintained at all costs to the detriment of African countries (Ansre 1979).

The inadequacy of scientific and technical vocabulary. It has been argued that African languages do not have the right level of development to guarantee that vocabulary in all scientific and technical fields can assume the important role of expressing the intricacies of modern science and technology, therefore languages of wider communication such as English and French should continue to be used in education as a gateway to modernism. All languages can be rapidly developed in terms of vocabulary by applying certain language engineering techniques such as borrowing (and loan adaptation), coinage, extension of coverage, lexical reanalysis to enable them to assume any academic function. All that is required to do this is the will, the means and the know-how (see Chumbow and Tamanji 1994). It should be realized that the same adverse arguments could have been used against English, French, Spanish and German at some point in history. These languages, which are world languages of communication today, were once considered 'languages of barbarians', unfit for the communication of knowledge at the time when Greek and Latin were the languages of civilization par excellence.

Once African languages have been recognized by policy and assigned some function (in education, government business, information dissemination, etc), *language standardization* efforts can be initiated by the appropriate experts to provide the language with an orthography (or a reform of the existing orthography) as well as undertake the expansion of the lexicon (by appropriate techniques) to make the language ready to assume the function allocated to it by government policy. Even the smallest language of the nation (in terms of numbers of speakers) can in this way be raised to the status of a national language if it is so desired by the people.

The multiplicity of languages renders the ideals of mother-tongue medium impracticable. Many African nations are multilingual in varying degrees, ranging from a few languages in Somalia to about 286 in Cameroon and 400 in Nigeria. This fact presents a number of problems in terms of the use of African languages in education, including the practical problem of providing education in so many languages (in terms of cost and human resources). Experts consider this a serious problem but one that is surmountable in the long run by adopting a gradual approach. First of all, mother-tongue education may begin with a few selected languages based on demographic considerations, i.e. languages spoken by the widest population, or on considerations of standardization, i.e. languages already committed to writing and effectively used and having the most developed literature. Subsequently the policy can be gradually extended to other smaller languages as resources permit. At any rate, experts agree that implementation of the policy to use African languages in education should be guided by the general principle that 'to ease the burden of the child in education, the mother tongue should be used as medium of instruction as far up the ladder of education as conditions permit' (UNESCO 1953; Chumbow 1987).

Another variant of this solution proposed by some African scholars is to introduce selected zonal languages so that all children within a region have to learn the zonal language irrespective of their mother tongue. Thus, Bot Ba Njock (1960) suggested ten zonal languages for Cameroon out of a total of about 286 languages. It has been argued that learning a zonal language for one who speaks a different mother tongue from the zonal language amounts to learning a foreign language (such as English). This is not entirely true if the zonal language chosen is closely related to the child's mother tongue. For example, because of 'deep' intrinsic relations between Bantu languages of the same sub-group such as Bakweri and Duala (Cameroon), it would be much easier for a Bakweri to use Duala as medium in the school system (and vice versa) than English or French. The same is true for genetic relations between languages of various African countries.

Cost and resources. Perhaps the most potent obstacle to the use of African languages in education is the cost of providing educational materials (textbooks and literacy materials, etc.) as well as trained teachers in all African languages. Many (including Bull 1964) have argued that for African countries with meagre resources and faced with problems of national development it will be a 'waste of resources' to give attention to education in African languages. As pointed out in Chumbow (1987, and above), the problem of cost can be greatly reduced if language planning (involving the use of African languages in education) is conceived as a long-term project. First, different economically viable stages of implementation can be outlined, each tied to and concomitant with other projects of the national development plan (since most countries in Africa have national development plans). Subsequently, each stage of the project will be implemented with the resources allocated for that stage until much is achieved (in terms of the adopted plan) over a period of time. It is, however, necessary to take the decision to use African languages now and envisage

177

its gradual implementation over a period of time. Even if the ultimate results are not achieved in our lifetime posterity will have reasons to be grateful (ibid.).

Another cost-reducing procedure is the one applied by the Rivers Readers Project (Williamson 1979) and popularized by many language planning committees. Rather than having textbook designers and writers for each language of the state, by pooling resources the same set of texts can be designed for all languages with much the same pictures and illustrative designs and as far as possible with the same content messages translated into and adapted to the various languages. Initially, teaching materials could be mimeographed rather than printed until funds are available.

The use of African languages in education will nevertheless require a considerable amount of funding, but what good cause has been achieved without a cost? Evidence has been adduced in the preceding section to show that the use of the mother tongue as medium is a good cause.

Shortage of adequately trained teachers to teach in African languages. This is a real problem also and is, in fact, tied to the previous problem of cost. Once the overriding importance of mother-tongue education is taken into consideration then all efforts should be made to train language teachers within the context of a language plan for national development.

The language factor in the development of science and technology

Science and technology are crucially relevant to national development in that they provide the scientific knowledge and the technologies relevant to the transformation of natural resources.

The relative underdevelopment of African countries can be attributed in part, at least, to the absence of a science and technology culture in most countries in Africa. Science and technology are mystified and pursued by a privileged few. This can be shown to be due to the neglect of the language factor and the use of an exoglossic language as the means of accessing scientific knowledge.

Forje (1989) provides a catalogue of recommended strategies to redeem science and technology (S&T) in the African context as follows:

- There is a need to incorporate S&T within the components of the national development plan in order to enhance public understanding of S&T and its role in the development process.
- The academic community has to be more active and demystify existing views of S&T.
- There should be optimal use of the resources of the nation.

- Measures should be taken to ensure the more effective diffusion of technologies and of domestic industries that are receptive to new S&T ideas.
- The educational system must be made more accessible and efficient so as to ensure that the new generation has confidence in science.
- Emphasis should be placed on research and development (R&D).

In Chumbow (1995) we demonstrate that fundamental to the implementation of these and other strategies in the service of the development of S&T in Africa is the recognition of the language factor, which is seldom considered in the analysis of obstacles to effective development of S&T in Africa.

Language and science and technology Language is the means by which cognition is developed and expressed; the means by which all knowledge is acquired and expressed. As Chomsky (1968) has observed, language and the mind are inextricably linked. Thus, we cannot think without language (in its most fundamental form of Piagetan abstract mental symbols that can be expressed verbally or visually). Thus, the acquisition of knowledge in general and S&T in particular is carried out through the medium of language. This also means that all knowledge, techniques and skills of the educational system (formal, non-formal and informal) are transmitted and/or acquired through a language medium.

Language and the acquisition of scientific knowledge The rapid development of S&T in the developed world is due in part to the fact that the educational system seeks to maximize the development of the intellectual potential of the child (i.e. his/her natural genius). This has led to the availability of high-level researchers, engineers, technicians, etc., in the service of the development of S&T. As observed by Hallak for advanced studies, 'sound basic literacy and numerical skills, middle level technical and organizational skills and to an increasing degree, high level cognitive skills, abstract reasoning and problem solving will be the cornerstones of the mastery of technological advances' (Hallak 1990: 48). Language is therefore crucial in the cognitive skills, etc., which ultimately determine the mastery of technological skill.

Indigenous knowledge, science and technology

VALIDITY OF INDIGENOUS KNOWLEDGE S&T is being practised by local people in villages, homes, farms and in small-scale industries such as pottery, carving and weaving. Methods of food conservation discovered out of necessity are transmitted from generation to generation. The curative powers of various herbs are well known to village herbalists. Indigenous

179

knowledge (IK) permeates every aspect of life in the African traditional society. Apart from a few anthropological essays on some aspects of this knowledge, African IK's potential remains largely untapped. One reason for this is the myth of the inferiority of African culture and African knowledge, which has led to a condescending attitude towards indigenous knowledge in general.

INDIGENOUS KNOWLEDGE AS A FOUNDATION FOR SCIENCE AND TECH-
NOLOGY Why do villagers in many traditional societies live to be so old? How did they envisage life? What did they eat and drink and what remedies did they use to combat tropical diseases? When questions of this type are asked, then the search for IK has begun in earnest. This research is important. Importation and implantation of Western science and techno-logy without a sound knowledge of the S&T culture of the local terrain may be counter-productive, just as introducing foreign bodies into the human body may be.

The lofty ideal of *sustainable development*, sought after by African countries and preached by donor agencies, ought to begin by exploring IK as a starting point for the development of a viable culture of modern S&T. IK systems in S&T, such as the distilling of alcohol and local methods of pasteurization, preservation and conservation of food and meat, as well as crafts such as carving, pottery, weaving and functional and artistic art, should be integrated into development programmes if African countries are to achieve desired levels of production (in agriculture, for instance) by using natural resources in a sustainable manner. Research in IK should therefore be pursued as a foundation for the take-off of science and techno-logy culture.

LANGUAGE, IK, S&T The reality of IK has been demonstrated, and it is necessary to draw attention to the fact that indigenous languages, which are vectors or carriers of indigenous science and culture, are the most ap-propriate media to express IK in all its vibrancy and dynamism. Indigenous languages constitute the best medium for harnessing this knowledge, in its riches, for ultimate translation into languages of wider communication (English, French, etc.). For instance, pastoral nomads living close to their cattle, and the products of cattle-related rural technology, have a richer lexical stock as regards dairy production and different breeds of cows than many exoglossic languages, since these languages do not share the same cultural, scientific and technological experience.

Therefore, contributions by Africa to universal knowledge in S&T is possible on a large scale if, and only if, IK is identified, developed and elaborated in the language medium in which it has been conceptualized, before being made available in a language of wider communication.

Layton (1992), looking at future perspectives in the conceptualization of S&T, proposed a movement towards the convergence of the *academic* and the *vocational* (or the school and the community) to produce a new realism which he terms *the technological school* – that is, an institutional setting more open to work and community influences than hitherto present. This perspective, which seeks to have the student confront the academic perception of S&T practice and the reality of the community, envisions a symbiosis that makes the *community language* all the more important in the development of S&T.

Dissemination of S&T New principles of S&T are generated or acquired in Africa for socio-economic development. These have to be disseminated, adopted and adapted as appropriate, however. The dissemination of new knowledge and the adoption of innovations in S&T is a process that goes through a number of stages, involving changes in the habits and the life of the potential adopters with respect to the innovation. These include:

- Awareness of the existence of the innovation and its usefulness.
- Knowledge of the innovation; use of the innovation, i.e. experiencing the innovation in a practical way.
- Functional autonomy in the innovation (which indicates adoption of the innovation).

The diffusion of new knowledge regarding S&T and its dissemination to the widest spectrum of the population – i.e. the potential agents of change – require the use of an appropriate language medium: the language accessible to the various levels of the population. The use of exoglossic languages (English, French, Spanish and Portuguese), to the exclusion of African languages, in dissemination clearly limits the number of people that S&T will reach, since only about 40 per cent of the African population has attained functional literacy in these official languages.

THE ACCEPTABILITY FACTOR IN THE ADOPTION OF APPROPRIATE TECH- NOLOGY The key to the diffusion and adoption of any innovation is *acceptability*. In the area of agricultural technology, for instance, appropriate innovation is available in the sorghum, millet, maize and other mills, but there are obstacles to its acquisition by the women who handle most food production and food-processing activities in African villages. Carr (1984) reports that in Burkina Faso and Botswana women have failed to see the benefit of purchasing and using hand-held maize shellers, however cheap

181

they may be. They have rejected the improved stove, which requires only finely chopped wood for fuel. The fact is that there is a breakdown in communication, which can be resolved by using the vernacular to convey to village women the advantages of the new technology and demonstrate that the advantages outweigh the disadvantages.

LANGUAGE RESEARCH AND DEVELOPMENT (R&D) Trends in the area of R&D favour the satisfaction of the needs of the local population. Thus, for instance, the agricultural geographer Richards argues for a peasant-focused decentralized approach to R&D in West African agriculture in order to take advantage of informal innovations, including those realized by women in the countryside. This people-oriented direction of research in S&T, in the service of development, needs the concomitant development of the language(s) of the people to ensure that they are well served by research findings. Quite often African research institutes come out with results that are confined to research reports and journals gathering dust on the shelves instead of being made available to those who need it most.

Access to the educational system is a priori limited when it is made available in a language used by a minority of the population. Japan was quick to realize the importance of language in the development of S&T, in particular, and human resource development in general. Kayuki (1989) reports that early in this century Japan ensured that the Japanese language was revived and developed to convey knowledge in modern S&T while English was reserved for international marketing and access to international S&T. The consequence was that the Japanese people as a whole, rural and urban, could be involved in the national development enterprise, propelled by the acquisition of science, transfer of technology and R&D that incorporated indigenous knowledge. The miracle of the Japanese industrial revolution is explained, in part at least, by a resolution of the language question in S&T in favour of the codification and development of the Japanese language to enable it to become the vector of S&T for the Japanese people.

To develop a culture of science and technology in Africa requires the demystification of science and technology, and this in turn requires the democratization of access to knowledge in science and technology by the use of community languages in education and the delivery of social services for natural development.

African languages and inter-African cooperation

Mention has been made of the fact the one of the fundamental ultimate goals of the pan-African ideology was achievement and consolidation of African unity. In this respect, as in the area of development, the results obtained are below expectations. African languages, especially trans-border languages, have an important role to play in this respect.

Border zones and trans-border languages The situation is excerbated by socio-political tension and conflict in African border zones defined as regions at the frontier of (national or) international boundaries. Examples abound throughout Africa, such as between Senegal and Mauritania, Mauritania and Morocco, Nigeria and Cameroon, Democratic Republic of Congo (DRC) and Uganda, DRC and Rwanda, etc. An analysis of the situation in Chumbow (2000) indicates that the underlying cause of these conflicts is the arbitrary imposition of an artificial boundary that is neither congruous nor coterminous with the more natural, older ethnico-cultural groups and nationalities that pre-date the modern nation-states in Africa (the result of the Berlin conference). Following the arbitrarily imposed boundaries, millions of African people of the same ethnic identity, sharing the same language and governed by deep-seated historical and cultural bonds, suddenly found themselves partitioned, divided and shared out to different colonial powers, and today belong to different nations.

Despite the disruptive effect of arbitrary boundaries on the cultural and ethnic unity of partitioned peoples, however, they quite often cultivate and reinforce the pre-partition networks of intra-group or intra-ethnic relations and in some cases (at least historically) they consider the boundary as binding only on the colonial powers or present-day governments and not on their own internal relations with their kith and kin, which they consider 'inviolable'.

Thus, there is at the border zones an invisible but clearly discernible ethnico-cultural boundary underneath the visible national boundaries. The former clearly undermines the latter as it penetrates into the various national territories and defiantly crosses national boundaries. This invisible boundary is maintained and nourished by the linguistic identity that cuts across the well-safeguarded national frontier. Linguistic identity across the border is therefore a powerful force to be reckoned with in the dynamics of nation-building and the development of border zones.

Border zones are characterized by *trans-border languages*, i.e. languages whose domain of usage straddles international boundaries (Chumbow and Tamanji 1997; Chumbow 2000) because of the linguistic and ethnic identity of its users, victims of the arbitrary split.

Perspectives on border cooperation In dealing with the problems of tension at the border, the traditional mode of border management by implementing or imposing regulatory mechanisms, leading to excessive

183

policing and militarization of frontier zones in order to impose *state authority*, has proved to be negative and counter-productive. A generally accepted approach to boundary management should emerge based on 'the principle of simplification of the boundary function' from a line of demarcation and separation to a line of contact and cooperation (Asiwaju 1984), a meeting point, a line of inclusion (Phiri 1984).

In Chumbow and Tamanji (1992) we proposed that international frontiers should be transformed into *bridges of cooperation* by exploiting shared ethnic, cultural and linguistic identities across the border. The principle of *bridges across the border* is best achieved by a comprehensive trans-border cooperation policy between nations.

Trans-border cooperation should seek to establish and consolidate inter-state cooperation at the political, cultural and economic levels with visible manifestations along the border in the form of development projects that will benefit people across the common border.

More specifically, this may involve at the political and administrative levels a joint consultative board to examine and monitor boundary problems and make recommendations to be jointly applied as a tension-diffusing measure. At the economic level, *joint economic and social development projects* in the interests of the welfare of the border people, such as border markets, healthcare units, schools, etc., may be undertaken.

At the cultural level, cultural exchanges or joint organization of cultural activities could be envisaged under a joint cultural committee functioning within the comprehensive policy of inter-state cooperation.

All these measures are best handled alongside the language issue.

Trans-border language cooperation and continental unity Within the perspective of a comprehensive policy of inter-state cooperation, trans-border languages have a crucial role to play, particularly in diffusing border tension, because these languages constitute the common property of the people of the two nations. Furthermore, language is the element of culture par excellence and the means by which people with a common cultural heritage express their common culture and ethnic identity. Trans-border languages can therefore be made to undergo the process of *language development* and used as the means of accomplishing the new perspective of bridges of cooperation at the frontier, specifically, as the vector of the new-found spirit of trans-border cooperation.

Peace and harmony can be achieved by such use of African trans-border languages. When it is considered that some of these languages are spoken by millions of people across several countries (e.g. Fula or Fulfude, spoken across several countries of West and Central Africa), then the potential role of trans-border languages in achieving some of the pan-African ideals can be fully appreciated.

Prospects and perspectives

Given the overwhelming evidence supporting the use of the mother tongue in education, some African countries flirted with the idea in the 1950s and 1960s, spurred by the many UNESCO-inspired conferences on the issue. Many countries today are involved in the process, and it is not our intention to examine details of national achievements in this area here.

Despite several years of work, however, in selling the idea and making its advantages plain, only very few African countries have demonstrated sufficient commitment to the use of African languages in education to evolve and pursue a vigorous policy in this regard.

Suffice it to say that some countries, such as Tanzania, Nigeria, Mali and recently South Africa, have language policies and implementation strategies that have yielded and are yielding palpable results in the area of the use of African languages for educational and national development. Several other countries have adopted the policy but have not demonstrated a sufficient level of commitment in terms of allocation of resources to the implementation of language policies in favour of a greater use of African languages in education and national life. In some countries, such as Cameroon, Côte d'Ivoire, etc., despite a low level of government engagement with the policy, individual NGOs have been encouraged to undertake appreciable work in the standardization and empowerment of local languages.

What are the prospects and perspectives for the future? There has been much concern about the future of Africa's economic development over the years, both from within Africa (see, for instance, Ali Mazrui's television serial *The African*) and from without (Dumont's *L'Afrique noire est mal partie*). Social scientists have made proposals for the economic development of Africa based on a critical analysis of identified problems of economic development.

The United Nations Economic Commission for Africa formulated an economic recovery plan in 1995 after an insightful analysis of the crippling impact of the Structural Adjustment Plan (SAP) of the Bretton Woods institutions (the World Bank and the International Monetary Fund). The list of plans and proposals is not exhaustive. The recent efforts by Presidents Mbeki of South Africa, Obasanjo of Nigeria and Wade of Senegal to present yet another putative panacea in the form of the 'New Partnership for African Development' (NEPAD) has left no one indifferent. Hailed by some for its insights and roundedly criticized by others for being less self-reliant and

185

more tragically dependent on initiatives of the North, NEPAD is nevertheless the one plan on the drawing board for the moment.

In Chumbow (1987) we proposed that language planning for national development should be envisaged as a concomitant component of national (economic) development plans. Neither NEPAD nor any of its ancestors (or simply predecessors) has given any thought to the language question. Given the pertinence and importance of the language issue as a factor in national development, as articulated in this paper and elsewhere, we submit that NEPAD and/or any other programmes of economic recovery and long-term sustainable development of Africa need to address the language question by integrating language development proposals into economic development plans for national development. More specifically, the Language Plan of Action for Africa adopted by the Organization of African Unity (now the African Union) in 1986 is still a viable basis for the language component of economic development planning as proposed in Chumbow (ibid.). The development and use of African languages for academic and intellectual purposes have recently been referred to as 'the intellectualization of African languages'.

While European languages of wider communication are essential in Africa for maintaining international communication and exchange, particularly in the era of globalization, there is an increasing awareness among some African scholars and intellectuals that limiting African intellectual, academic, technical and scientific discourse to these languages is inadequate and in fact counter-productive. It is fraught with a number of undesirable consequences.

Over 70 per cent of the masses of the rural population, because they speak only African languages, are *ipso facto* marginalized and disempowered from actively participating in relevant activities of nation-building and excluded from benefiting from the avalanche of new knowledge and useful information available from the 'global village' and the information superhighway. Limiting intellectual life and activities to exoglossic (foreign) languages to the exclusion of African languages is a barrier to tapping the *indigenous knowledge system* available in African traditional societies and articulating such knowledge within current scientific and technological paradigms for the benefit of the populations and national development at large. It further limits original contributions of the African continent to universals in science and technology.

While some countries in Africa have evolved language planning policies that seek to develop and assign functions to African languages in the enterprise of national development, others are yet to engage in any meaningful action beyond lip-service to the use of African national languages for national development. There are, however, *continental networks* of scholars committed to the *intellectualization* of African languages by envisaging and implementing processes and mechanisms for the accelerated development of such languages. To the extent that these activities are congruent with and constitute further elaborations of the 1986 Language Plan of Action for Africa, we shall call them the Language Plan of Action for African Development (LAPAD).

Some priorities put forward by one such continental network (to which the author belongs), at a recent workshop sponsored by the Project for African Education in South Africa (PRAESA) and the Ford Foundation in Cape Town in July 2003, are presented below as an illustration of the type of engagement that can be undertaken in favour of the intellectualization of African languages within the context of the Language Plan of Action for African Development (LAPAD).

A continuing series of workshops on several topical issues relevant to the development and use of African languages in education, science and technology should be organized. Suggested topics include:

- The proposed activities of the Academy of African Languages (ACALAN) as an umbrella organization at the level of the African Union to conceive and programme action on the standardization and use of African languages to be implemented by member countries.
- Development of materials for teaching mathematics in a variety of African languages as a pilot project, transferable to other science subjects.
- Comparative studies of constitutional provisions and a legal framework and regulations concerning national languages and language institutions across Africa.
- Investigation of the extent to which the specification and articulation of these IK systems is dependent upon close analysis of written and oral African language texts.
- Terminology construction: principles, mechanism and techniques for developing terminology to express new knowledge in science and technology in African languages.
- Comparing differences in language planning practices and dynamics in the anglophone, francophone, lusophone and hispanophone countries of Africa and their consequences for the advancement of the language planning enterprise.
- Working with or on the African Union to declare the Year 2007 'The Year of African Languages' and institute programmes designed to demonstrate their importance to African culture, development and the world community.

187

- Developing a large-scale, continent-wide translation programme to make available in the major African languages key texts from all over the world. These would include important histories, literature and classics as well as volumes on contemporary issues. Short stories might be prioritized as part of the broader effort of the translation programme to encourage a 'culture of reading'.

- Encouraging national competitions and prizes for literature in African languages. Several different categories might be identified: scholarly, fiction, poetry, children's books, etc. The goal would be to focus public attention on these books, create markets for them, encourage writers to use African languages and, again, to help develop a culture of reading. The translation programme might then translate the best of this literature in each of the categories into other African languages.

- Establishing a collaborative multi-university, multi-country MA programme on bilingual and multilingual education at all levels of education. Such a programme would provide training for both young academics and practitioners and build skilled cohorts and colleagues committed to developing the educational potential of African languages. Language, literature and linguistics departments should be encouraged to identify students with strong language interests and skills, and encourage them to apply for the MA programme. The universities participating in the programme might also develop a series of short-term training and refresher programmes on specific topics.

- Making use of the popular media, both electronic and print, to make the case for the wider use of African languages in cultural, political and economic discussions, as well as in educational contexts. Again, 'success stories' in the use of bi- and multilingual education would be particularly useful.

- Linking up African language and literature departments with counterpart linguistics departments, and then whenever possible creatively linking them with the frequently multiple, campus-based, language-oriented student clubs and similar organizations in the larger community.

- Pressing the case for university leadership in the intellectualization and academic use of African languages through incentives for teaching and publishing in these languages. Active university support for and encouragement of the publication of African language academic journals would seem particularly useful and important.

- Conducting coordinated national language audits to provide better information than currently available on actual language use: bi- and multilingualism, code-switching, degrees of literacy (reading and writing), urban/rural, gender and generational differences, spreading, declining or dying languages, contexts for the use of local, national and colonial languages, etc. Such efforts would require a combination of carefully constructed surveys, intensive interviews and observation in a variety of settings (homes, offices, schools, marketplaces, stores, sports facilities, etc.). Audits of this sort would seek to illuminate current language dynamics and constraints and opportunities in education, the media and national policy for further developing and expanding the use of African languages.

- Conducting a series of experimental pilot projects, both technical and pedagogic, in teaching African languages at different levels of education and among different categories of learners (e.g. children, youths, adults, mother-tongue and second-language students). These pilot projects might involve different settings (formal classrooms, smaller learner circles) and a variety of different materials and teaching techniques.
- Developing high-quality, standardized, computerized teaching materials for the major African languages which can then be used (and marketed to generate income) in other countries in Africa and beyond.

The programmatic proposals presented here are adopted and adapted from our network's workshop report edited by Neville Alexander and David Zvanton. The proposals are certainly not exhaustive, but rather are indicative of how a language plan of action can be conceptualized for execution or implementation. These ideas should ultimately be converted into a strategic plan with a time frame for the various activities projected in the plan.

Conclusion

An objective assessment of the achievements of pan-African ideals and aspirations for African development after forty years indicates that there has been more growth than development. It has been shown that the *language factor* is a contributory factor to the snail pace of education (formal, informal and lifelong) as well as all forms of training of human resources needed as viable *agents of change* in the national development enterprise. Education is carried out essentially in a foreign or exoglossic language (English, French, etc.) which *ipso facto* marginalizes the masses of the rural population (who do not speak these languages) and excludes them as active elements in the process of development. To mobilize and maximize the use of available human resources in the enterprise of national development, education and available scientific knowledge and technological know-how must be made available to the masses in an African language, a language they know best.

As for practical problems associated with the implementation of this

189

policy, it has been argued that the advantages outweigh by far the disadvantages and therefore appropriate measures must be taken to surmount all obstacles and solve relevant problems.

Ultimately, the issue boils down to this: given the fact that mother-tongue education has psychological and educational advantages, should the psychological and pedagogical needs of the child be sacrificed in favour of political and economic expediencies? It may be politically and economically more expedient to use a foreign language in education now, but in the long run the adverse effect of such a policy, which diminishes and retards the development of the intellectual potential of the African child, will take its toll on the ability of African economies to develop and the ability of Africans to make original contributions to knowledge. Given the educational advantages to the child and the long-term benefits of developing the child's intellectual ability by using a familiar medium in education (at least in the formative years), African governments should endeavour to allocate the funds necessary for the enterprise.

In light of the above we submit that no paradigm proposed for African development that fails to address the language question can succeed in ushering in much needed national development in Africa. Several five-year economic development plans have failed to achieve desirable levels of national development after forty years.

A Language Plan of Action for African Development (LAPAD), properly conceptualized for each nation-state, needs to be integrated in the economic development plans of African states as a concomitant input to the overall national development plan. Considering the latest in the series of economic plans, the NEPAD, it follows from our submission that *there can be no successful implementation of NEPAD without LAPAD.*

References

Afolayan, A. (1976) 'The Six Year Primary Project in Western Nigeria', in Bamgbose (1976)

Ansre, G. (1979) 'Four Rationalisations for Maintaining European Languages in Education in Africa', *African Languages*, 5(2): 10–17

Asiwaju, A. I. (ed.) (1984) *Partitioned Africans*, Lagos University Press

Bamgbose, A. (1976) *Mother Tongue Education: The Africa Experience*, Paris: UNESCO

— (1991) *Language and the Nation: The Language Question in Sub-Saharan Africa*, Edinburgh University Press

Bot Ba Njock, H. M. (1960) 'Le Problème linguistique au Cameroun', *Afrique et l'Asie*, 73

Bull, W. (1964) 'The Use of Vernacular Languages in Education', in D. Hymes (ed.), *Languages in Culture and Society*, New York: Harper and Row

Carr, M. (1984) 'Intermediate Technology in Botswana: A Review of the Botswana Technology Centre', Occasional Paper no. 10, London: Intermediate Technology Groups

Chomsky, N. A. (1968) *Language and the Mind*, New York: Harcourt Brace Jovanovich

Chumbow, B. S. (1982) 'The Use of African Languages in Education', in B. S. Chumbow (ed.), *Introduction to Applied Linguistics in Africa* (unpublished)

— (1987) 'Towards a Language Planning Model for Africa', *Journal of West African Languages*, XVI(1)

— (1990) 'The Place of the Mother Tongue in the (Nigerian) National Policy in Education', in N. Emenanjo (ed.), *Multilingualism, Minority Languages and Language Policy in Nigeria*, Agbor, Nigeria: Central Books

— (1995) 'The Language Factor in the Development of Science and Technology', in N. Pilai et al. (eds), *The Development of a Culture of Science and Technology in Africa*, Pretoria: Human Science Research Council

— (1997) 'Thematic Glossaries and Language Development', in B. Smieja and M. Meische (eds), *Human Contact through Language. Papers in Honour of René Dirvin*, Frankfurt: Peter Lang, pp. 271–90

— (1999) 'Transborder Languages of Africa', *Social Dynamics*, 25(1)

Chumbow, B. S. and P. Tamanji (1992) 'Linguistic and Ethnic Identity across the Nigerian-Cameroon Border', Paper presented at the International Symposium on Trans-border Cooperation, Yola

— (1994) 'Development of Terminology in African Languages: Mechanisms of Lexical Expansion', paper presented at the First Mozambican Workshop on Educational Use of African Languages and the Role of LWLs, Maputo, Mozambique, November, to appear in the proceedings edited by Christopher Stroud, Centre for Bilingualism, University of Stockholm

— (1997) 'Transborder Languages of the Cameroon Triangle', in K. Prah (ed.), *From Extinction to Diction: Language Standardization and Harmonization*, Johannesburg: University of Witwatersrand Press

Engles, P. (1975) 'The Use of Vernacular Languages in Education. Language Medium in Early School Years for Minority Language Groups', Washington, DC: Center for Applied Linguistics

Forje, J. W. (1989) *Science and Technology in Africa*, London: Longman

Hallak, J. (1990) *Investing in the Future: Setting Educational Priorities in the Developing World*, UNESCO/International Institute for Educational Planning/Pergamon Press

Kayuki, A. (1989) 'Human Resource Development in Japan', paper presented at a symposium on Human Resource Development in Yaounde, Cameroon, IDRC

Krashen, S. (2001) 'First Language in a Second Language Environment', *Journal of the Sociology of Language*, 2(1)

Lambert, W. and G. Tucker (1972) *The Bilingual Education of Children. The St Lambert Experiment*, Rowley, MA: Newbury House

Layton, D. (1992) 'Reconceptualizing Science and Technology Education for Tomorrow', *Science, Technology and Development*, 10(2)

Mincer, T. (1975) *Education, Income and Human Behavior*, National Bureau of Research, New York: McGraw-Hill

Modiano (1968) 'An Experiment in Language Learning in Mexico', Washington, DC: ERIC Clearing House, Centre for Applied Linguistics

Phiri, S. H. (1984) 'National Integration, Rural Development and Frontier Communities. The Case of the Ngoni Astride the Zambian Boundary with Malawi and Mozambique', in Asiwaju (1984)

Ramos, G. et al. (1967) *The Determination and Implementation of Language Policy*, Quezon City: Alemar-Phoenix

Saville, M. and R. Troike (1971) *A Handbook on Bilingual Education*, Washington, DC: Teachers of English to Speakers of Other Languages

Striner, H. (1979) 'The Pay-off of Lifelong Education and Training', in H. Gilden (ed.), *Policies for Lifelong Education*, report of the 1979 Assembly, American Association of Community and Junior Colleges

Tadadjeu, M. (1990) 'Le Défi de Babel au Cameroun', University of Yaounde, Collection PROPELCA no. 53

UNESCO (1953) *The Use of Vernacular Languages in Education*, Monograph on Fundamental Education, Paris: UNESCO (Report of the 1951 UNESCO meeting of specialists on the subject)

Williamson, K. (1979) 'Small Languages in Primary Education. The Rivers Readers Project as a Case History', *African Languages*, 5(2)

9 | Historians, nationalism and pan-Africanism: myths and realities

HANNINGTON OCHWADA

This chapter analyses the role African historians have played in interpreting and producing knowledge on nationalism and pan-Africanism.[1] The historical interpretation of nationalism and pan-Africanism has been shrouded in myths of various kinds. Many critics have argued that the twin ideology of proto-nationalism and pan-Africanism informing the production and teaching of history in the early years of independence merely celebrated the founding of African nations – largely ignoring the social-based contradictions in the political economy. As a result, political leaders of the nascent nations of Africa were absolved of the responsibility of aggravating economic miseries and hardships among the masses in the period immediately after independence.[2] In their assessment of the nationalist historiography, D. Denoon and A. A. Kuper put it more bluntly:

> ... the new historiography has adopted the political philosophy of current African nationalism, and has used it to inform the study of African history. The commitment inclines the school towards rhetoric in defense of narrowly selected themes and interpretations, and the stereotyping and total rejection of other views.[3] The essence of their argument is that nationalist and pan-Africanist scholarship was designed to meet ideological needs of nascent states and the ideals they forged of uniting Africa.[4] The main concern of nationalist and pan-Africanist scholarship was to celebrate and glorify African past achievements amid critiques that social and economic disparities dogged political relations in Africa as ever.[5]

Thus, the scholarship of the 1960s searched for heroes in the African past. The search for and production of historical knowledge indirectly or directly consolidated the colonial legacy by maintaining the existing colonial institutions in independent Africa, including the government administration, education, housing, health and the legal system.

Having considered the propitious conditions in which the nationalist historiography flourished, I will argue that the production of social and historical knowledge obliges one to define one's ideological position from which one proposes to proceed. One is compelled to consciously select those aspects of social knowledge one wishes to popularize and inculcate.[6]

For such social and historical knowledge to be worthwhile, it must address the burning issues of the day in the society in question. I will also argue in the following pages that intellectuals and political leaders could use the nationalist and pan-Africanist ideals in the African renaissance as they used nationalism and pan-Africanism to consolidate their newly independent states in Africa.

Bethwell Alan Ogot reminds us that 'political independence could only have meaning if it was accompanied by historical independence'.[7] This summarizes what African scholars perceived their role in intellectual leadership to be. Indeed, African social scientists were faced with the challenges of building institutions to decolonize the minds of their compatriots and the masses by deliberately producing usable past knowledge. They were charged with the responsibility of producing the history of ideas relating to the socio-political and economic realities obtaining in the early years of independence. Ali Mazrui has such a tale to tell: in the 1960s, as professor of political science at Makerere University in Uganda, he was challenged by a high-placed government official to state the role of the African intellectual in the new nations.[8]

The fact that the decade of the 1960s marked a high noon in the discourse and debates on nationalism and pan-Africanism as rallying points in the memory and social awareness of Africa cannot be overstated. Caroline Neale has argued that:

> The coming of independence was not seen as any ordinary change of government. It was to entail a fundamental change in the relationship of black nations to white nations, and of black to white Africa, and it called for a new representation of the relationship that had obtained up to that point. There had been a political statement that black and white were to be treated as equals; now there was needed a cultural demonstration that something was possible.[9]

Thus, the first decade of independence was a time when African historians across the continent celebrated the event of independence. The endeavour was described as the 'new historiography' because historians laid emphasis on nationalism and pan-Africanism – ideals largely ignored by colonial historiography save for the Afrikaner nationalist historiography in the racially segregated South Africa.[10] If social science scholars produced knowledge that came to be known as 'usable pasts', it was because of the roles the knowledge played in generally consolidating the gains of independence and restoring the lost African dignity during the colonial period.

African political leaders urged historians to produce a new historiography whose role would be to serve newly independent nations. On the occasion of opening the international congress of African historians held at the University College of Dar es Salaam from 26 September to 2 October 1965, President Julius Nyerere of Tanzania advised African historians at the African university and other institutions of higher learning to take a leading part in the recovery of an edifying African past. In Nyerere's perception:

> The primary sources are here in Africa, and the primary interest is not really other people's desire to understand us, but our own desire to understand ourselves and our societies, so that we can build the future on a firm foundation ... I believe that in this forward looking discussion the Africans among you have a very special responsibility. Because they are of this continent, and concerned so intimately with its future as well as its past, the citizens of Africa should be able to indicate where our needs for historical knowledge press most heavily upon us.[11]

The new historiography provided the impetus for Africans to find pride in their past achievements in all spheres of life. This included demonstrating that Africans contributed to the cultural, political, social, historical, religious, scientific and philosophical realms of their own societies.[12] Therefore historians needed to explain African achievements in world civilization in their writings. The 1960s and the early 1970s witnessed a growth in historical research on the so-called recovery of African initiatives in history.

African scholars, like other black scholars across the globe, argued that Africans erected pillars of their own civilization devoid of patronage from outside.[13] They worked within the popular framework of the day – the 'Ebonics' – and the concern to locate social progress and civilization on the historical plane. They saw Ebonics as a viable discourse that informed the place of historical memory and cultural continuity in the production of social and historical knowledge on Africa.[14]

Working from the assumption that Africans had a rich cultural past, this paper draws on the canonical works of historians and other African researchers who espoused nationalist and pan-Africanist ideals.[15] I will also consider the works by critics of the nationalist school of historiography, chiefly Marxists and right-wing or liberal Western scholars.[16]

African historians and the past at independence

With the triumph of the nationalist ideology over colonialism a foundation was laid for developing a forceful, but dignifying, nationalist political perspective. It was obvious that the political status of Africa had reordered social and economic relations. An African historiography followed closely on its heels as the politics of African universities were redefined by the event of independence, thanks to the liberation struggles of the 1950s and 1960s, which were concerned with the mental and physical decolonization of Africans.[17] It is no wonder, then, that Patrice E. Lumumba prophetically asserted that 'History will have its say one day – not the history they teach in Brussels, Paris, Washington or the United Nations, but the history taught in the countries set free from colonialism and its puppet rulers. Africa will write her own history, and both north and south of the Sahara it will be a history of glory and dignity.'[18] Arguably, African historians and social scientists of the period generally aimed at enhancing nationalist and pan-Africanist ideals on the continent following on the heels of independence leaders such as Kwame Nkrumah, Abdel Nasser, Julius Nyerere, Modipo Keita, Haile Selassie, Léopold Sédar Senghor, Jomo Kenyatta, Kenneth Kaunda and Ahmed Sékou Touré among others.[19] Their goals were to rally the citizens of the individual African countries towards nurturing the ideals of nationalism, the consolidation of black solidarity, and uniting the entire continent of Africa. Nkrumah, Nasser, Selassie and Touré believed in the pan-Africanist ideal and how it could be used in the efforts of nation-building and to enhance social, political and economic institutions in independent Africa.

During 5–13 December 1958, the above-mentioned 'philosopher-kings' convened the first All-African Peoples' Conference (AAPC) in Accra, Ghana. The conference was regarded as the successor to the Pan-African Congress held in Manchester, England, in 1945. In attendance were 500 trade unions and party political delegates from twenty-eight African countries. This meeting followed the twelfth General Assembly of the United Nations held on 26 November 1957 when it was resolved to establish the Economic Commission for Africa (ECA).[20] Thus, the idea of functional pan-Africanism gelled in the minds of African political leaders and intellectuals.

Led by Nkrumah, African political leaders came out strongly in support of the pan-Africanist idea of establishing a continental government. The idea of an African government did not come to fruition, however, owing to individual ideological differences dogging African political leadership. Instead, the differences gave way to a loose idea of a compromise continental body, the Organization of African Unity (OAU), in 1963. The founders of the organization wanted to put aside their ideological differences and complete the process of decolonization, to dismantle the apartheid system in South Africa and lay a firm foundation of African unity.[21]

But the OAU proved to be less effective in consolidating pan-Africanism as a basis for forging solid continental unity. With the lukewarm reception of pan-Africanist ideas and the erosion of a basis of continental solidarity, nationalist ideals and sentiments found fertile ground on which to flourish.

Different leaders of African states opted to pursue national programmes, giving rise to the various strands of African socialism across the continent. For example, on 27 April 1967, the United National Independence Party (UNIP) of Zambia under the leadership of Kenneth Kaunda adopted Zambian humanism as its official ideology at a meeting held at Matero in Lusaka.[22] One can argue that Zambian humanism was adopted against the background of nation-building and cultivating a national identity.

Thus, African leaders who seemed to be less radical and believed in celebrating and glorifying African past achievements, or what has been described as 'merrie' Africa within the confines of colonial-inherited boundaries, chose to pursue purely nationalist programmes. Nyerere, Senghor and Keita, like Kaunda, opted to experiment with African communalism and the various shades of socialism. They emphasized how indigenous institutions could be useful in spurring economic and social development through community-based self-help programmes. This explains, for instance, why, at the launch of his policy on African socialism, Nyerere came up with his paper entitled *Arusha Declaration*.

African intellectuals reinvented different national traditions by postulating that African socialism was the most appropriate ideology in the process of charting out strategies for the development of the continent.[23] In 1967, Nyerere undertook an experiment in African communalism (*ujamaa*), while Kenyatta and Keita among others adopted African socialism and applied it as a development strategy of their respective countries.[24] On the other hand, Senghor strove to nurture the ideals of negritude by integrating values espoused by black and white as the basis for creating a new African personality in Senegal and beyond its boundaries.[25] Senghor's type of Negritude presupposes ontologically that it has two aspects, one constituted of the old and dead past, the other being the newly created or invented Africa.[26] According to Senghor both aspects were important in the African gnosis.

Working in alliance with white liberal scholars, therefore, African historians and social scientists would interpret the past as a way of consolidating nationalism and pan-Africanism. Three distinct centres of academic debate seem to have emerged in the late 1950s and early 1960s in Africa. These were the Cheikh Anta Diop school of thought under Abdoulaye Ly and Joseph Ki-Zerbo, based at the University of Dakar in Senegal; the Ibadan nationalist school of historiography at Ibadan University in Nigeria under K. O. Dike, S. O. Biobaku, A. E. Afigbo, E. A. Ayandele and Jacob Ajayi; and the Dar es Salaam school of historiography under Terence Ranger at University College, Dar es Salaam, in Tanzania. The dominating theme of the early period of African independence was African resistance versus African oppression.

Less important but still forceful, however, was a school of historiography that emerged within the national boundaries of the South African apartheid system. This school promoted the study of bourgeois nationalist history in South Africa for the privileged Afrikaner settler community. But Afrikaner nationalism was not without its detractors. There were contradictory ideologies and social philosophies in southern Africa. In fact, there was no consensus on how citizenship of the country ought to be defined in the absolute sense. The main contradictions in socio-political and economic projection are neatly captured in five schools of historical thought, namely the British settler, Afrikaner settler, South African settler, indigenous African (or Africanist) and liberal or multiracial schools of thought. These schools of thought did not develop at the same time, however – they were a product of the historical and social conditions obtaining in the country.

The appearance of competing ideologies and the histories of these schools of thought are a function of the changing patterns of contradiction within South African social relationships. The British settler tradition had its roots in the British settler colonies of the Cape and Natal. The Afrikaner settler communities seeking to establish independent Afrikaner republics gave rise to this version of nationalism. The South African settler community celebrates the role of all European settlers in South Africa. The liberal or multiracial school tends to handle the issue of race using a pluralist approach. The Africanist approach engages in an uncritical celebration of anti-imperialist history.[27] Essentially they all represented different ideologies based on race and class, reflecting the power struggles inherent in South Africa.

In the meantime, however, many a scholar came to do research on the roles of African heroes such as Samori Touré of West Africa, Shaka of the Zulu state, Kinjiketile of the Matumbi and the resistance movements of Chimurenga of Southern Rhodesia and the Herero/Nama of Namibia.[28] The nationalist school of historiography, with its variant strands, was chiefly concerned with establishing chronology and reconstructing the political and military activities of Africans in the past. Whether in South Africa or other parts of the continent, the researchers were less concerned with social and economic changes than they were with establishing chronology and progress. It is my contention that, as much as an ideology that facilitated the struggle for independence, they wanted knowledge that was useful for enhancing their position in society. Paul E. Lovejoy has argued that research on '"Kings and battles" was the order of the day; only to the extent that Africans as a collectivity were the oppressed people of a European-dominated world order did those other than the mighty and powerful enter into the historical record'.[29]

It was important that African scholars of the 1960s sought to place African history within a chronological and modernization framework in order to account for their political past. Their efforts largely impinged on nationalism given that they celebrated the triumph of nationalist struggles in the liberation of Africa. Whereas the mainstream nationalist historiography emphasized African choice, African initiatives, African adaptations, among other issues, the South African historiography was steeped in a peculiar variant of nationalist historiography that reflected competing currents in power relations – the place of race and class in national identity.

Critique of nationalist historiography: which way forward?

The nationalist period was an important epoch in modern African history because it provided intellectuals on the continent with various strands of nationalist and pan-Africanist frameworks. They used these frameworks to assess their own conditions. Different African socialisms, including *ujamaa*, consciencism, the concepts of *harambee* and Negritude, emerged and were seized upon by African scholars as a framework of analysis.[30] We noted above that while the nationalist schools of history in South Africa reflected the competing socio-political voices and economic contradictions, the mainstream nationalist historiography in the rest of sub-Saharan and Arab Africa provided newly independent African states with an ideology that inspired collective responses towards efforts in building nascent nations and consolidating their newly won independence.

Bethwell Alan Ogot has argued that in the 1960s historians had to demonstrate that African societies had, for instance, well-organized states and engaged in long-distance trade with properly organized markets. Thus, social science scholars proceeded to argue that Africans had developed religions, philosophies, military organization, legal systems, medicine and technology, among other things.[31] The critics of the nationalist historiography have been quick to point out, however, that in the process of highlighting these achievements historians and other social scientists romanticized the past, stripping African history of its dynamism, contradictions and antagonisms, class struggles, and the socio-political and economic transformations that people experienced at various levels.[32] For example, K. O. Dike's study of commerce among the Niger Delta communities treated African peoples' involvement in the trade as a political event and not merely as a commercial activity. Dike belaboured the fact that Africans were also traders in their own right and, therefore, deserved a place in the history textbooks. Likewise Ogot's own work on the history of southern Luo considered the different communities as a homogenous entity that did not exhibit remarkable social contradictions and dynamism.[33]

The first generation of African historians overlooked many factors that constrained and impinged upon social and political relations in past African experience. These included the dictatorial and authoritarian nature of some of the indigenous leaders.[34] In their concern to produce usable knowledge African historians believed they could help to nurture African personhood and a vibrant sense of nationhood across the continent. European authorship from the Enlightenment period to the early years of African independence argued that Africa was eclipsed by darkness, and that 'darkness was no suitable subject for history'.[35] Buoyed by the nationalist spirit, however, and employing the same concepts that characterized pan-Africanism, they problematized African identities in their own terms. In effect they helped to reclaim the African past that some Western scholars had banished to the dustbin of history.

Yet by the same token (in using the same methodologies as their mentors) African historians remained trapped in the problems of the colonial or bourgeois history they so vehemently criticized. In fact, they did not engage in serious theoretical analyses that placed them 'at the service of masses in the effort to understand their past against the forces of exploitation'.[36] Writing on the theoretical poverty of the nationalists' historiography, Henry Slater has observed that:

> 'bourgeois nationalist' historiography was criticized for its concentration on politics conceived in a vacuum, and for its romantic emphasis upon the role of African initiative, both of which singularly failed to provide a historical explanation of the present condition of African economic and political powerlessness. How then could such knowledge contribute to Africa's contemporary struggles to overcome these conditions of powerlessness?[37]

Slater's argument underscored the all-important fact of the historians' partial representation of the different forces at work in the colonial past. Only by identifying the social and economic contradictions and the relations of power in society could historians contribute to finding solutions for the numerous problems that the new states were facing. Few historians, however, seriously analysed the contradictions in society. What, then, are some of the pertinent issues to be considered?

One needs to examine the role of the OAU, and several other sub-regional groupings and intellectual consortiums such as Casablanca, Monrovia and the front-line states whose aims were to liberate the entire continent from the colonial yoke and end minority white settler rule in southern Africa. Pan-Africanists looked forward to a dispensation whereby Africans would redeem themselves from a world system that largely marginalized them because of their skin pigmentation. Certainly these were positive indicators of the nationalist and pan-Africanist intellectual effort to grapple with issues of national and continental concern.[38] The more relevant question that remains on our minds is: whither nationalist historiography?

Given the cultural and economic marginalization that Africa is suffering currently, it behoves historians and other social scientists to revisit the role of nationalism and pan-Africanism in debates and discourses on the African condition. Already debates are emerging on the immediate challenges facing Africa as it seeks to forge new social and political initiatives in the implementation of policies to enhance development in the face of the ravages of global capitalism.[39] My argument is that African historians should delve deep into the African past in order to bring to the fore the knowledge that could be used to rejuvenate the socio-political and economic institutions of the continent.

Indeed, it is important that our reflection on the future of African societies be firmly based on objective analyses and evaluations of our past. Suffice it to state again that proto-nationalist historiographers recognized the power of history in awakening the political consciousness of Africans during the colonial period and the independence struggles. To them, an African renaissance was the way to go in rallying the masses. They were convinced that every nation was charged with the responsibility of building its future based on its past. Thus, they immersed themselves in historical research on pre-colonial institutions.[40] As we have noted above, the Diops, Ogots, Ajayis, Vansinas and Dikes played a great role in exhuming the past that colonial writers ignored.

Now, as in the early years of independence, African political leaders are yearning for a renaissance after decades of institutional decay and the wastage of resources of every kind by post-independence political leaders and service managers. Instead of merely glorifying the so-called undifferentiated African past, historians should reconceptualize and theorize the institutions of governance by promoting concepts of human rights as seen by Africans themselves – the ideals that would enhance African citizenship.[41] The main question here is to rethink the place of civil society in creating an African citizenship – how did historians problematize regional citizenship? How did historians interpret the experiences of peoples living in proximity? What did communities borrow from each other in their attempts to create regional citizenship? What were the constraints on regional citizenship that people experienced and what was the interpretation of historians regarding them? What role should historians play in the renaissance of Africa?

Most of Africa possesses an interlinked historical heritage dating back into the remote pre-colonial period. During pre-colonial times people intermingled freely without the restrictions of artificial boundaries of country-specific laws. Africans traded among themselves in short- and long-distance commercial activities, intermarrying and relating at various social and political levels provided by host communities. For instance, in the nineteenth century prior to colonialism Waswahili traders from the East African coastal region established chiefdoms and kingdoms in areas as far away as the Great Lakes of East Africa. There were long-distance trading activities between different peoples of West Africa, such as the Hausa, the Yoruba and the Dyula. They also intermarried, in the process creating a viable citizenship. Paul Tiyambe Zeleza has described the interactions African were involved in as follows:

> Family, clan and ethnic associations, both real and affected, played an
> important role in the provision of trading skills, capital and credit, and in-
> formation. Traders formed alliances in foreign countries through marriage
> and blood brotherhood. The careers of the famous Swahili and Nyamwezi
> traders, such as Tippu Tip and Msiri who created commercial empires in
> Kasongo and Katanga respectively, were built on shrewd alliances with local
> rulers or people based on either marriage or fictional kinship ties.[42]

There is no doubt that the reason why the rulers created the empires was to secure important scarce items and products in daily use, which were not otherwise readily available in their local environments. Furthermore, they needed to purchase goods for exchange in the vibrant export and import trade of the nineteenth century. We need to explain why some regions in Africa enjoyed well-connected local and long-distance trade. For instance, in present-day Uganda, around Kibero on Lake Kyoga and Bunyoro, there were specialized activities in the production of salt and iron respectively.[43] The inhabitants of the sub-regions promoted inter-regional trade among themselves. This leads one to conclude that African states could promote regional trade by drawing from the lessons provided by pre-colonial historical experiences.

It is crucial that historians undertake comparative studies on different social systems of the past in view of the theoretical significance of such studies to the social terrain of interaction as illuminants for economic development. Historians ought to study the constitutionality of integra-tion with a view to explaining how African citizenship could be built in the hope of having a shared space to pursue socio-political and economic activities across national borders. An explanation of efforts of integration could help to chart avenues for the region's stability through enhanced citizenship and the full realization of the potential of human resources for progress and development. Such an endeavour could also lessen the problem of refugees, which has severely affected security and the process of development in Africa. African nations have in the past concentrated refugees from Sierra Leone, Liberia, Sudan, Rwanda, Burundi, Uganda and Somalia in the various camps within the region. In other instances, refugees and immigrants have been denied employment because of their citizenship of individual countries.[44]

African historians are cognizant of an unjust international economic order, otherwise known as the New International Economic Order (NIEO). The NIEO favours developed countries over developing ones. As a consequence, developing countries, particularly those of Africa, have been trapped in the negative effects of the deteriorating terms of trade and high interest rates, a situation that made it difficult for them to earn much needed foreign exchange resources for the purposes of development. In the light of these developments African leaders appear to have adopted new tactics to deal with the unfavourable economic relations.

In the late 1970s African leaders began to change their strategies regarding the management of their economies. They sought appropriate solutions to their dire economic and social problems. Working with this understanding in mind, African intellectuals and policy specialists met in Monrovia in February 1979 to discuss development prospects in Africa. They were concerned with the type of development and the means that would transform the functionality of African social and economic systems as they approached the twenty-first century. Other meetings followed thereafter, the most important of them, perhaps, being the sixteenth session of the OAU Assembly of Heads of State and Government in July 1979 in Monrovia. The outcome was what was known as the 'Monrovia Declaration of Commitment'. The strategy that they adopted laid emphasis on three basic principles, namely self-reliance, self-sustainment and economic cooperation and integration. According to them this strategy would help African leaders solve their social, political and economic problems. Yet the most glaring omission is the role that historians could play in efforts to reignite an African renaissance.

Conclusion

In this ongoing conceptual paper I have attempted to explain the roles African historians have played in using nationalist and pan-Africanist concepts in the African renaissance. I have tried to explain their efforts in the period immediately after *uhuru* (independence) and the challenges they faced – the task of rallying citizens of individual countries towards building national identities. I have, however, noted that in their efforts to rally citizens towards nationalism they did not consider the fact that

Africa was not an undifferentiated entity. Thus, they ignored the dangers of authoritarian rule and dictatorship that led to wastage of national resources.

There is a new spirit of reviving African institutions, calling upon historians, among other social science scholars, to problematize African citizenship anew. This entails the recognition of individual and civil rights as a security guarantee within the region, a factor that would facilitate free movement of people and their interactions and help in policing criminal activities across borders. It is my proposal that the previous approaches to nationalism and pan-Africanism be rethought to give more attention to the bottom-up approach, an approach that considers a broader, but more responsible, African citizenship. What this calls for is grounding debates in the essence of constitutionalism and the possibility of constitutional consensus by way of debate. The assumption is that if consensus can be achieved in the process of politics within the region, the politically established boundaries will be rendered inconsequential with time and natural integration will take place. My assumption is that there would be greater respect for human rights and the possibility of achieving the much-sought economic development by harnessing human resources and capital freely across the continent.

Notes and references

1 For definitions of nationalism and pan-Africanism see S. Randrianja, 'Nationalism, Ethnicity and Democracy', in S. Ellis (ed.) (1996) *Africa Now: People, Policies and Institutions*, London: James Currey, pp. 20–4. Randrianja defines nationalism as an anti-colonial ideology 'extolling unity against the foreign oppressor'. It was progressively transformed into the all-important ideology of consolidating independence in Africa. Pan-Africanism, on the other hand, is solidarity based on racial principles. There is yet another definition of pan-Africanism as the idea and programme of an envisioned continental unity. See B. Davidson (1994) *The Search for Africa: A History in the Making*, London: James Currey, pp. 65–74.

2 E. S. Atieno-Odhiambo (1974) 'Synthesizing Kenya History', *Africa Thought and Practice*, 1(1); E. Wamba-dia-Wamba (1993) 'African History and Teaching of History in Dar es Salaam', *Tanzania Zamani*, 1(3).

3 D. Denoon and A. Kuper (1970) 'Nationalist Historians in Search of a Nation: The"New Historiography" in Dar es Salaam', *African Affairs*, 69, p. 348.

4 See J. S. Saul (1970) 'Radicalism and the Hill', *East African Journal*, 7; E. S. Atieno-Odhiambo (1974) *The Paradox of Collaboration*, Nairobi: East African Publishing House; B. Swai (1980) 'The Use of History: Towards the Sociology of Africanist Historiography', University of Dar es Salaam mimeograph; B. Swai (1980) 'An Inquiry into the Idea of the African University', *Taamuli: A Political Science Forum*, 10(1).

5 H. Bernstein (1976) 'Marxism and African History: Endre Sik and His

Critics', *Kenya Historical Review*, 4(1); E. Wamba-dia-Wamba (1980) 'Brief Theoretical Comments on the Quest for Materialist History: Concerning the Article "The Object of History"', unpublished paper, Department of History, University of Dar es Salaam; A. J. Temu and Bonaventure Swai (1981) *Historians and Africanist History: A Critique*, London: Zed Press.

6 E. S. Atieno-Odhiambo, 'Synthesizing Kenya History', p. 36.

7 B. A. Ogot (1976) 'Towards a History of Kenya', *Kenya Historical Review*, 4, p. 1.

8 See A. A. Mazrui (1978) *Political Values and the Educated Class in Africa*, London: Heinemann. Mazrui was challenged by Akena Odoko, chief of staff, to debate publicly what the role of the intellectual in Africa was. This followed an earlier lecture that Mazrui had given in which he defined an intellectual as a person fascinated with ideas. According to state officials in Uganda an African intellectual had to be committed to his/her society. They thought that African intellectuals had no place engaging in what they perceived to be meaningless juggling with ideas for the sake of it; they were required to produce useful social knowledge.

9 C. Neale (1986) 'The Idea of Progress in the Revision of African History, 1960–1970', in B. Jewsiewicki and D. Newbury (eds), *African Historiographies: What History for Which Africa?*, Beverly Hills, CA: Sage Publications, p. 112.

10 H. Slater (1989) 'Southern Africa and the Production and Dissemination of Historical Knowledge', in J. R. Mlahagwa, L. M. Sago, F. Lutatenekwa and G. T. Mishambi (eds), *Landmarks in Southern African History*, Dar es Salaam: The Historical Association of Tanzania, pp. 27–8. According to Afrikaner nationalism racial differences were markers of socio-political and economic development in South Africa. Thus, the proposal for the segregated policy of separate development known as apartheid.

11 J. K. Nyerere (1968) 'Opening Speech', in T. O. Ranger (ed.), *Emerging Themes of African History*, Nairobi: East African Publishing House, pp. 3–4. For further reading see also J. K. Nyerere (1968) *Ujamaa: Essays on Socialism*, Oxford University Press; J. K. Nyerere (1970) *Freedom and Socialism*, Oxford University Press.

12 See Denoon and Kuper, 'Nationalist Historians', pp. 329–49; T. O. Ranger (1971) 'The New Historiography in Dar es Salaam: An Answer', *African Affairs*, 70, pp. 50–61; J. N. K. Mugambi (1974) 'The African Experience of God', *Africa Thought and Practice*, 1.

13 G. G. M. James (1954) *Stolen Legacy: The Greeks were not the Authors of Greek Philosophy, but the People of North Africa, Commonly Called Ethiopians*, New York: Philosophical Library.

14 See B. Davidson, *The Search for Africa*, pp. 65–74; I. Amadiume (1997) *Re-inventing Africa: Matriarchy, Religion and Culture*, London: Zed Books, p. ix.

15. P. Tempels (1959) *Bantu Philosophy*, Paris: Présence Africaine; C. A. Diop (1974) *The African Origin of Civilization: Myth or Reality*, Westport: Lawrence Hill & Co.; C. A. Diop (1987) *Black Africa: The Economic Basis for a Federated State*, Westport: Lawrence Hill & Co.; P. M. Mutibwa (1977/78) *African Heritage and the New Africa*, Nairobi: East African Literature Bureau; M. Bernal (1986) *Black Athena: The Afroasiatic Roots of Classical Civilization*, vol. 1, *The*

Fabrication of Ancient Greece 1785–1985, London: Free Association Books; C. A. Diop (1987) *Precolonial Black Africa: A Comparative Study of the Political and Social Systems of Europe and Black Africa, from Antiquity to the Formation of Modern States*, Westport: Lawrence Hill & Co.

16 Jacques Depelchin (1977) 'African History and the Ideological Reproduction of the Exploitative Relations of Production', *Africa Development*; G. T. Mishambi (1977) 'The Mystification of African History: A Critique of Rodney's How Europe Underdeveloped Africa', *Utafiti*, 2(2), pp. 201–28; J. Mlahagwa (1978) 'Towards a Functional Materialist History: The Dar es Salaam Experience', mimeographed paper, Dar es Salaam; N. N. Luanda (1979) 'The Negative Mrror Images of African Initiative: Colonial Resistance and Collaboration', Dar es Salaam; J. R. Mlahagwa (1989) 'Epistemology and the Weapon of Theory', in Mlahagwa et al., *Landmarks in Southern African History*.

17 H. Ochwada (1993) 'An Appraisal of the Development of African Historiography in East Africa since 1960', unpublished MA thesis, Kenyatta University, Nairobi, p. 257.

18 P. E. Lumumba cited in Wamba-dia-Wamba, 'African History and Teaching of History in Dar es Salaam', p. 1; P. T. Zeleza (2003) *Rethinking Africa's Globalization*, vol. 1, *The Intellectual's Challenges*, Trenton: Africa World Press, pp. 65–9.

19 See J. Reed and C. Wake (eds) (1965), *Léopold Sédar Senghor: Prose and Poetry*, London: Oxford University Press; K. D. Kaunda (1966), *Humanist in Africa*, London: Longman; B. Zewde (1999/2000) 'African Historiography: Past, Present and Future', *Afrika Zamani*, 7 & 8.

20 T. Mboya (1993) *The Challenge of Nationhood*, Nairobi: East African Educational Publishers, pp. 127–9.

21. T. Drame (1996) 'The Crisis of the State', in S. Ellis (ed.), *Africa Now: People, Policies and Institutions*, London: James Currey, p. 208.

22 See H. Meebelo (1973) *Main Currents of Zambian Humanist Thought*, Oxford University Press. Like African socialism now in vogue elsewhere on the continent of Africa, Zambian humanism drew its principles from indigenous African social systems. Its character traits were adjusted, however, to accord with conditions for the ideology to be workable. Zambian humanism drew from both indigenous and the foreign cultures that Zambians encountered.

23 See W. H. Friedland and C. G. Rosberg, Jr (1964) 'Introduction: The Anatomy of African Socialism', in W. H. Friedland and C. G. Rosberg, Jr (eds), *African Socialism*, Stanford University Press; E. Hobsbawm and T. Ranger (eds) (1983) *The Invention of Tradition*, Cambridge University Press.

24 Tom Mboya (1986) *Freedom and After*, Nairobi: East African Educational Publishers.

25 See Mutibwa (1977) *African Heritage and the New Africa*, pp. 216–18; D. A. Masolo (1994) *African Philosophy in Search of Identity*, Nairobi: East African Educational Publishers, pp. 25–8.

26 Masolo, *African Philosophy*, pp. 29–30.

27 Slater, 'Southern Africa and the Production and Dissemination of Historical Knowledge', pp. 26–9.

28 E. S. Atieno-Odhiambo (1999–2000) 'From African Historiography to an African Philosophy of History', *Afrika Zamani*, 7 & 8, p. 45.

29 P. E. Lovejoy (1986) 'Nigeria: The Ibadan School and Its Critics', in B. Jewsiewicki and D. Newbury (eds), *African Historiographies: What History for Which Africa?*, Beverly Hills, CA: Sage Publications, p. 198.

30 H. Ochwada (1995) 'Men of Literature and Kenya's Historiography: an Appraisal of Ngugi-wa-Thiong'o', *TransAfrican Journal of History*, 24: 152; K. Nkrumah (1970) *Consciencism: Philosophy and the Ideology for Decolonization and Development with Particular Reference to the African Revolution*, London: Panaf Books.

31 B. A. Ogot (1978) 'Three Decades of Historical Studies in East Africa, 1947–1977', *Kenya Historical Review*, 6(1 & 2): 25.

32 Y. Q. Lawi (1988) 'A History of History Teaching in Post-colonial Tanzania, 1961–1986', unpublished MA dissertation, University of Dar es Salaam, p. 207.

33 See K. O. Dike (1956) *Trade and Politics in the Niger Delta, 1830–1885*, Oxford: Clarendon Press; B. A. Ogot (1967) *A History of Southern Luo: Migration and Settlement 1500 to 1900*, vol. 1, Nairobi: East African Publishing House.

34 C. Odegi-Awoundo (1992) *The Rise of the 'Cheering Crowd': Fiction and Kenya's Political History*, Nairobi: Casper Odegi-Awoundo.

35 Atieno-Odiambo, 'From African Historiographies to an African Philosophy', p. 42.

36 Mlahagwa, 'Epistemology and the Weapon of Theory', p. 11.

37 H. Slater (1989) 'Dar es Salaam and the Postnationalist Historiography of Africa', in Mlahaqur et al., *Landmarks*, p. 254.

38 See A. A. Mazrui and M. Tidy (1984) *Nationalism and New States in Africa from about 1935 to the Present*, Nairobi: Heinemann.

39 See C. Ake (1996) *Democracy und Development in Africa*, Washington, DC: Brookings Institution; C. Leys and M. Mamdani (1997) *Crises and Reconstruction – African Perspectives: Two Lectures*, Uppsala: Nordiska Afrikainstitutet; J. S. Saul (2003) 'Africa: the Next Liberation Struggle', *Review of African Political Economy*, 96: 187.

40 C. Wondji (1986) 'Towards a Responsible African Historiography', in B. Jewsiewicki and D. Newbury (eds), *African Historiographies: What History for Which Africa?*, Beverly Hills, CA: Sage Publications, p. 269.

41 I. G. Shivji (1989) *African Concepts of Human Rights*, Dakar: CODESRIA; I. G. Shivji (1991) 'State and Constitutionalism: A New Democratic Perspective', in I. G. Shivji (ed.), *State and Constitutionalism: African Debates on Democracy*, Harare: Sapes.

42 P. T. Zeleza (1993) *A Modern Economic History of Africa*, vol. 1, *The Nineteenth Century*, Dakar: CODESRIA, p. 303.

43 E. Gimode (1996) 'Attempts at Economic Integration in East Africa: Memories, Problems and Prospects', paper presented at the 4th Historical Association of Kenya Symposium at Kenyatta University, Nairobi, 6–8 December, p. 3.

44 L. H. Malkki (1994) *Purity and Exile: Violence, Memory, National Cosmology among the Hutu Refugees in Tanzania*, Chicago University Press; M. Turshen and C. Twagiramariya (eds) (1998) *What Women Do in Wartime: Gender and Conflict in Africa*, London: Zed Books; M. Mamdani (2001) *When Victims Become Killers: Colonialism, Nativism, and the Genocide in Rwanda*, Princeton University Press.

10 | The academic diaspora and knowledge production in and on Africa: what role for CODESRIA?

PAUL TIYAMBE ZELEZA

The African academic diaspora, however defined, has never been larger than it is now, and it continues to grow rapidly. According to some estimates, since 1990 an average of 20,000 highly educated Africans, among them academics, have been migrating to the North every year. That much is clear, but far less so are the causes, courses and consequences of this expansion, specifically the implications for knowledge production in and on Africa. Depending on one's developmentalist anxieties, globalist or cosmopolitan affectations, pan-Africanist aspirations, or analytical predispositions towards international skilled labour migration (the 'brain drain' of popular and policy discourse), the academic diaspora can be seen as either a liability depriving Africa of desperately needed professionals trained at enormous cost, or an asset providing the continent with crucial connections to the North that can facilitate transfers of capital (technological, financial, cultural and political), and help mediate, in terms of knowledge production, the globalization of African scholarship and the Africanization of global scholarship.

This essay seeks to discuss the role that the academic diaspora plays and can play in African knowledge production. Needless to say, as a social formation this diaspora is quite complex in its composition and it exhibits contradictory tendencies in its practices, so that it is difficult to make generalizations about its politics or engagements. Nevertheless, I am inclined to argue that in general the diaspora, both the historic and contemporary diaspora – and its intelligentsia in particular – has the potential, which it has exercised during some key moments of modern African history, through the pan-African movement, for example, for a productive and progressive engagement with Africa. The challenge is to decipher the tendencies and instances among the academic diaspora in contemporary times – a conjuncture characterized by the vast and complex processes and projects of capitalist globalization, technological change, and new economics of knowledge production and the production of knowledge economies – which can be mobilized for African intellectual development at multiple spatial and social scales, from the local to the global and across generation and gender.

The essay is divided into four parts. It begins by trying to define the diaspora, for it seems to me that it is important to distinguish between dispersal and diaspora and the historic and contemporary diasporas and the connections between them. This is followed by an attempt to contextualize the academic diaspora, to map the institutional, intellectual, ideological and individual dynamics of diasporic knowledge production. The third part makes an effort to historicize diasporic academic production and linkages with Africa during two crucial periods, the colonial and early post-independence eras. The final part focuses on current trends and interrogates some of the typologies that have been advanced to characterize the orientations of the contemporary African academic diaspora.

In conclusion, the essay suggests the ways in which intellectual communities and networks based both in the diaspora and on the continent, such as CODESRIA, can most productively engage each other. It cannot be overemphasized, as I have argued elsewhere, that

> the rising international migration of Africa's professional elites and intellectuals may indeed be a curse if dismissed and ignored, but it can be turned into a blessing if embraced and utilized. It is generated by, and inserts Africa into, contemporary processes of transnationalization and globalization, which follow and reinforce the old trails of Pan-Africanism ... The challenge for Africa is how to rebuild the historic Pan-African project, spawned by the global dispersal and exploitation of African peoples over the centuries, by creatively using the current migratory flows of African peoples, cultures, capacities, and visions and the contemporary revolution in telecommunications and travel technologies. It is an old challenge in a new age that requires responses and solutions that are both old and new. (Zeleza 2003a: 170)

Defining and debating African diasporas

There are several conceptual difficulties in defining the African diaspora, indeed in defining the term diaspora itself, for it simultaneously refers to a process, a condition and a discourse: the continuous processes by which a diaspora is made, unmade and remade, the changing conditions in which it lives and expresses itself, and the contentious ways in which it is studied and discussed. Also embodied in the term diaspora are temporal, spatial and cultural considerations, the connections and divides of the diaspora from the times, spaces and cultures of the putative homeland. Clearly, the temporality, spatiality and culturality of the African diaspora are more problematic than might appear at first sight. When and why did the dispersal of the Africans start, to where and what did they spread, which and whose culture(s) did they share?

Dispersal does not automatically create a diaspora. A diasporic identity implies a form of group consciousness constituted historically through expressive culture, politics, thought and tradition, in which existential and representational resources are mobilized, in varied measures, from the minds of both the old and the new worlds. A diaspora is constructed as much in the fluid and messy contexts of social existence, differentiation and struggle as in the discourses of the intellectuals and political elites. Its development involves the mobilization and appropriation of what Jacqueline Brown (1998) calls 'diasporic resources' – cultural productions, people and places and their associated iconography, images, ideas and ideologies.

Given the multiplicity of historical conditions in which diasporic identities can be moulded, there cannot but exist different African diasporas whose complex relationships and exchanges, including the trafficking of the notion of diaspora itself, or blackness, are entwined in the very construction of the various diasporas. It is in the metropolitan centres, in the interstices of the 'overlapping diasporas', to use Earl Lewis's (1995) term, that different diasporas connect and compete most intimately, thereby refashioning themselves and creating and commodifying new trans-national diasporic cultures mediated by national, ethnic, religious, class, and gender identities.

There are several dispersals associated with African peoples over time. Colin Palmer (2000) has identified at least six, three in prehistoric and ancient times (beginning with the great exodus that began about 100,000 years ago from the continent to other continents), and three in modern times, including those associated with the Indian Ocean slave trade to Asia, the Atlantic slave trade to the Americas, and the contemporary movement of Africans and peoples of African descent to various parts of the globe. Our tendency to privilege the modern diasporic streams, especially the last two, is a tribute to the epistemic and economic hegemony of the Euro-American world system that spawned them and created what Tiffany Patterson and Robin Kelly (2000) call 'global race and gender hierarchies' within which African diasporas are situated and often discussed.

It is quite instructive that the term African diaspora emerged only in the 1950s and 1960s in the United States, although African diasporas existed long before then in different parts of the world, and the mobilization of African peoples was described in other terms, such as pan-Africanism. One author complains that the discursive politics of the term diaspora has 'imposed a US and English language-centered model of black identity on the complex experiences of populations of African descent' (Edwards 2000: 47). But even African diasporic histories focused on the wider Atlantic world are partial in so far as African migrations and diaspora communities

211

also emerged in the Mediterranean and Indian Ocean worlds of southern Europe and Asia (Blakely 1986; Alpers 2000; Hunwick and Powell 2002; Jaysuriya and Pankhurst 2003). Michael West (2000: 62–3) has even suggested that if black internationalism, in the ontological sense, did not originate in Africa, we also need to think of a 'Black Pacific', an entity that, if 'properly constructed, would include not just communities of African descent along the Pacific coast of North, Central, and South America, but also, presumably, black communities with no known ties to Africa – in historic times, that is – elsewhere in the South Pacific, such as Fiji, Papua New Guinea, and Australia, communities that only began to join the black internationalism, in the ontological sense, in the 1960s'.

Thus, the conflation of hegemony and discourse can be seen in the pre-eminent position occupied by African Americans in diaspora studies, despite the fact that the largest community of diaspora Africans in the Atlantic world, indeed globally, is in Brazil, not in the United States. Such is the popular fascination and scholarly preoccupation with the African American diaspora that its members remain foregrounded even in texts that set out to dethrone them, such as Paul Gilroy's *The Black Atlantic*, itself a monument to anglophone self-referential conceit and myopia. If Africa is largely a silent primordial presence in Gilroy's *Black Atlantic*, the historic Atlantic African diaspora is pilloried by Kwame Appiah's (1992) *In My Father's House* in his ill-tempered attack on the supposedly racialist pan-Africanisms of Alexander Crummell and W. E. B. Dubois. In fact, it can be argued that, except in the obligatory histories of pan-Africanism and nationalism, the historic African diaspora tends to be ignored in much African scholarly discourse. Instead, far greater concern is expressed for the travails of the contemporary African diaspora in the North, but even here the discourse is firmly rooted in the economistic preoccupations of development studies, rather than the culturalist thrust of diaspora studies (Zack-Williams 1995).

It is critical for African scholars on the continent to become more engaged in diaspora studies, to help in mapping out the histories and geographies of African global migrations, dispersals and diasporas that are so crucial to deepening our understanding of both African history and world history for intellectual and ideological reasons, as well as in terms of developmental and cultural considerations. As I have demonstrated elsewhere, African migrations to the North, especially western Europe and North America, are increasing (Zeleza 2000, 2002). Many of these migrants are constituting themselves into new diasporas, whose identities involve complex negotiations with the host African diaspora communities and their countries of origin. If the diaspora of enslavement – the historic diaspora

– had no choice but to see itself in pan-Africanist terms whenever it identified with Africa, the diaspora of colonialism and neo-colonialism – the contemporary diaspora – is more disposed to see itself in pan-national, or even pan-ethnic, terms. It cannot be taken for granted, therefore, that the contemporary diaspora is more pan-Africanist than the historic diaspora, which is one more reason for the different diasporas to engage each other and for institutions on the continent to engage both.

In a country such as the United States, there are in fact at least four waves of African diasporas. First, the historic communities of African Americans, themselves formed out of complex internal and external migrations over several hundred years; second, migrant communities from other diasporic locations, such as the Caribbean, which have maintained or invoke, when necessary or convenient, national identities as Jamaicans, Puerto Ricans, Cubans, and so on; third, the recent immigrants from the indigenous communities of Africa; and finally, African migrants who themselves form diasporas from Asia or Europe, such as the East African Asians or South African whites. Each of these diasporas, broadly speaking, has its own connections and commitments to Africa, its own memories and imaginations of Africa, and its own conceptions of the diasporic condition and identity. The third group is, in turn, sometimes divided by the racialized codifications of whiteness and blackness, sanctified in the colonial cartographies of North Africa and sub-Saharan Africa, and by US immigration law under which North Africans are classified as white.

This merely points to the complexities of the African diasporas and the challenges of studying them, and underscores Kim Butler's (2000: 127) point that 'conceptualizations of diaspora must be able to accommodate the reality of multiple identities and phases of diasporization over time'. She offers a simple but useful schema for diasporan study divided into five dimensions: '(1) reasons for, and conditions of, the dispersal; (2) relationship with homeland; (3) relationship with hostlands; (4) interrelationships within diasporan groups; (5) comparative study of different diasporas'. For Darlene Clark Hine (2001) black diaspora studies need to have three features: a transatlantic framework, an interdisciplinary methodology, and a comparative perspective.

Contextualizing the academic diasporas

Knowledge production by the African academic diaspora, as for other academics, is conditioned by various structural and epistemic imperatives over which they do not always have much control. The contexts and constraints that shape academic production are subject to changes emanating as much from the academy itself as from the wider society. As is well known by now, in recent years the academy almost everywhere has been undergoing massive transformations tied to shifting internal and external mandates and missions. Since it is not possible in a short essay such as this to discuss these changes in much detail, I will try to outline an analytical framework that might help us capture their essential features and dynamics. Knowledge production systems involve the intricate interplay of institutional, intellectual, ideological and individual factors.

Academic institutions can be classified according to their physical location (rural, urban or metropolitan), fiscal base (private, public or for-profit), academic structure (doctorate-granting, masters, baccalaureate, associates, or specialized),[1] and cultural composition (historically white, historically black, or women's). The intellectual enterprise itself can be distinguished in terms of its disciplinary organization (humanities, social sciences, sciences or professions), theoretical orientation (positivist, post-structuralist, feminist, etc.), and methodological considerations (empirical, experimental, ethnographic, textual, etc.). Ideology in the academy, often reflecting the ebbs and flows of wider social thought and movements, shapes intellectual discourses and practices from research and teaching to faculty hiring and publishing.

The dominant ideologies have included, among many others, racism and liberalism in the American academy and nationalism and developmentalism in the African academy, while Marxism has found succour in both at certain times. Besides these ideological tropes, for Africanists in the American academy, including African diaspora academics, the knowledge they produce might also be framed by their attitudes to the grand ideas and images of the 'West', 'Africa', the 'Third World', 'the North', 'the South', 'globalization' and 'trans-nationalism', or the diasporic demands and dreams of pan-Africanism or Afrocentricism. As for the last factor, there can be little doubt that individual traits, values and idiosyncrasies, especially the social inscriptions of gender, class, race, nationality, ethnicity, age and even religion and sexuality, influence academics' ideological and theoretical proclivities, their institutional and disciplinary preferences, and their research and publication practices.

Clearly, the variables to consider in charting the contours of knowledge production by academics in general and African diaspora academics in particular are too complex for glib generalizations, whether those inspired by the solidarities of pan-Africanism or the solitudes of Afropessimism. To my knowledge, no comprehensive data have been collected identifying the location of the African diaspora academics, from all the four diasporic waves I identified earlier, in the matrix of institutional, intellectual, ideological and individual factors outlined above. Much of what is known even about contemporary African academic migrants in the United States is anecdotal, for little systematic research has been conducted on their demographic and social composition or occupational and institutional affiliations, let alone their ideological orientations and personal inclinations. The data problems are compounded by the fact that the universities are losing their monopoly over scholarly production to other institutions and agencies, thanks to the changes associated with capitalist globalization, namely the liberalization and privatization of the universities themselves and the commercialization and commodification of knowledge in the wider economy and society, so that academics are no longer confined to the universities and tracking them is no easy task. For example, I know of many African diaspora academics working for NGOs, foundations and think tanks in the United States.

Notwithstanding these limitations, several broad observations can be made about African diaspora academics. It is quite evident that their numbers in the American academy are relatively small and their influence is rather limited.[2] If this is true of the historic diaspora as a whole, it is even more so for the contemporary academic diaspora. According to the 2003 *Almanac* of *The Chronicle of Higher Education* (2003a: 22–3), the total number of full-time black faculty members (US citizens and resident aliens) at US universities and colleges (of which there were 4,197 in 2000–3) was 29,222 out of 590,937 in 1999, or a mere 4.9 per cent, far below their share of the national population, estimated at 12.3 per cent. Interestingly, Asians, with only 3.6 per cent of the total US population, outnumbered black faculty by nearly five thousand. No less telling is the fact that only 3 per cent of the black faculty were professors. The 4,784 black professors comprised 16.4 per cent of the total black faculty, while 22.1 per cent were at the rank of associate professor, 28.9 per cent were assistant professors, 18.4 per cent were instructors, and 14.3 per cent were lecturers and other.[3]

The exact share of the contemporary African academic diaspora among black faculty is not known, but it is most likely small, although it is growing. The proportion of African migrant academics at historically black colleges and universities (HBCUs) is within the range of the 13 per cent that make up 'other minorities and foreigners' at these institutions (58 per cent of HBCU faculty are African American and 29 per cent white) (Johnson and Harvey 2002: 298). Needless to say, the HBCUs tend to be a lot poorer and have heavier teaching loads than the white research universities. While courses on Africa are taught regularly at many HBCUs, compared to the latter the HBCUs are less internationalized in terms of their curricula, study abroad and faculty exchange programmes. Furthermore, they seem to place a higher premium on the professions and sciences than the humanities and social sciences. It has also been said that they are generally conservative politically, ideologically and socially, a lingering tribute to their vocational and religious foundations, precarious funding and mission to vindicate and improve the 'race', to build a black professional elite.[4]

Black faculty continue to find themselves relatively marginalized in the historically white universities (HWUs), despite all the rhetoric about affirmative action in the aborted promises of civil rights. Robin Wilson (2002: A10) tells us that about half of the black faculty 'work at historically black institutions. The proportion of black faculty members at predominantly white universities – 2.3 per cent – is virtually the same as it was 20 years ago.' It is not unusual on the large campuses with more than 30,000 students and thousands of faculty to find less than a hundred black faculty, or entire departments without a single black faculty member, especially among the Eurocentric bastions of the humanities (philosophy and classics), the aspiring queen of the social sciences (economics), the assorted mandarins of the natural sciences (physics, chemistry, mathematics and biology), and the new high-tech interdisciplinary frontiers from information technology and biotechnology to nanotechnology and environmental technology.

While much is heard, and sometimes done, about internationalization, and African studies courses and programmes have expanded remarkably in the last three decades, Africa and recent African migrants find themselves engulfed in America's eternal racial war, buffeted between the competing demands of white hegemony (manifested in the much bemoaned control of African studies programmes by European Americans) and black struggle (articulated in the often beleaguered efforts to build viable and respected African American studies programmes).[5] I have written at length elsewhere of the frequently bitter contestations – which are simultaneously political, pecuniary and paradigmatic – between migrant Africans, African Americans and European Americans in the study and construction of Africa (Zeleza 2003b: ch. 5).

If the relations between the contemporary African academic diaspora and European Americans are marked by questions of race and intellectual authority, between migrant Africans and African Americans they centre on nationality and institutional access. It is not uncommon for the historically white universities to hire recent African immigrants over African Americans in order to serve affirmative action and save themselves from combative race relations. As immigrants and indigenes, the two African diasporas are driven by the different memories and materialities of colonized and underdeveloped Africa and racialized and developed America, of being abroad and at home, by different motivations and moralities of personal and public engagement, national and trans-national sentiments and solidarities. Not surprisingly, relations between these diasporas are characterized by the conflicting emotions and realities of accommodation, ambiguity and animosity.[6]

Historicizing diasporic academic production and linkages

The diaspora has been a critical site of knowledge production on Africa for a long time, and this history might hold salutary lessons as we seek to strengthen the engagements among the different waves of the diaspora and between them and Africa. As both a place and a project, a cultural and cognitive community, the diaspora has provided an unusually fertile space for imagining and writing on Africa. Pan-Africanism, the progenitor of the numerous territorial nationalisms in Africa and the Caribbean, emerged out of the diasporic condition of enslavement and the diasporic experience of colonialism. During the late nineteenth and early twentieth centuries, as colonialism reconfigured the global civilizational presence of Africans and reconnected Africa to its diaspora, the diaspora became crucial to the (re)constructions of Africa as an idea, Africa as an object of study, Africans as academics, and pan-Africanism as a project.

The idea of Africa – descriptions, meanings, images and discourses about Africa – as inscribed by both Africans and non-Africans, has mutated in various historical and geographical contexts from ancient times to the present. By the end of the nineteenth century, in the emerging 'colonial library', as V. Y. Mudimbe (1994) calls it, the African paradigm of negative difference was firmly entrenched, as immortalized in Hegel's imperious dismissal of Africa as the incarnation of the 'Unhistorical, Undeveloped Spirit'. Assaulted for centuries by European racial and epistemic violence, it is not surprising that Africans in the diaspora, rather than those on the continent, were the first to launch protracted and passionate struggles for epistemological and political liberation, in which the vindication of Africa, as a human and historical space, was central. To be sure, there were those who reproduced the narratives of derision, who yearned for unconditional assimilation and Africa's erasure from their memories and bodies. And even among those who longed for Africa's redemption many had internalized the civilizational binaries of the Western epistemological order and believed that Africa would only be liberated from its current backwardness by the modernized diaspora returning to the motherland.

Notwithstanding such ambiguities, or even contradictions, so well noted by several commentators,[7] the vindicationist tradition, represented most powerfully in the writings of W. E. B. Dubois, William Leo Hansberry and Edward Blyden, to mention just a few, sought to emancipate African societies and cultures from the cognitive and colonial apparatuses of European imperialism, a struggle that still continues.[8] It is quite remarkable, indeed, how little the defamations and defences of Africa have changed since the late nineteenth century, a tribute to the enduring power of Euro-centricism, thanks to Western hegemony in the world capitalist system, a sobering reminder that the struggles to liberate Africans at home and abroad must continue.

The texts of the vindicationist writers constituted one foundational stream for contemporary African studies. This is the pan-African tradition, whose analytical scope and scheme differed from the Africanist tradition that emerged after the Second World War. 'Rejecting the dichotomies on which Africanist scholarship would later be constructed', Michael West and William Martin (1997: 311) state, African diaspora scholars 'connected ancient Africa to modern Africa, Africa north of the Sahara to Africa south of the Sahara, and, especially, the African continent to the African diaspora. They tended to concentrate on broad political, religious, and cultural themes that transcended national and continental boundaries in the black world.'

They were preoccupied with the fundamental questions of Africa's purity and parity, as Kwaku Korang (2004) has so perceptively observed; purity in terms of Africa's autonomy and authenticity and parity in terms of Africa's progress and modernity, of creating what Blyden called an 'African per-sonality', an African ontology and epistemology that was both distinctly African and worldly in the context of an overriding European epistemic and existential presence that constantly sought to create and consume an African difference inscribed with inferiority. These large civilizational and cultural questions were generally shed from the African studies of the post-war Africanist tradition, in which the modernization paradigm – packaged in a variety of ideological and theoretical but decidedly positivist trajectories – assumed ascendancy, which resonated with the developmentalist pre-occupations of post-colonial Africa.

In pre-civil rights America, where segregation was legal, and colonial Africa, where universities were few (mostly concentrated in South Africa and North Africa), the HBCUs provided the most auspicious home for the study of Africa by both African Americans and Africans from the continent. It was at these colleges and universities that the serious and systematic study of Africa was pioneered, courses on African peoples established, and monographs and journals published, long before the historically white universities, in pursuit of national security, disciplinary excitement or be-lated multiculturalism, discovered African studies or diaspora studies. As is clear from Joseph Harris's (1993) masterly collection *Global Dimensions of the African Diaspora*, there are few significant intellectual or political figures in early-twentieth-century African American or anglophone African history who did not study, teach or were not inspired by or had some dealings with an HBCU. The cases of Kwame Nkrumah and Nnamdi Azikiwe at Lincoln University in Philadelphia, Pennsylvania, or medical doctors such as Hastings Kamuzu Banda at Meharry medical school in Nashville, Tennessee, are emblematic of the thousands of Africans who received their university education in the United States during the first half of the twentieth century, when segregation kept the doors to the white universities shut (Veney 2002, 2003).

Thus, diaspora academic institutions were in the forefront of producing both knowledge and personnel, counter-hegemonic discourses and developmental capacities for the diaspora itself and Africa. The transformative role of the diaspora in terms of knowledge production is nowhere as evident as it is in the settler and receptive settlements of Liberia and Sierra Leone during the late nineteenth and early twentieth centuries. Much has been written about the initiatives, choices and adaptations the Americo-Liberian and Sierra Leonean Krio intelligentsia, both secular and religious, made as teachers and evangelists to reconcile their dual, and in some cases triple, heritage as a community with claims to Africa, the West and sometimes Islam, to nativity, modernity and difference. They were led by the indomitable iconoclast Edward Blyden, whose voluminous writings laid the foundations of twentieth-century pan-Africanist thought. As Toyin Falola (2001) has demonstrated in his history of *Nationalism and African Intellectuals*, Blyden was eagerly emulated and debated by his contemporaries and later by the Negritudists and independence nationalists.

The thought and praxis of these intellectuals (there were as yet not many academics on the continent because there were few universities) demonstrated the umbilical relationship between pan-Africanism and nationalism, the intricate web of ideas, images, individuals, values, visions, expressive culture and institutional practices circulating in the elite cosmopolitan, not to say globalized, circles of Africa and the diaspora. Pan-Africanism would later develop different spatial and social referents, but in the late nineteenth and early twentieth centuries it was pre-eminently a transatlantic phenomenon. As I have argued elsewhere, 'the lead taken by the African diaspora in the Caribbean and the United States in organizing Panafricanism can be attributed to the fact that racial ideologies there were more severe than in Latin America. Also, Britain was a colonial superpower and later the United States became a global superpower' (Zeleza 2003b: 416).

Transatlantic pan-Africanism was articulated most concretely in the first half of the twentieth century through political movements and the traffic in expressive culture. The movements included W. E. B. Dubois' elitist Pan-African Congresses, Marcus Garvey's populist conventions and bungled 'Back to Africa' scheme, and a whole range of organizations formed by African students and African American activists, such as Paul Robeson's Council on African Affairs, especially in the aftermath of the 1935 Italian invasion of Ethiopia – the beacon of successful African resistance and freedom from colonialism – which enraged and galvanized the African world. The transatlantic circulation of expressive cultural practices, from music to dress to language, were powerful signifiers of black cosmopolitanism, and in highly racialized colonies such as South Africa, African American cultural forms were adopted as performative tools that disconnected modernity from whiteness by subverting, mocking and reversing the 'racial time' of white modernity 'that locked Africans into static "uncivilized native" categories' (Kemp and Vinson 2000: 141).

Clearly, pan-Africanism involved far more than transatlantic political discourse and engagement. It also represented the globalizing cultural flows between Africa and its diaspora, in which cultural imports and exports were traded in complex circuits of exchange throughout the transatlantic world. The circulation of many forms of popular music from rumba and jazz to reggae and rap is a fascinating story that has been told by many. So too is that of the connections between the literary movements of Africa and the diaspora, most significantly the Harlem Renaissance and the Negritude movement in the 1920s and 1930s, as well as the religious linkages from the role of diaspora missionaries and models in the spread of Christianity and the growth of Christian independence (also called independent churches) to Africa's contribution to the development of diaspora religions, such as Candomble, Santeria, Voodoo and Rastafarianism. In short, an African cosmopolitanism emerged in the transatlantic world. Cosmopolitanism here refers to a cultural phenomenon that is both local and trans-national, social islands of practices, material technologies, conceptual frameworks and lifestyles that circulated internationally but were localized in their production and consumption.[9]

As the storms of decolonization gathered momentum in Africa and the Caribbean and that of desegregation in the United States, transatlantic pan-Africanism entered a new phase, in which it was increasingly supplanted by new pan-Africanisms and territorial nationalisms. To be sure, there were continued reverberations between these nationalisms and pan-Africanisms. For example, the nationalist achievements in Africa and the Caribbean inspired civil rights struggles in the USA, while civil rights activists in the USA provided crucial support to liberation movements fighting against recalcitrant settler regimes in southern Africa by applying pressure on the American state and capital. But there was no denying that other pan-Africanisms were rising, both in practice and in discursive terms.

The most significant discursive intervention was Gilroy's notion of the 'Black Atlantic', a form of pan-Africanism that is largely confined to celebrating the creativity and construction of new cultures among the African diasporic communities in the Americas and Europe, excluding continental Africa. The other pan-Africanisms were as much conceptual as they were organizational, namely continental, sub-Saharan, pan-Arab and global. The first has focused primarily on the unification of continental Africa. The second and third have restricted themselves to the peoples of the continent north and south of the Sahara, and in the case of pan-Arabism has extended itself to western Asia or the so-called Middle East. Gamal Abdel Nasser proudly saw Egypt at the centre of three concentric circles linking the African, Arab and Islamic worlds. The last, which seeks to reclaim African peoples dispersed to all corners of the globe, is the weakest in organizational terms, although it is assuming intellectual salience as diaspora scholars seek to map out the dispersal of Africans in the Indian Ocean and Mediterranean worlds and configure their African diasporic identities.

The political transformations associated with the nationalist and civil rights struggles transformed the institutional bases of pan-African academic knowledge production and linkages. The terrain changed significantly for the independence generation of African students both at home and abroad. In their countries they were no longer confined to the woefully few regional universities belatedly set up by the colonial states as new national universities were established, while in the United States they were no longer limited to the HBCUs as the white universities were officially desegregated. What they gained in access, they lost in scope. In other words, unlike the pre-independence generations, the post-colonial generations of African students and even faculty often lacked exposure to the pan-Africanizing experiences of the old regional universities and the HBCUs, even if they might express pan-African sentiments about Africa's common future and the need for greater unity and sympathize with civil rights struggles in the diaspora.

Despite its proverbial failures to realize the fruits of *uhuru*, territorial nationalism succeeded in turning the cartographic contraptions bequeathed by colonialism into objects of desire and discord for the increasingly despondent citizens and professional elites – including academics – of the post-colonial state. If decolonization engendered nationalist identities (notwithstanding the fissiparous tendencies of ethnicity) for continental Africans, the enfranchisement that came with desegregation in the United States strengthened national identity among African Americans (even though racism persisted). Thus, encounters between post-colonial Africans and post-civil-rights African Americans were increasingly mediated by territorial nationalisms that were far more muted during the era of Nkrumah and Dubois.

Tendencies of the contemporary academic diaspora

The contemporary African academic diaspora has to engage and negotiate with multiple constituencies as academics, as immigrants in another country, and as emigrants from specific African countries.[10] As predominantly academics of colour, to use the American nomenclature for racial minorities, its members must learn to climb the slippery poles of the highly racialized American academy and come to grips with the complex institutional, intellectual and ideological imperatives of the largest and most diversified and differentiated higher education system in the world.

As immigrants, they confront, on the one hand, the legal issues of their resident status, now further complicated by the imposition of a stringent homeland security regime following the terrorist attacks in New York and Washington on 11 September 2001.[11] On the other hand, there are the infinitely thorny challenges of social adjustment, which require them to navigate the contours of race, ethnic and gender relations in America, to negotiate relations with the dominant white society and with African Americans as well as other immigrants (including those from their own countries, other African countries and elsewhere in the African diaspora, especially the Caribbean), and to assure their participation in the country's social and political affairs.

As emigrants, they face unending demands from home, both real and imagined, ranging from the intimate obligations to family and friends, often to provide financial and moral support, to the more abstract compulsion to defend and promote Africa in a country where things African are routinely denigrated and demonized. In fact, the devaluation of Africa frequently seems to parallel the depreciation of their own qualifications and status, a condition that induces acute agonies and tortured adaptations, as they are forced to pay an additional cultural tax for being African – usually on top of the racial tax that African Americans have always paid for being black, while for the women among them there is an extra gender tax.

The number of African immigrants in the United States has been increasing steadily since 1970 for reasons we cannot go into here, except to point out that this is related to changes in migration pressures in Africa itself and immigration conditions and law in the United States. According to the latest US census, there were 700,000 African-born residents in the

United States. While this number may appear large and has nearly doubled since 1990, it represents a mere 2.5 per cent of the foreign-born population (estimated at 28.4 million, accounting for 10.4 per cent of the total US population, the highest since 1930). An indication that many African residents are recent migrants is demonstrated by the fact that the median length of their residence is 10.2 years while the proportion of naturalized citizens is 37 per cent, both of which figures are lower than for most of the other major regions.[12]

Where African migrants trump everybody else, including native-born Americans, is in education. In 2000, 94.9 per cent of African-born residents aged twenty-five and over had completed high school or further education, compared to 86.6 per cent for native-born Americans and 67 per cent for all foreign-born residents. Among the African-born residents, 49.3 per cent had a bachelor's degree or higher as compared to 25.6 per cent for the native-born population and 25.8 per cent for the foreign-born population as a whole.[13] Clearly, African residents in the United States constitute the most educated population in the country, while residents from America's historic back yard in Mexico, Central America and the Caribbean have the lowest educational levels.

Not surprisingly, African residents are mostly to be found in the professions, despite the proverbial stories of Africans with PhDs driving taxis in New York, Washington or other major American cities. More than a third, 36.5 per cent to be exact, were in a managerial and professional speciality, 22.1 per cent in technical, sales and administrative support, 19.6 per cent in service occupations, 4.2 per cent in precision production, craft and repair, and the remaining 17.1 per cent labourers, fabricators and operators. In contrast, the occupational distribution for residents from (using the census classifications) Latin America, the Caribbean, Central America, Mexico and South America is weighted to the less professional and managerial occupations and include sizeable groups in farming, forestry and fishing. Yet, in terms of household income and poverty rates, African residents tend to do less well than their educational levels would seem to suggest.[14]

The irony cannot escape anyone: Africa, perhaps the least educated and most underdeveloped continent in the world, has the most educated population in the world's most developed country. This gaping mismatch, a testimony to the asymmetrical linkages between Africa and the North, is undoubtedly a tragedy, but it can potentially be turned in Africa's favour if effective strategies are developed to transform the 'brain drain' into 'brain gain', or to turn it into what some have called 'brain mobility'. The latter involves building expatriate knowledge networks and establishing connections between the migrant professionals and their countries or regions of origin, which can facilitate the exchange of information and knowledge and the transfer of skills (Granovetter and Sweedberg 1992; Murdoch 1997). The African academic diaspora, I have argued at length elsewhere,

> as cultural producers, have an important and specific role to play in brokering relations between Africa and the North, in [Africanizing] the Atlantic. They must resist the seductions of the Northern academies to become native ventriloquists, complicit 'others' who validate narratives that seek to marginalize Africa. Nor should they let themselves be manipulated as a fifth column in the North's eternal racial wars by disavowing the protracted struggles of historic African diaspora communities for the full citizenship of racial equality, economic empowerment, and political power. (Zeleza 2003b: 162–3)

And I proceed to outline some of the possible strategies, which need no repeating here, that might be used to turn the contemporary African academic diaspora from a liability into an asset for African intellectual development in terms of the triple mission of the academic enterprise – research, teaching and service (ibid.: 161–70).

Prescriptions, which Africa always gets in abundance, often of course sink in the quicksands of reality, in this case the realities of both the African and American academies and knowledge production systems. One issue is to look at the actual linkages that have been established between the two, and the other the profile of the members of the contemporary African academic diaspora in the United States, who are by no means homogenous and whose tendencies can facilitate or hinder productive and progressive linkages with their colleagues on the continent. Earlier I alluded to linkages between the HBCUs and Africa. These linkages continue, of course, although since the 1950s and 1960s they have increasingly been eclipsed by the entry of the historically white universities, bankrolled by the foundations and the state itself (for example, through the federally funded Title VI area studies programmes), into African studies and academic exchanges with African institutions.

Briefly, as I have also shown elsewhere, the patterns of academic exchange between the United States and Africa have been unequal, patterns that the contemporary processes and projects of globalization are helping to reinforce and recast. Historically, academic exchanges between the United States and Africa have involved student and faculty exchange programmes, short-term training programmes, and technical assistance for specific projects. Since the 1990s new patterns of academic exchange and mobility between American and African universities began to emerge. Three can be identified. First, the growth of what is called 'trans-national' education (often involving the establishment of overseas branches of American universities). Second, the globalization of American scholarly societies (expanding their global reach by aggressively recruiting foreign members, including from Africa). And third, the expansion of online education (using the Internet to export curricula and instructional expertise, especially in the lucrative fields of science, engineering and business) (Zeleza 2003b: ch. 3).[15]

It is not easy to identify the tendencies among the contemporary African academic diaspora. There is of course no shortage of impressionistic accounts of their politics and scholarship. For example, Falola (2001: 282) has observed that 'like all communities they have their tensions, petty rivalries, and resentments toward members who are perceived to be especially successful', and he discusses how they deal with the questions of identity politics and scholarly audience, singling out the experiences of Manthia Diawara, Es'kia Mphahlele and Nawal el Saadawi. His tantalizing distinction between 'migrants as revolutionaries', as people with 'alternative allegiances', and as 'agents of culture', however, is not further developed (ibid.: 281–93).

The Kenyan scholar Francis Njubi Nesbitt offers a more compelling typology of the African academic diaspora. He has argued that the Duboisian 'double consciousness' of African migrant intellectuals in the North, which is spawned by the contradiction between their high academic achievements and an inferiorized identity in America's unyielding racial hierarchy and between their alienation from Africa (where they are often condemned for abandoning their countries) and the need to come to terms with their Africanity and to promote Africa, produces three 'types' of migrant intellectuals: the comprador intelligentsia, the post-colonial critic and the progressive exile.

Members of the comprador intelligentsia cynically use their Africanity to authenticate the neo-colonial and neo-liberal agendas of the international financial institutions. They are infamous for defending the global order and condemning African countries for corruption, 'tribalism' and ineptitude. For their part, the post-colonial critics see themselves in a mediating role, as expert interpreters of the African experience to the West and transmitters of the ever changing panorama of Euro-American perspectives – liberalism, modernization, Marxism, dependency and the 'posts' (postmodernism, post-structuralism and post-coloniality) – to Africa and in 'explaining' the African experience. The progressive exiles seek to use their space of exile to develop a dignified pan-African identity by unabashedly promoting African knowledges and participating in the liberation struggles of both the diaspora and their countries of origin. Njubi suggests Ngugi wa Thiong'o as the paragon of the progressive exile and Kwame Anthony Appiah as the post-colonial critic, and one could point to a George Ayittey (1992, 1998) as the quintessential comprador intellectual.

When Njubi presented his paper at CODESRIA's 10th General Assembly in December 2002 in Kampala, some participants pointed out that the categories could be expanded or were not mutually exclusive, a point the author himself in fact emphasized. 'Intellectuals who consider themselves progressives in one context', he wrote,

> find themselves allied with global capital and neocolonial forces in another. Take the case of the independence generation ... It is this generation that gave us hopeful theories like African personality, Consciencism, and African Socialism. Yet, once they returned home from exile and seized the reins of power, an alarmingly large number of them abandoned their progressive politics for the worst forms of neocolonial clientilism and despotism. (Nesbitt 2004: 74)

Undoubtedly, one could come up with other typologies based on different criteria. Njubi's classification primarily refers to the contemporary African academic diaspora's ideological positioning towards African liberation. They could also be classified in terms of their disciplinary orientation – as humanists, social scientists, scientists and professionals, each of which has a bearing on the kinds of research they conduct and the possible collaborations they can establish with colleagues and institutions on the continent, because each of these organizational branches in the academy has its own intellectual requirements and institutional and reputational resources. For example, research in the humanities is more poorly financed than in the sciences, and scholars in the literary disciplines can conduct their textually based research without ever going to Africa, which would be frowned upon for historians or anthropologists, who need to conduct empirical and ethnographic research. Also, in many social science and humanities disciplines it is common to work individually, while in many of the sciences collaboration is often necessary given the cost of the research apparatus and the academic culture that has evolved in the sciences.

The permutations and implications of the disciplinary schema as a basis for organizing knowledge production and classifying academics and assessing the nature of their potential or actual engagements with Africa obviously deserve consideration. Yet one cannot resist the search for a more comprehensive typology that incorporates as many of the dynamics that frame academic knowledge production as possible. Earlier we identified four of these – the institutional, intellectual, ideological and individual factors. With this in mind I would propose, very tentatively it must be stressed, three broad classifications of African diaspora academics: the pan-Africanists, the Americanists and the globalists, based on the organization and content of their research, publishing and teaching practices. Members of the first group conduct their research and derive their research agendas, and do their publishing and sometimes their teaching (conventional and electronic), in both Africa and the United States, while the second are largely focused on the United States in their research, publishing, and teaching practices, and the third are connected to multiple sites besides the United States and Africa. Needless to say, these 'choices' are driven as much by ideological and individual predispositions as by institutional and intellectual predilections.

It cannot be overemphasized that this is a rather rudimentary typology, that many people straddle these categories at different times in their careers. Indeed, many African academics circulate between Africa and the United States as students, faculty or visitors. It simply underscores the fact that for African diaspora academics located in the United States, it is not just their *personal politics* towards Africa and its struggles which are important as far as knowledge production is concerned. Equally important, perhaps even more so, are their *academic practices*, which do not always coincide with their personal inclinations or ideologies. A more comprehensive typology would in fact also help us to differentiate among those in the historic African diaspora who are engaged in African studies, and identify the tendencies among the two diasporas that continental research networks and organizations such as CODESRIA might fruitfully engage for mutual benefit. Beyond these 'natural constituencies' of Africa in the United States, there are of course the European American Africanists, and many others who have more than a nodding acquaintance with or interest in knowledge produced in and on Africa. The African knowledge production enterprise in the North is indeed a house of many mansions.

Conclusion: what role for CODESRIA?

There can be little doubt that the contemporary African academic diaspora in the United States and elsewhere in the North is becoming a force to reckon with in knowledge production on Africa. It is also becoming more conscious of itself as a diaspora, of the many ties that bind it together and to the historic diasporas and to Africa, but also of the many tensions that tear it apart internally and from the other diasporas and the continent. This is a diaspora often brought to the United States through chain migration (after studying or working in other countries, including foreign countries in Africa), so that it has rich reservoirs of trans-national experiences and empathies.

227

Indeed, the revolution in telecommunications and travel, which has compressed the spatial and temporal distances between home and abroad, offers this diaspora, unlike the historic diasporas from the earlier dispersals, unprecedented opportunities to be trans-national, to be people of multiple worlds, perpetually translocated, physically and culturally, between several countries or several continents. They are able to retain ties to Africa in ways that were not possible to earlier generations of the diaspora. Lest we forget, let us note that many of the people who have worked for CODESRIA, including the current and past two executive secretaries, have had their sojourns in the diaspora. Thus, CODESRIA is not only a pan-African institution, but a beneficiary and beacon of intellectual energies from and for the diaspora.

The challenge for CODESRIA is to recognize and strengthen its diasporic communities and commitments. Institutionally, this entails giving the diaspora, both the contemporary and historic, a formal voice in CODESRIA's governance and deliberations, a subject that was raised forcefully by several participants at CODESRIA's 10th General Assembly. The mechanics of doing this are of course problematic, but the principle should not be. Intellectually, the challenge is also to incorporate diaspora academics in CODESRIA's research networks, institutes and publishing programmes. There might be reluctance if resources are seen in zero-sum terms, but this need not be so if it is understood, and insisted upon, that the diaspora has access to and should harness and channel its resources to these research activities.

As the premier African social science research network on the continent, CODESRIA has a responsibility to promote critical and informed public debate and discussion about African issues globally and relations between Africa and its diaspora. In building more effective linkages with the African diaspora, it might be necessary to expand the boundaries of research by integrating more actively research domains associated with the sciences, the so-called professional fields and the new interdisciplinary areas, not only because it makes eminent intellectual sense in this era of furious disciplinary reconfigurations, but also to tap into the intellectual energies of the African academic diaspora working in these areas, which is seeking active collaborations with African social scientists in addition to those they may already have with academic fellow-travellers. I am often quite amazed by the exciting research being conducted on the burning issues confronting Africa today by diaspora academics outside the traditional humanities- and social-science-dominated circles of North American African studies.

Many of these academics already collaborate with colleagues and institutions on the continent. Indeed, many of us in the diaspora maintain strong personal linkages with colleagues in Africa and we will continue to do so. The challenge and opportunity for CODESRIA and for us is to channel and enrich these engagements under CODESRIA's inclusive and energizing intellectual umbrella, which has prevailed and prospered during thirty years of trials, tribulations and triumphs in building a viable African research community. It is time CODESRIA set its sights to help (re)shape the world of Africa's own academic diaspora. This might be its singular contribution to pan-Africanism in the new century.

Notes

1 This is the classification used by the Carnegie Foundation for the Advancement of Teaching, and is the leading typology of American colleges and universities. See <www.carnegiefoundation.org/classification>. Needless to say, different classifications of higher educational systems operate in different countries.

2 For studies of blacks in the American academy see Washington and Harvey (1989), Jones (2000) and James and Farmer (1993).

3 Of 29,222 black faculty, 14,660 are men and 14,562 are women; and women made up 35.7 per cent of the professors, 44.3 per cent of the associate professors, 54 per cent of the assistant professors, 56.2 per cent of the instructors, and 57.7 per cent of the lecturers and other.

4 For histories of the HBCUs see Willie and Edmonds (1978), Garibaldi (1984), Anderson (1988), Roebuck and Murty (1993) and Sims (1994).

5 For some interesting analysis of the struggles of African American, Afro-American, Africana or black studies – the nomenclature is itself indicative of the field's contestations and continued search for a viable identity – see some of the following: Alkalimat (1990), Azevedo (2003), Marable (2000), Skinner (2000), Kasonde (2001), Hamilton (2003) and Barrett and Carey (2003).

6 Recent examples of conflict between African migrants and African Americans include the widely publicized altercations at Virginia State University, an HBCU, in which the institution's black president was accused of demoting African American heads of department in favour of foreign-born faculty, including Africans, under a reorganization. See Wilson (2001). In a different twist an African-Lebanese man from West Africa sued Loyola College in Maryland in the federal court after he was turned down for a position allegedly on the grounds that black faculty members were pressing for the hiring of an 'African-American that was visibly black'. See Clegg (2002).

7 See, for example, Mudimbe (1988), Davidson (1992) and Korang (2004).

8 See Blyden (1857, 1967, 1971); Dubois (1970, 1976, 1994); Hansberry (1974, 1977).

9 On the influence of African American cultural practices in South Africa see Magubane (2003) and on cosmopolitanism in Zimbabwe as expressed through music see Turino (2000, 2003).

10 See the following recent studies on African immigrants in the United States: Lewis (1995), Ashabranner and Ashabranner (1999) and Arthur (2000).

11 For a discussion of the implications of this see Mazrui (2002), Veney (2003), Zeleza (2003a), and the special issue of *The Chronicle of Higher Education* (2003b).

12 The median length of residence years for US residents born in the following regions is as follows: Europe 25 years, Asia 14.3 years, Latin America 13.5 years, Caribbean 17.6 years, Central America 12.9 years, Mexico 12.8 years, South America 13 years, Northern America (mostly refers to Canada) 24.8 years, and other 13.2 years. Comparable figures for naturalized citizens among the foreign-born resident population from the other regions are as follows: Europe 52 per cent, Asia 47.1 per cent, Latin America 28.3 per cent, Caribbean 46.5 per cent, Central America 21.1 per cent, Mexico 20.3 per cent, South America 38.6 per cent, Northern America 43.1 per cent, and other 24.3 per cent (US Census Bureau 2001: 19–21).

13 Comparable figures for the other regions in terms of the proportion of those with high school or further education are: Europe 81.3 per cent, Asia 83.8 per cent, Latin America 49.6 per cent, Caribbean 68.1 per cent, Central America 37.1 per cent, Mexico 33.8 per cent, South America 79.7 per cent, Northern America 85.5 per cent, and other 50.8 per cent. As for the proportions of those with a bachelor's degree or higher the figures are: Europe 32.9 per cent, Asia 44.9 per cent, Latin America 11.2 per cent, Caribbean 19.3 per cent, Central America 5.5 per cent, Mexico 4.2 per cent, South America 25.9 per cent, Northern America 36.2 per cent, and other 10.5 per cent. See ibid.: 36–7.

14 In 2000 they earned an average $36,371 as compared to $41,733 for residents from Europe, $51,363 for Asians, $36,048 for the foreign-born all together, and $41,383 for native-born Americans. In terms of poverty rates, it was 13.2 per cent for African-born residents, 9.3 per cent for European-born, 12.8 for Asian-born, 21.9 per cent for Latin American-born, 20.6 per cent for Caribbean-born, 24.2 per cent for Central America-born, 25.8 per cent for Mexico-born, 11.5 per cent for South America-born, 7.4 per cent for Northern America-born, and 17.8 per cent for other. See ibid.: 36–7.

15 For a detailed examination of linkages between African and American institutions of higher learning, see Samoff and Carrol (2002).

References

Alkalimat, A. (1990) *Paradigms in Black Studies. Intellectual History, Political Meaning and Political Ideology*, Chicago, IL: Twenty-first Century Books and Publications

Alpers, E. (2000) 'Recollecting Africa: Diasporic Memory in the Indian Ocean World', *African Studies Review*, 43(1): 83–99

Anderson, J. D. (1988) *The Education of Blacks in the South, 1860–1935*, Chapel Hill: University of North Carolina Press

Appiah, K. A. (1992) *In My Father's House: Africa in the Philosophy of Culture*, New York: Oxford University Press

Arthur, J. A. (2000) *Invisible Sojourners: African Immigrant Diaspora in the United States*, Westport: CT, Praeger

Ashabranner, B. K. and J. Ashabranner (1999) *The New African Americans*, North Haven, CT: Linnet Books

Ayittey, G. B. N. (1992) *Africa Betrayed*, New York: St Martin's Press

— (1998) *Africa in Chaos*, New York: St Martin's Press

Azevedo, M. (ed.) (2003) *African Studies: A Survey of Africa and the African Diaspora*, 3rd edn, Durham, NC: Carolina Academic Press

Barrett, M. and P. Carey (2003) *Diaspora: Introduction to Africana Studies*, Dubuque, IA: Kendall/Hunt

Blakely, A. (1986) *Russia and the Negro: Blacks in Russian History and Thought*, Washington, DC: Howard University Press

Blyden, E. W. (1857) *A Vindication of the African Race: Being A Brief Examination of the Arguments in Favor of African Inferiority*, Monrovia: G. Killian.

— (1967 [1887]) *Christianity, Islam and the Negro Race*, Edinburgh University Press

— (1971) *Black Spokesman: Selected Published Writings of Edward Wilmot Blyden*, ed. Hollis R. Lynch, London: Frank Cass

Brown, J. N. (1998) 'Black Liverpool, Black America, and the Gendering of Diasporic space', *Cultural Anthropology*, 13(3): 291–325

Butler, Kim D. (2000) 'From Black History to Diasporan History: Brazilian Abolition in Afro-Atlantic Context', *African Studies Review*, 43(1): 125–39

Chronicle of Higher Education (2003a) *Almanac*, 29 August

— (2003b) 'Special Report, Closing the Gates', 11 April, pp. A12–A25

Clegg, R. (2002) 'When Faculty Hiring is Blatantly Illegal', *The Chronicle of Higher Education*, 1 November, p. B20

Davidson, B. (1992) *The Black Man's Burden: Africa and the Curse of the Nation-state*, New York: Times Books

Dubois, W. E. B. (1970) *Black Reconstruction in America*, New York: Atheneum

— (1976) *The World and Africa*, Millwood, NY: Kraus-Thomson

— (1994) *The Souls of Black Folk*, New York: Dover

Edwards, B. H. (2000) '"Unfinished Migrations": Commentary and Response', *African Studies Review*, 43(1): 47–50

Falola, T. (2001) *Nationalism and African Intellectuals*, University of Rochester Press

Garibaldi, A. (ed.) (1984) *Black Colleges and Universities: Challenges for the Future*, New York: Praeger

Gordon, A. (1998) 'The New Diaspora – African Immigration to the United States', *Journal of Third World Studies*, 15(1): 79–103

Granovetter, M. and R. Sweedberg (1992) *The Sociology of Economic Life*, San Francisco, CA: Westview Press

Hamilton, K. (2003) 'Challenging the Future of Black Studies', *Black Issues in Higher Education*, 20(2): 38–9

Hansberry, W. L. (1974) *Pillars in Ethiopian History*, ed. J. E. Harris, Washington, DC: Howard University Press

— (1977) *Africa and Africans as Seen by Classical Writers*, Washington, DC: Howard University Press

Harris, J. (ed.) (1993) *Global Dimensions of the African Diaspora*, 2nd edn, Washington, DC: Howard University Press

Hine, D. C. (2001) 'Frontiers in Black Diaspora Studies and Comparative Black History: Enhanced Knowledge of Our Complex Past', *Negro Education Review* 52(3): 101–8

Hunwick, J. and T. Powell (2002) *The African Diaspora in the Mediterranean Lands of Islam*, Princeton, NJ: Markus Wiener

Jaysuriya, S. de S. and R. Pankhurst (eds) (2003) *The African Diaspora in the Indian Ocean*, Trenton, NJ: Africa World Press

Johnson, B. and W. Harvey (2002) 'The Socialization of Black College Faculty: Implications for Policy and Practice', *Review of Higher Education*, 25(3): 297–314

Jones, L. (ed.) (2000) *Brothers of the Academy: Up and Coming Black Scholars Earning Our Way in Higher Education*, Sterling, VA: Stylus

Joy, J. and R. Farmer (eds) (1993) *Spirit, Space and Survival: African American Women in (White) Academe*, New York: Routledge

Kasonde, M. (2001) 'African American Studies: An African Scholar's View', *Contemporary Review*, 278(1,624): 272–5

Kemp, A. D. and R. T. Vinson (2000) 'Professor James Thaele, American Negroes, and Modernity in 1920s Segregationist South Africa', *African Studies Review*, 43(1): 141–60

Korang, K. L. (2002) 'Intellectuals: Colonial', in P. T. Zeleza and D. Eyoh, (eds), *Encyclopedia of Twentieth Century African History*, London/New York: Routledge, pp. 268–74

— (2004) *Writing Ghana, Imagining Africa: Nation and African Modernity*, University of Rochester Press

Lewis, E. (1995) 'To Turn as on a Pivot: Writing African Americans into a History of Overlapping Diasporas', *American Historical Review*, 100 (3): 765–87

Magubane, Z. (2003) 'The Influence of African American Cultural Practices on South Africa, 1890–1990', in P. T. Zeleza and C. R. Veney (eds), *Leisure in Urban Africa*, Trenton, NJ: Africa World Press, pp. 297–319

Marable, M. (2000) *Dispatches from the Ebony Tower: Intellectuals Confront the African American Experience*, New York: Columbia University Press

Mazrui, A. A. (2002) 'Brain Drain between Counterterrorism and Globalization', *African Issues*, xxx(1): 86–9

Mudimbe, V. Y. (1988) *The Invention of Africa: Gnosis, Philosophy, and the Order of Knowledge*, Bloomington and Indianapolis: Indiana University Press

— (1994) *The Idea of Africa*, Bloomington and Indianapolis: Indiana University Press

Murdoch, J. (1997) 'Towards a Geography of Heterogeneous Associations', *Progress in Human Geography*, 21(3): 321–37

Nesbitt, F. N. (2004) *Race for Sanctions: African Americans against Sanctions, 1946–1964*, Bloomington and Indianapolis: Indiana University Press

Palmer, C. (2000) 'The African Diaspora', *Black Scholar*, 30(3/4): 56–9

Patterson, T. and R. D. G. Kelly (2000) 'Unfinished Migration: Reflections on the African Diaspora and the Making of the Modern World', *African Studies Review*, 43(1): 11–45

Roebuck, J. B. and K. S. Murty (1993) *Historically Black Colleges and Universities: Their Place in American Higher Education*, Westport, CT: Praeger

Samoff, J. and B. Carrol (2002) 'The Promise of Partnership and the Continuities of Dependence: External Support to Higher Education in Africa', paper presented at the African Studies Association Annual Meeting, 5–8 December

Sims, S. J. (1994) *Diversifying Historically Black Colleges and Universities: A New Higher Education Paradigm*, Westport, CT, Greenwood Press

Skinner, E. P. (2000) 'Transcending Traditions: African, African-American and African Diaspora Studies in the 21st Century – the Past Must be the Prologue', *Black Scholar*, 3(4): 4–11

Turino, T. (2000) *Nationalists, Cosmopolitans, and Popular Music in Zimbabwe*, University of Chicago Press

— (2003) 'The Middle Class, Cosmopolitanism, and Popular Music in Harare, Zimbabwe', in P. T. Zeleza and C. R. Veney (eds), *Leisure in Urban Africa*, Trenton, NJ: Africa World Press, pp. 321–41

US Census Bureau (2001) *Profile of the Foreign Born Population in the United States*, Washington, DC: US Census Bureau, pp. 19–21

Veney, C. R. (2002) 'The Ties that Bind: The Historic African Diaspora and Africa', *African Issues*, XXX(1): 3–8

— (2003) 'Building on the Past: African and American Linkages', in P. T. Zeleza and A. Olukoshi (eds), *African Universities in the Twenty-first Century*, vol. 1, *Liberalization and Internationalization*, Dakar: CODESRIA

Washington, V. and W. Harvey (1989) *Affirmative Rhetoric, Negative Action: African-American and Hispanic Faculty at Predominantly White Institutions*, Washington, DC: George Washington University

West, M. (2000) '"Unfinished Migrations": Commentary and Response', *African Studies Review*, 43(1): 61–4

West, M. O. and W. G. Martin (1997) 'A Future with a Past: Resurrecting the Study of Africa in the Post-Africanist Era', *Africa Today*, 44(3): 297–326

Willie, C. V. and R. R. Edmonds (eds) (1978) *Black Colleges in America: Challenge, Development, Survival*, New York: Teachers College Press

Wilson, R. (2001) 'A Battle over Race, Nationality, and Control at a Black University. At Virginia State U., Black Americans and Black Africans Each See Bias from the Other Side', *Chronicle of Higher Education*, 27 July, p. A8

— (2002) 'Stacking the Deck for Minority Candidates? Virginia Tech Has Diversified Its Faculty, but Many Professors There Doubt the Efforts are Fair – or Even Legal', *Chronicle of Higher Education*, 12 July, p. A10

Zack-Williams, A. (1995) 'Development and Diaspora: Separate Concerns?', *Review of African Political Economy*, 65: 349–58

Zeleza, P. T. (2000) 'African Labor and Intellectual Migrations to the North: Building New Transatlantic Bridges', paper presented to the African Studies Interdisciplinary Seminar, Center for African Studies, University of Illinois at Urbana-Champaign, 4 February

— (2002) 'Contemporary African Migrations in a Global Context: Towards Building the Black Atlantic', paper presented at the 10th CODESRIA General Assembly, Kampala, 8–12 December

— (2003a) 'Academic Freedom in the Neo-liberal Order: Governments, Globalization, Governance, and Gender', *Journal of Higher Education in Africa*, 1(1): 149–94

— *Rethinking Africa's Globalization*, vol. 1, *The Intellectual Challenges*, Trenton, NJ: Africa World Press

About the contributors

Beban Sammy Chumbow, Agrégé ès Lettres (Lovanium) and PhD (Indiana, USA), is Professor of Linguistics (1982) and currently Vice-Chancellor of the University of Yaounde I (Cameroon). For over ten years he served as Deputy Vice Chancellor and Vice Chancellor of three other universities. He has to his credit over sixty scientific publications in the field of linguistics (phonology, applied linguistics and language planning), and has played a leadership role in a number of academic and learned societies, as well as serving as consultant for several international organizations, including LICCA, UNESCO and UNECA. He is presently a member of the ILPAA Steering Committee, a select continent-wide group of language experts charged with devising strategies for the Implementation of the Language Plan of Action for Africa (ILPAA) in conjunction with the activities of the Academy of African Languages (ACALAN) and the African Union (AU).

Joseph Ki-Zerbo is professor of history, action researcher, politician and advocate for endogenous development. He founded the Centre d'Études pour le Développement Africain (CEDA) in Ouagadougou, Burkina Faso.

Amina Mama has occupied the chair in Gender Studies at the University of Cape Town since 1999, where she is responsible for offering intellectual leadership in the field of gender and women's studies. She is based at the African Gender Institute, home of Africa's first regional gender studies journal, *Feminist Africa*. She previously worked in a number of European-based international research and teaching institutions, and was a founder member of the Centre for Research and Documentation in Kano, Nigeria, and the Network for Women's Studies in Nigeria. She has held visiting positions at St Anthony's College, Oxford, Wellesley College, Massachusetts, and the Development and Project Planning Centre, University of Bradford.

Ali A. Mazrui is director of the Institute of Global Cultural Studies and Albert Schweitzer Professor in the Humanities at the State University of New York and Binghamton; Albert Luthuli Professor-at-Large at the University of Jos, Nigeria; Andrew D. White Professor-at-Large Emeritus and Senior Scholar in African Studies at Cornell University, Ithaca, New York; and Chancellor of the Jomo Kenyatta University of Agriculture and Technology, Kenya.

Thandika Mkandawire is the Director of the United Nations Institute on Social development (UNRISD) based in Geneva, Switzerland. He is a previous Executive Secretary of CODESRIA (1986–96). He has published extensively on problems of adjustment, democratization and the social sciences in Africa. His current work is focussed on social policy in the context of development.

Hannington Ochwada is involved in the African Studies Program at Indiana University, Bloomington. He was formerly lecturer in African history at Kenyatta University, Nairobi. His work has appeared in (among other publications) *African Sociological Review*, *African Development* and the *Journal of Eastern African Research and Development*.

Raymond Suttner is based at the Faculty of Social Sciences and Humanities, University of South Africa, Pretoria.

Ngugi wa Thiong'o is Distinguished Professor of English and Comparative Literature and director of the International Center for Writing and Translation, University of California at Irvine.

Paul Tiyambe Zeleza, a historian, literary critic, novelist and short-story writer, is professor of African studies and history at the Pennsylvania State University. Until recently he was professor of history and African studies and director of the Center for African Studies at the University of Illinois at Urbana-Champaign. He is the author of scores of essays and more than a dozen books, including most recently *Rethinking Africa's Globalization*, *Routledge Encyclopedia of Twentieth Century African History* and *Leisure in Urban Africa*. He is the winner of the 1994 Noma Award for his book *A Modern Economic History of Africa* and the 1998 Special Commendation of the Noma Award for *Manufacturing African Studies and Crises*.

Index

11 September attacks, 222

academic autonomy, 62, 100
academic exchange between US and
    Africa, 224–5
academic freedom, 22, 26, 43
academic institutions, classification
    of, 214
Academy of African Languages
    (ACALAN), 187
accountability, 35, 44
activism, critique of, 39
Adoko, Akena, 56, 59
affirmative action, 100, 216
Afigbo, A.E., 197
Afrabia, concept of, 65, 66–7, 73
Africa: devaluation of, 222; in
    Western mythologies, 104, 105;
    marginalization of, 201; natural
    and human resources of, 156,
    168–9, 180; pre-colonial period
    of, 201–2; purity and parity of,
    218; role in the production of
    knowledge, 156; seen as zone of
    darkness, 200; systematic study
    of, 218
African Americans, 68–73, 74, 212
African Association of Political
    Science, 64
African Claims in South Africa, 130
African cosmopolitanism, 220
African culture, myth of inferiority
    of, 180
African Gender Institute, 102, 106–12
African heroes, histories of, 198
African intellectuals *see* intellectuals,
    African
African National Congress (ANC), 3–4;
    as collective intellectual, 141–5;
    banning of, 141; formation of, 122;
    intellectuals within, 117–54; M-
    Plan, 131–2; Radio Freedom, 139,
    144; relations with CPSA, 129–31;
    viewed as broad church, 145;
    women's membership of, 125

African personality, 6, 18, 218, 226
African Renaissance, 64, 73, 88–93,
    201
African scholarship, victimology of,
    38
African Security Council, 75
African Studies programmes,
    dominated by Europeans, 216
African Union, 65, 66, 74–6, 186, 187;
    creation of, 73
African Union Security Council, 76
African unity, 163, 165, 183
Afrika Zamani, 64
Afrikaner nationalism, 198
Afrocentrism, 214
Afro-pessimism, 37, 44
Afro-World Wide Web, 68
Afwerki, Isaias, 14
agents of change, 169, 181, 189
aid donor establishment, 42–3
Aidoo, Ama Ata, 163
AIDS, 40; spread of, 101
Ajayi, Jacob, 197, 201
Ake, Claude, 26
Alexander, Neville, 160
Algeria, 23, 27–8, 32, 72, 85
Ali, Muhammad, 70
All-African People's Conference
    (AAPC), 58, 196
American Africans, 68–73, 74
American personality, 67–8
Americanism, 227
Amin, Idi, 59, 61
Amin, Samir, 20, 23, 163
Anderson, Benedict, 38; *Imagined
    Communities*, 15
Annan, Kofi, 70
anthropology, in European studies of
    Africa, 160
anti-colonialism, 21
anti-imperialism, 3, 15, 25, 45
Anyoku, Eleazar Emeka, 71
apartheid, 8, 9, 64, 87, 120, 134
Appiah, Kwame Anthony, 18, 25, 34,
    226; *In My Father's House*, 212

Index

245